GUILTY ROBOTS, HAPPY DOGS

GUILTY ROBOTS, HAPPY DOGS

THE QUESTION OF ALIEN MINDS

David McFarland

OXFORD
UNIVERSITY PRESS

OXFORD

UNIVERSITY PRESS

Great Clarendon Street, Oxford OX2 6DP

Oxford University Press is a department of the University of Oxford.
It furthers the University's objective of excellence in research, scholarship,
and education by publishing worldwide in

Oxford New York

Auckland Cape Town Dar es Salaam Hong Kong Karachi
Kuala Lumpur Madrid Melbourne Mexico City Nairobi
New Delhi Shanghai Taipei Toronto

With offices in

Argentina Austria Brazil Chile Czech Republic France Greece
Guatemala Hungary Italy Japan Poland Portugal Singapore
South Korea Switzerland Thailand Turkey Ukraine Vietnam

Oxford is a registered trade mark of Oxford University Press
in the UK and in certain other countries

Published in the United States
by Oxford University Press Inc., New York

British Library Cataloguing in Publication Data

Data available

Library of Congress Cataloging in Publication Data

Data available

Typeset by SPI Publisher Services, Pondicherry, India
Printed in Great Britain
on acid-free paper by
Clays Ltd, St Ives plc

ISBN 978-0-19-921929-2

1 3 5 7 9 10 8 6 4 2

CONTENTS

LIST OF ILLUSTRATIONS

PREFACE

TRAFFIC ROBOT

The traffic was heavy. As I approached the intersection I heard the frantic whistles that indicate traffic police. I signalled left. Then I saw the policeman—not a human policeman at all—a robot. Although it wore a policemen's cap on its spherical head, the resemblance ended there. It had two protruding lens-like eyes and a whistle for a mouth. Its head swivelled on a thin neck, supported by a torso that rotated on a pedestal, not on two legs. Two long arms directed the traffic: the hands on the ends of them pointed to, beckoned, and stopped the traffic in the time-honoured manner. I slowed to take a good look. One hand pointed at me; a short blast of the whistle and a brusque hand signal promptly sent me on my way.

It took me a while to recover my breath. The questions were tearing through my head. How could a robot be allowed to direct traffic? Was it supervised? What if there was an accident? How could a robot, possibly, do the job safely and effectively?

It was a simple automaton, presumably, a glorified set of traffic lights. But why install such an expensive traffic director? To free up police for other duties, maybe. But surely it had to be more than a simple automaton. It had to be able to react to any eventuality the way a human traffic policeman would do. It had to be trusted to direct the traffic in an efficient and proper manner, and in the event of an accident or other kind of mishap to take some kind of responsibility for its actions.

'TRUST?' Yes of course. But how can a robot be trusted? I trust my alarm clock to wake me up on time, but I do not hold it responsible if it fails to do so. An alarm clock is a very simple automaton. When it goes wrong I blame myself for failing to set it properly or the manufacturer for selling me faulty goods. I do not blame the clock itself. So what about the robot? What kind of robot would it have to be to take responsibility for its actions? If the robot caused an accident, either directly or indirectly, then it would be responsible in the direct causal sense, but this would imply nothing more than a fault *in* the robot, not a fault *of* the robot.

The distinction here is an important one, legally. If the traffic-director is an automaton and if it fails, then the fault would be the responsibility of whoever was legally responsible for the well functioning of the robot: the designer, or the maintenance engineer, and so forth. If the traffic-director is a person, and the accident is judged to be their fault, then questions of *legal responsibility* and *moral responsibility* apply. To be legally responsible is to fulfil the requirements for accountability under the law. To be morally responsible, an agent—that is the person performing or failing to perform the function in question—has as a rule a moral obligation, and so is worthy of either praise or blame. The person can be the recipient of what are sometimes called by philosophers their 'desert'. But a robot is not a person, and for a robot to be given what it deserves—'its just deserts'—it would have to be given something that mattered to it, and it would have to have some understanding of the significance of this. In short, it would have to have some sense of its own identity, some way of realising that *it* was deserving of something, whether pleasant or unpleasant.

Does this mean that it would have to have a mind? Is it conceivable that a robot—a traffic robot—any other kind of robot—could have what we might call a mind? What is a mind, anyway?

Questions about the mind have been asked in the past by any number of philosophers and scientists. An obvious starting point for our attempt to answer them would be to look at what they have had to say. On the other hand there is always a danger in starting out on well-trodden paths. Most philosophers and scientists have been concerned with the human mind, whereas our robot, assuming it has a mind at all, must have an *alien mind*, one, possibly, quite different from a human mind.

In fiction, aliens come in many forms: gods and devils, fairies and gnomes, aliens from outer space, man-made monsters and robots. They all have one property in common: they all have some human attributes. Usually, they are somewhat humanoid in a visual sense. Usually, they can communicate in a human language, and they have some recognisably human emotions. Mary Shelley's monster created by Frankenstein is one of the best and best-known examples. But we don't have to resort to fiction in our quest for answers to such questions. Real aliens have always been with us. They were here before us, and have been here ever since. We call these aliens animals.[1]

Animals are not like us. Yet we have persistently attributed human-like qualities to them, in our ordinary thought, in folklore, in any number of stories. This is pure myth. We have no sound basis for assuming animals have minds, let alone if their supposed minds are anything like human ones. Fundamentally we don't know anything about them. We don't know because animals are aliens. To understand the mind of an animal, if it has one at all, we would have to understand an alien mind.

In this book we will look at animal behaviour and at robot behaviour. We will ask what it might mean for an animal or robot to have a mind. We will ask how we might come to know whether a particular animal or robot could or might have a mind. We will ask whether it makes any sense for us to wonder whether animals or robots have minds like human minds. We will ask whether we are capable of imagining what an animal or robot mind might be like.

I thank Penelope Farmer for setting the tone of this book. I also thank Michel Cabanac, Matthew Elton, Latha Menon, Susan Prospere, and Colin Tudge for their helpful comments on the first draft.

MINDLESS MACHINES

In this chapter we look at the behaviour of some simple robots, from both a scientific and a philosophical viewpoint. Although such robots, unlike our traffic-police-robot, are very simple machines they can exhibit quite complex behaviour. The interpretation of such behaviour depends very much on the viewpoint of the observer. From a scientific viewpoint, if the design of the robot is well understood its behaviour will be no surprise. From the viewpoint of naïve observers, however, the behaviour may seem baffling, mysterious, and much more complicated than it really is.

The interpretation of the behaviour of other beings is commonly influenced either by inside knowledge or by lack of it. The engineer, who has inside knowledge about the design and capabilities of a robot, and our naïve observer, who does not, tend to interpret its behaviour quite differently. It is just the same with observations of animal behaviour, which the expert—the biologist—may interpret in one way, the non-biologist in another. A classic example occurred in 1961 when a chimpanzee called Ham was launched into space, on a suborbital trip, from the USA. On the space capsule's return to Earth Ham was photographed grinning widely, and the press concluded that he had enjoyed his trip. However, a young zoologist, Gilbert Manley, who had studied the facial expressions of chimpanzees, concluded that Ham had found the experience very frightening.

Although none of this may seem surprising, it does have philosophical implications for our quest into the alien mind. Historically, interpretations of animal behaviour have varied greatly over the ages, whereas interpretation of human behaviour has been rooted in folk psychology, and has probably changed relatively little. Folk psychology is a philosophers' term for the subject matter of our everyday understanding of one another in psychological or mental terms, such as 'I believe, I want, or I intend something.' In contrast to scientific experimental psychology, folk psychology is usually regarded as a theory that we know implicitly, and that we use to predict the behaviour of others. For example, if I see my spouse putting on a coat, picking up an umbrella, and making for the door, I may think (or say) that my spouse wants to go out and believes that it might rain. If I see my dog wagging its tail and following my spouse, I may think (or say) that the dog believes that it is to be taken for a walk. My thoughts about my spouse are perfectly normal interpretations of behaviour in folk psychology terms. It may be true that my spouse really does believe that it might rain. On the other hand, my thoughts about the my dog's behaviour are somewhat inappropriate. I may assume that my dog is capable of having beliefs, and this assumption may be based upon a particular *philosophical stance* that I take towards the possibility of canine beliefs, but it is more likely to be based on nothing more than attribution by me of human characteristics to my dog.

Let me introduce you to my dog. Along with our traffic-robot she will figure in this book from time to time. Named appropriately 'Border', she is a continuously busy border terrier of very strong character, addicted to digging up mice and lizards—and in the process gardens—to her own timetable rather than her owner's. This leads to altercations not just between her and me but also at times between me, my neighbours, and my spouse, who cannot understand why, even while she is yelling her name, Border continues to head—busily—in the opposite direction. Border will figure as representative of what we usually call an intelligent animal. We will interpret her behaviour in various (alternative) ways, as the occasion arises. Whether she is capable of having beliefs will in particular be a matter for discussion. 'From my naïve perspective,' says my maddened—and unashamedly anthropomorphic—spouse, when we invoke the issue, 'she certainly seems to have motives. I wouldn't put it past her to have beliefs.'

It is not only the behaviour of animals that gets interpreted in such ways. I was in a laboratory in Bristol one day where a student of mine was doing an experiment with some simple mobile robots engaged in building a wall. Some members of the public had been invited by a colleague to have a look around. They were fascinated by the robots and spent a long time watching them and talking about them amongst themselves. It was quite clear to me that they were interpreting the robots' behaviour in terms of folk psychology. To them, the robots were like little people cooperating in building a wall. They asked how the robots were communicating with each other. When told that there was no communication between the robots they were incredulous. In other words, to the naïve observer, the behaviour of very simple machines no less than that of animals can appear quite sophisticated; it, too, may be viewed anthropomorphically.[1]

3

This can be illustrated by considering *automata*, an early example of robot technology. 'Automata' are machines with concealed motive power and life-like actions. Historically, they took the form of a doll or animal, operated by clockwork and performing particular operations in a life-like manner. An example might be a wind-up tin soldier that walks along and beats on a drum. Another seemingly more complex one would be the clockwork doll in the ballet 'Coppelia', a doll so lifelike men thought she was human and fell in love with her. This kind of automaton has a fixed behavioural routine that proceeds unconditionally once started. It has what zoologists call a fixed action pattern. An example of a fixed action pattern from human behaviour is swallowing. Another would be laughing when tickled. Tickling triggers a series of actions over which the actor has little or no control, the kind performed automatically following an external or internal stimulus.

Other more complex automata are capable of acting conditionally. That is, when in one state they behave in one way, and when in another state they behave in a different way. The change in state may result from having accomplished a particular activity. For example, a car-washing machine starts off in a particular state, and consequently starts a particular behavioural routine, such as spraying and brushing the car from front to back. Having finished this routine, the machine arrives in a different state, and starts a new routine. Depending upon the type of car, the machine is able to vary its behaviour to some extent, each variation triggered by a change in state.

We can improve behavioural flexibility by providing an automaton with sensors. This is particularly so for mobile automata. Thus a toy clockwork mouse has a fixed action pattern and will run along the ground so long as it does not collide with something. Watching such a toy one day I concluded that if the mouse could sense obstacles and avoid them, then it could have an uninterrupted run. With the help of an engineering colleague, I made a mobile robot from a radio-controlled toy car to see if I could improve on the toymaker's product.

At the front, the robot had a single ultrasound sensor removed from a widely available room-measuring device that provided information about the distance of an object directly in front of the robot. This was the only sensory information available to it. Even so it was now able to move around at high speed without hitting objects. How was it done? Firstly, by making the speed of the robot proportional to the distance to an obstacle: the robot slows down as it approaches an object. Secondly, by making the angle of the front wheels proportional to the distance to an obstacle: the nearer it gets to an object, the more sharply the robot turns. Thirdly, if the robot is turning to avoid an object but the distance is getting smaller, then the robot must be turning the wrong way. By changing the direction of steering when the distance is getting smaller, but not when it is getting larger, the robot turns away from the obstacle. To summarise, the robot is able to avoid objects at high speed by following the three simple rules described above. The robot is purely reactive in the sense that its behaviour is determined solely by reaction to external stimuli. The robot's place in the world at any instant ('its situation') determines its behaviour. Finally, the robot follows rules, but this does not mean that it looks up the rules and then follows them (which would be explicit rule-following). The rules are embedded in the robot circuitry, so the rule following is implicit.

This simple example illustrates two important features of simple mobile automata. Firstly, they are *reactive*. That is, all their behaviour can be accounted for in terms of information they gain from the outside world. In contradistinction to pre-programmed robots which simply ignore the world (like the clockwork drummer-boy and the doll Coppelia) and motivated robots whose response to the world is partly determined by their internal state (as we shall see

5

later), the behaviour of reactive robots consists of a series of responses to external stimuli. Secondly, they are *situated*. Situated
actions are actions taken in the context of particular concrete
circumstances.[2] The concrete circumstances partly determine the
action to be taken, and largely determine the consequences of the
action. For example, in an automatic car, gear changes are entirely
situated, because they are determined by the current circumstances
relating to the engine revs, speed, etc., and they are carried out
automatically as circumstances dictate.

The situatedness of animal behaviour is well illustrated by the
behaviour of ants and termites. When termites start to build a nest
they modify their local environment by making mud balls, each of
which is impregnated by a pheromone. Initially, the termites deposit
their mud balls at random. The probability of depositing one
increases as the sensed concentration of pheromone increases.
After the first few random placements, the other termites, responding to the pheromone, tend to deposit their mud balls in the same
place, so that small columns are formed. The pheromone from
neighbouring columns causes the tops of columns to lean towards
neighbouring columns. Eventually the tops meet, forming
arches, the basic building units of the nest. This kind of process is
called *stigmergy*. The principle of stigmergy was first discovered
by the French biologist Pierre-Paul Grasse in 1959. It is essentially
the production of behaviour that is a direct consequence of
the effects produced in the local environment by previous behaviour. In the case of termites, the effects produced by previous
behaviour are indicated by the pheromones. As other stigmergic
processes come into play, involving water vapour, carbon dioxide
concentrations, and the presence of the queen, the whole complex
nest structure is produced. This may include the royal cell, brood
nurseries, air conditioning, larders, and communication and
foraging tunnels.

Once, when staying at the University of Bielefeld in Germany, I wandered into a laboratory where Owen Holland and Ralph Beckers were involved in an experiment with three small mobile robots. These robots were pushing around a number of small pucks (actually wax night-lights), apparently at random. As I watched, the robots gradually gathered the scattered pucks into a single close-packed group. This experiment was repeated many times, and whatever the starting configuration, and whatever the number of robots (1 to 5), the result was always the same—the pucks ended up in a single group. How was it done?

Each battery-powered robot had a motor-powered wheel at the mid-point of each side, with a single castor wheel at the front. This arrangement allows the robot to move forwards or backwards in a straight or curved trajectory, and to turn on the spot. Each robot carried an aluminium forward-facing C-shaped horizontal scoop with which it could push small objects along the floor. The robots were equipped with two IR (infrared) sensors for obstacle avoidance, and a microswitch (a very small switch) that was activated by the scoop when an object above a certain weight was pushed by the scoop.

Typically, the robots are placed in an arena where there are circular pucks that the robots can push around. Three pucks are required to trigger the microswitch. The robots move in a straight line if they are receiving no sensory information. On detecting an obstacle (with the IR sensors), the robot executes obstacle avoidance behaviour of turning on the spot away from the obstacle and through a random angle. Now free of the obstacle, the robot moves off in a straight line in the new direction. If the robot is pushing pucks when it encounters an obstacle, the pucks will be retained by the scoop throughout the turn. When the scoop contains three or more pucks, their weight activates the microswitch, and this triggers puck-dropping behaviour. This consists of backing up for one second, thus releasing the pucks from the scoop, and then executing a turn through a random angle. Matters are so arranged that the obstacle-avoidance behaviour has priority over the puck-dropping behaviour.

The results of experiments with these robots show that eighty pucks, initially set out in a grid pattern, always end up in a single clump, irrespective of the number of robots present in the arena. Each experiment has three phases. At the beginning the pucks are not touching each other, and the robot typically moves forward collecting pucks into its scoop one at a time. When three have been collected the robot drops them, leaving them in a cluster of three, and moves off in another direction. After a while, the pucks are in small clusters which cannot be pushed around. In the second phase, a robot removes one or two pucks from a cluster by striking the cluster at an angle with the scoop. The pucks removed in this way are added to other clusters when the robot collides with them. Some clusters grow rapidly in this phase, and in due course there will be a small number of relatively large clusters. The third and most protracted phase consists of the occasional removal of a puck or two from one of the large clusters, and the addition of these pucks to another cluster, or sometimes to the same cluster. The process eventually results in the formation of a single cluster. In every case, however many robots are involved, the experiment begins with the pucks set out in a grid pattern, and ends with them in a single cluster. To the naïve onlooker, the behaviour of the robots seems purposive. The robots work on the grid pattern, transforming it into a single cluster of pucks, an obvious and easily identifiable endpoint.

This is an example of stigmergic behaviour in simple mobile robots. In principle it is the same kind of behaviour found in termites, ants, bees, and wasps. Each robot (or animal) follows a few very simple rules. In an appropriate situation (e.g. a smooth floor and the presence of pucks) the environment is transformed by the *collective behaviour* of the robots (or animals). Collective behaviour is essentially self-organising, and there is no direct communication between the participants. There is, however, indirect communication via the environment, in the sense that the environment is used as a kind of external memory. One robot (or animal) alters the environment in such a way (e.g. by injecting a mudball with a pheromone, or leaving three pucks in a particular place) that the behaviour of another robot (or the same robot on another occasion) is affected. The whole scenario hangs together in such a way that progress is inevitably made towards the endpoint.

A number of types of stigmergic behaviour in mobile robots, including collecting objects, sorting different kinds of objects, and building a wall in the manner of ant behaviour, have been demonstrated.[3] In all cases, a few very simple rules and an equally simple repertoire of behaviour is all that is required.

The experiment with puck-pushing robots is instructive in many ways. Although the behaviour of the robots seems haphazard, it also seems purposive. The robots are persistent, and they make steady progress towards an end-configuration that is relatively stable. But what do we mean by saying the behaviour is purposive? What is usually meant by this is that the behaviour is adapted to some purpose or end. From the design point of view, we can see that the designer of the automata might have intended (for example) that the mobile robots push all the pucks into a single group. In the case of animals, we can imagine that natural selection acts as a designing agent of the stigmergic rules used by termites in building their nest. Finally, a human example of stigmergic behaviour could be my spouse's diary note 'Take Border to vet', which acts as a kind of external memory and influences her future behaviour, provided she consults her diary at the appropriate time.

My spouse makes the entry in the diary on purpose, knowing that she is likely to forget about the vet. But what about the robots?

Can they be said to do things on purpose? So far we have used the word purpose to stand for what biologists usually call *function*, that is, the role of the structure or behaviour in question. In the case of a naturally evolved item, the function is the contribution to *fitness* of that item, as we see in Chapter 2. In the case of a man-made item, the function has to do with the designer's intentions (see above). When we talk about a person doing something 'on purpose' we usually mean that it is intentional—the result of some mental activity. Here we are referring, not to the role of the item, but to its mechanism.

At this point we need to investigate the precise implications of a robot's (or animal's) achievement of a goal or end purpose: amassing pucks, building a termite mound, taking dog to the vet; asking, in other words, what such seemingly purposive behaviour implies about the inner workings of the agent in question. We need first to distinguish between different kinds of goal-attaining behaviour.

Firstly, a *goal-achieving* system is one that can 'recognise' the goal once it is arrived at (or at least change the agent's behaviour when it reaches the goal), but the process of arriving at the goal is largely determined by environmental circumstances. Implicit recognition of the goal is sufficient. For example, our puck-pushing robots are equipped with a microswitch that is activated by the scoop when three or more pucks are pushed. The microswitch triggers the puck-dropping behaviour. So the microswitch provides a representation of the pucks that is implicit, and the designer has not provided the robot with any kind of explicit recognition system. The use made of the information provided by the microswitch is entirely procedural, in that the information is instrumental in changing the behaviour of the robot, and is not put to any other use. In other words, the information provided by the microswitch is part of a fixed procedure that leads to the robot changing its behaviour. This satisfies one criterion for goal-achieving behaviour. The second criterion of goal-achieving behaviour is the absence of processes within the robot that guide it towards the goal (of puck-dropping behaviour). The robot arrives in a situation of having three pucks in its scoop in an entirely haphazard manner. It switches among its three possible activities (straight run, obstacle avoidance, and drop pucks) on the basis of encountering environmental situations outside its control.

Goal-achieving behaviour in humans is probably more common-place than we tend to imagine. Consider the collector of old matchboxes, or any other artefact with a long and varied history. The collector does not deliberately set out to search for match-boxes, but relies upon serendipity—the habit of making sudden and unexpected discoveries by accident. The goal is achieved by hap-pening to be in the right place at the right time, and recognising a desirable matchbox for what it is.

Secondly, a *goal-seeking* system is one designed to seek a goal without the goal being represented within the system. Many phys-ical systems are goal-seeking in this sense. For example, a marble rolling around in a bowl will always come to rest in the same place. The marble appears to be goal-seeking, because the forces acting on it are so arranged that the marble is 'pulled' towards the goal. In the case of the puck-pushing robots, each experiment ends with the pucks being in a single cluster. The robots have no information about the existence of this cluster. They cannot distinguish between a cluster of three pucks and a cluster of thirty pucks. What the robots actually do is carry on as usual. Consequently they occasion-ally clip off a puck from the group, carry it about a bit, and then put it back again. From the robot's point of view, there is no represen-tation of the goal-to-be-achieved. From the point of view of the designer, however, the system is goal-seeking by virtue of the fact that the designer provides both the robots and their environment, just as the designer provides both the marble and the bowl. In the case of natural systems, the designer (evolution) provides an animal that is adapted to live in a particular type of environment. A simple example is habitat selection by the common woodlouse (*Porcellio scaber*). These animals move about in an irregular manner, but their movements are more rapid in dry than in moist air, with the result that the animals spend more time in damp places, thus achieving a very simple form of habitat selection.

Finally, a *goal-directed* system involves a representation of the goal-to-be-achieved, which is instrumental in guiding the behaviour. The term goal-directed applies to that behaviour (of a human, animal, or machine) directed by reference to an internal (implicit or explicit) representation of the goal-to-be-achieved. By directed we mean that the behaviour is actively controlled by reference to the (internally represented) goal. The behaviour will be subject to outside disturbances that will usually be corrected for. Thus by directed we mean that the behaviour is guided or steered towards the goal, despite disturbances.

For a robot to be goal-directed, it would have to have a representation of the state of affairs that would pertain if the goal were to be achieved. In the case of the puck-robots this would have to involve a representation of the pucks in a single cluster. These robots do not have such a representation, so their behaviour cannot be goal-directed. Of course, we could imagine a robot that did have goal-directed behaviour. For such a robot success would be signalled by comparison of the representation of the goal-to-be-achieved and the actual state of affairs. Any mismatch between the two is called the error. When the error has been reduced to zero, the goal has been achieved. Engineers call this type of system a *feedback control system*, and these are often employed in machines designed to track, or home-in on, desirable goals. Examples include guided missiles, radar tracking-systems, and thermostats. Thus a thermostat has a representation (often in the form of a dial with numbers on it) of the temperature desired by the user, and the temperature to be achieved by the device.

Now we can see that although the behaviour of robots or animals may seem purposive, it may not actually be purposive in the sense that it is deliberate, done on purpose, or intentional. Human behaviour can be said to be intentional when it involves some representation of a goal that is instrumental in guiding behaviour. Thus, if I have a mental picture of the desirable arrangement of books on my shelf, and if this mental representation guides my behaviour in placing books on the shelf, then I can be said to place them intentionally. If, however, I place the books haphazardly, or on the basis of simple habit rules, then my arrangement of the books may not be intentional. When my dog Border enters the kitchen, she invariably heads straight for the cat's food dish. Is this behaviour intentional? For it to be intentional in the normal common-sense meaning of the term, Border would have to have a mental representation of the cat's bowl as a desirable goal. However, it is not difficult to explain Border's behaviour in various other ways that do not involve mental representation, and therein lies the problem. If Border has a mind at all, Border has an alien mind. How could we discover whether Border has mental representations?

Future Robots

In this millennium we humans will be living with robots, and robots will be living with us. What will these robots be like? At present it is possible to buy toy robots and domestic robots that vacuum the house or cut the lawn. In the next decade other types of robot will come on to the market, maybe robot porters that carry luggage, or robot car park attendants. When motorcars first became available they were a novelty, but in time they became a necessity. Just as the motorcar evolved slowly, over decades, so will the robots. The mechanical typewriter evolved over decades, but now it is virtually extinct. Robots may follow the same pattern, or they may become indispensable. It is difficult to foretell.

The evolution of robots will be similar to that of animals. They will be designed according to whatever is best for their own ecological circumstances. These robots will be bought and sold and will therefore have to compete in the marketplace against other robots and against humans willing to carry out the same tasks. This ecological competition will lead to the evolution of certain attributes, among them robustness, speed of reaction, self-sufficiency, and autonomy.

The most useful robots of the future, the kind people would want to buy, would have to be both self-sufficient and autonomous to some degree. Only such robots would be able to carry out tasks that humans do not want to carry out. The current idea of a robot as a mindless slave will not really cut ice in the future marketplace. Such robots exist today (car-washing machines, assembly-robots, etc.), as do human-guided robots used in sewers and nuclear power stations. These will be superseded by robots able to take control of their own behaviour, so that we need not concern ourselves about them. They will carry out tasks, such as underwater survey, that are dangerous for people, and they will do so in a competent, efficient, and reassuring manner.

To some extent, some such tasks have traditionally been performed by animals. We place our trust in horses, dogs, cats, and homing pigeons to perform tasks that would be difficult for us to perform as well if at all. Horses pull vehicles; dogs retrieve birds, dig out foxes, kill rats, and find criminals and drugs; cats catch mice; homing pigeons carry messages. We recognise that some degree of autonomy is necessary for these agents to perform on our behalf. We do not worry about it, except when it becomes a nuisance ('Your dog!' cries my spouse; in her view Border has altogether too much autonomy). Should we worry about autonomous robots? To answer this kind of question we need to know what autonomy implies.

Autonomy implies freedom from outside control. There are three main types of freedom relevant to robots. One is freedom from outside control of energy supply. Most current robots run on batteries that must be replaced or recharged by people. Self-refuelling robots would have energy autonomy. Another is freedom of choice of activity. An automaton lacks such freedom, because either it follows a strict routine or it is entirely reactive. A robot that has alternative possible activities, and the freedom to decide which to do, has motivational autonomy. Thirdly, there is freedom of 'thought'. A robot that has the freedom to think up better ways of doing things may be said to have mental autonomy.

First let us look at *energy autonomy*. Robots require energy, and we usually think of this as being supplied by their human owners. But in the future, if they are to carry out such tasks as planetary and deep-sea exploration they will need to be energy self-sufficient. This development, besides making them more useful and marketable will make them more like animals.

Energy autonomy concerns the ability of the robot to obtain its own energy. The first person to demonstrate that this could be done was Grey Walter in 1950. His robot was a simple electro-mechanical device on wheels looking rather like a tortoise in that it had a shell. It was equipped with a single photoreceptive 'eye' that continually scanned the environment, enabling the robot to exhibit both positive and negative phototaxis (moving towards or away from light). Whenever the robot shell hit against an obstacle, a switch was activated, and this triggered reflex obstacle avoidance behaviour that overrode the response to light during its perambulations. Thus, if the path towards a light source was obstructed, the robot was able to circumvent the obstacle. The robot was attracted to light of moderate intensity, but avoided bright light. Consequently it tended to hover near a light source without approaching too close. As the battery ran down, the balance between positive and negative phototaxis shifted, and the robot became increasingly attracted to bright light. The robot had a 'hutch' or 'kennel' in its vicinity with a bright light inside. When low on fuel, it was attracted by the bright light, and entered the hutch where its battery was automatically recharged. My one-time colleague Owen Holland resurrected the original robot, and also made a replica.[4] He was able to demonstrate that a range of activities resulted from interaction of the two basic activities, phototaxis and obstacle avoidance, including self-recharging of the on-board batteries.

Energy sources provided by humans are a feasible proposition for robots and animals that inhabit a peopled environment. But the prime future scenario for robots—in outer space, for instance—involves environments in which human-supplied power would be uneconomic. So how could robots obtain energy by their own efforts? Robots that use solar power have been devised, and these are readily available in kit form. They have the advantage that the energy they obtain is readily transformed into an electrical supply of energy to the robot. However, there are many environments in which the sunlight is insufficient for this type of power. Plants obtain their energy from the sun, and they can do this without having to move around, but plants are limited to microenvironments that supply them with their vital resources. Although some robot tasks, such as cutting grass, make solar power a viable proposition there are many that do not. Robots required to move around and through a variety of environments must be more like animals than plants. They must forage for their fuel.

Natural selection favours efficient foragers, and most animals are extremely adept at searching for, and harvesting, food. Different species employ different foraging methods, some searching for food, some lying in wait for prey, some grazing, etc. Thus some species have a high rate of energy expenditure while foraging, but spend little time foraging, while other species have a low rate of energy expenditure, but spend a lot of time foraging. The rate at which energy is obtained depends upon the availability and accessibility of the food. These determine the rate of return on foraging. Animals usually consume their food on the spot, but if an animal has a nest, or comes from a colony, it may take food home. Such animals usually make an outward journey, spend some time searching, and then make a return journey. This type of foraging is called central place foraging.

The problem for robots is that sources of energy such as plant and animal organic matter pose the problem of converting the source energy into a form that can be used by the robot. Let us briefly consider some of the main issues. A robot needs to be mobile in order to forage for food. As with animals, the robot must either consume its food on the spot or take it home. The food supply may only be available at certain limited times and locations, depending upon climate, time of day, seasons, and so forth. Much depends upon the nature of the food. Static vegetation necessitates a foraging strategy different from that required for the hunting of mobile prey. Obtaining food is one thing; processing it is another. By whatever means the food is found it has thereafter to be converted and stored into a usable form; the conversion process constituting some kind of artificial metabolism. One could envisage a system incorporating the elements of a mobile robot and an energy conversion unit. They could be combined in a single robot or kept separate so that the robot brings its food back to the 'digester'. Such a robot would exhibit central place foraging.

An example is the 'slugbot', devised by a group of scientists in Bristol.[5] They decided to employ a strategy similar to that of leaf-cutter ants. These ants bring back leaf cuttings to a 'garden' where the organic material is converted into a fungus that the ants eat. Similarly the proposed robots would forage for organic material and bring it to a central 'digester' which converts the bio-mass into electricity to power the robots. The scientists chose slugs as the robot prey for the following reasons: the prey should be sufficiently plentiful and be of a sufficient energy density to justify the energy expenditure involved in searching, catching, transporting, and converting to usable fuel. The prey should not be capable of rapid movement since this would require the robot to expend considerable energy in catching the prey. Its control should also conform to ethical considerations. As a slow-moving invertebrate pest abundant on UK agricultural land—especially the slug *Deroceras reticulatum*—and already subject to lethal control measures, slugs fit both criteria perfectly. They represent a considerable threat to vegetation, doing most damage to crops requiring a well-cultivated seedbed, such as potatoes or wheat. UK farmers spend over £20 m per year on chemical measures to control them.

The slugbot is equipped with a long arm, with a grabber at the end. In the 'palm' of the grabber is a camera by means of which the robot can detect the presence of slugs. The robot's grabber picks up slugs and deposits them in its 'pocket'. When the robot needs to recharge its on-board battery, it homes in on the recharging station and docks. While it is recharging its battery, it unloads the slugs that it has collected. These enter a 'digestive system' that is part-and-parcel of the charging station. The product of digestion is a bio-gas that is fed into a fuel cell,[6] which produces the electrical energy that ultimately powers the robot.

The slugbot detects slugs visually using a low-powered (CMOS) camera mounted inside the grabber pointing through the fingers. The grabber is maintained at an optimal distance of 15 cm above the soil and perpendicular to the surface. This is realised by employing a passive gimbal system at the grabber 'wrist'. The gimbal can also be locked to prevent any unnecessary swinging. The robot sweeps its arm low over the ground searching for slugs on the surface. Even under the benign conditions of sparse crops in seed beds the detection of slugs represents a difficult practical problem. Slugs need to be differentiated from non-slug materials such as leaves, stones, and soil lumps. Since slugs are mainly active at night, the scientists developed a simple method of extracting slug images from the background by employing a form of filtering. An image is recorded with red light, and the camera is fitted with a matching red filter. Under these conditions the background material of vegetation and soil appear relatively much darker than the slug body of *D. reticulatum*. When the slugbot catches a slug it puts it in its pocket, a vessel containing water. When it has a pocketful of slugs, or when foraging in a particular area is no longer productive, the slugbot homes in on its digester-station and unloads its harvest. This foraging strategy means that the robot must operate within a particular territory, always keeping within range of its home base.

Other energy autonomous robots are under development[7] for deployment on land, in water, and in the air. Many of these use fuel cells. Such robots will be able to roam far from their home base, foraging for organic matter and digesting it on the move. All these robots will have one feature in common, namely a degree of motivational autonomy that enables them to decide by themselves when to do what.

We now come to *motivational autonomy*. The energy self-sufficient robot must have the freedom to utilise behaviour that is in its own vital interest. For example, a robot able to obtain its own energy by visiting some kind of recharging station must also be able to decide by itself when to discontinue its current behaviour and commence the foraging behaviour that leads to recharging. Ideally, the robot would base this decision partly upon information about its own on-board energy level, and partly upon other considerations, such as its current motivation for work, the likely time required for foraging for fuel, or other motivational alternatives. The ability of a robot to do this is an aspect of its motivational autonomy.

Autonomy implies freedom from outside control. The philosopher Daniel Dennett asks, 'What is control, and what is its relation to causation and determinism? Curiously, this obviously important question has scarcely been addressed by philosophers.'[8] In ordinary terms, he goes on, 'A controls B if and only if the relation between A and B is such that A can drive B into whichever of B's normal range of states A wants B to be in .... For something to be a controller its states must include desires—or something "like" desires—about the states of something (else).'

For example, for a boy to control a radio-guided airplane, the boy must want the plane to move in a particular way. However, to control the plane, the boy must also have some knowledge about the system (the radio-controller and the plane) and the ability to operate the controls. Moreover, the boy cannot control the plane without observing it. In some cases (for technical reasons) complete control is not possible, often because adequate observation of the effects of attempted control is not available to the would-be controller.

Motivational autonomy implies a degree of self-control. It follows from the above argument that a robot with self-control must have some motivation. That is, it must 'want' to move from its current state X to a new state Y. It is this self-motivation that makes the robot, or animal, relatively uncontrollable by outside agents. Thus the slugbot must want to catch slugs. It must decide for itself when to do so, and when to return home to deposit the slugs caught and to recharge its on-board battery.

For a robot to have motivation, it must have internal states capable of influencing its behaviour. This type of robot is not a pre-programmed automaton, nor is its behaviour entirely reactive. *Motivation* is usually defined as a set of internal reversible processes that influence behaviour, in contradistinction to learning which is irreversible. In animals, motivation covers such processes as hunger, thirst, sleep and sexual arousal. In robots it may include the state of the on-board energy store (usually a battery), the internal temperature (especially in aquatic robots), or the amount of work accomplished (relevant to the task that the robot is designed to accomplish). Thus the slugbot would keep a record of the number of slugs caught per foraging trip.

An animal or robot will usually have an overall motivational state relevant to a number of different activities that cannot be performed simultaneously. Thus an animal may be somewhat sleepy, somewhat thirsty, and somewhat hungry, all at the same time. Clearly it cannot sleep, drink, and forage simultaneously. These activities are said to be incompatible. Therefore, the animal must somehow make some decision about which activity to perform. My dog Border, for instance, may have to choose between chasing a lizard she has unearthed and responding to my calling 'time for a walk'. Her 'decision' hinges on whether her desire for a walk overrides her tendency to chase small moving animals. In robotics research, the mechanism that makes such decisions is called the *action-selection* mechanism. This is often a distinct mechanism that does the weighing up. In animal behaviour research, however, action selection is not usually seen as the role of a distinct mechanism, but as the outcome of the balancing act carried out by the motivational system as a whole. Research on action selection in both animals and robots has led to a variety of schemes, some of which perform better than others. The aim of such research is to find that scheme that performs best as judged by success criteria. What the success criteria should be we discuss in Chapter 2. For the present we will call them the costs and benefits.

Any course of action followed by the animal or robot has consequences, not only in terms of costs and benefits, but also in terms of changes in the state of the animal or robot. All behaviour depletes the on-board energy resources, and may also alter internal

21

temperature, etc. Moreover, doing one activity implies that other activities are postponed, and this in itself will cause changes in state. For example, sleeping animals do not feed, and grow hungrier while they sleep. Clearly, if there are five 'jobs to be done', the order in which they are done and the timing involved will have a consequential effect upon the state of the robot or animal.

Not only does a particular activity have costs and benefits, but being in a particular state has associated costs. It is more costly to be very hungry than to be moderately hungry, because there is a risk that when the time comes to feed, food may not be available. This type of risk is particularly important for refuelling robots. If the robot refuels too often it is wasting time that could better be spent on other activities. If it sets out to obtain fuel too late, then it may encounter unusual obstacles, and run out of fuel. The situation is much the same for a motorist. Stopping at every gas station is a time-wasting policy, and waiting until the warning light comes on is a risky policy. What then is the best policy? The answer depends partly upon the environmental situation. If refuelling stations are open round the clock and regularly spaced, a risk-prone policy will pay. If they are irregularly spaced and sometimes shut, a risk-averse policy is better. Out of all these considerations comes the notion of an optimum policy that offers the most beneficial trade-off amongst the alternatives. Such notions have been much employed in animal behaviour research, and are also being applied in robotics.

So far we have discussed energy autonomy and motivational autonomy, but what about mental autonomy? The whole issue of autonomy raises the possibility of an animal—or robot—becoming too autonomous. Border as I have indicated has often shown signs of this—to the irritation of her owner and his spouse. As robots become more complex autonomy will be ever more of an issue in them. The possibility of turned-autonomous robots taking control away from their human creators has already been addressed by writers of science fiction, as with the computer HAL imagined by Arthur C. Clarke and made still more famous by Stanley Kubrick's iconic film of Clarke's iconic book, *2001: a Space Odyssey.*

Some of the issues relating to autonomy will be discussed in the next chapter. These are the issues relating to automata, machines designed by humans that are constrained by the rules that govern their behaviour. As we shall see in Chapter 2, it is not difficult for the designer to place limits upon the energy and motivational autonomy of such machines. When it comes to mental autonomy, however, the matter becomes more serious. The serious—and philosophically most challenging—questions involved will have to be held over till towards the end of the book. Not till then will we seek to discover whether or how robots can be endowed with mental attributes, and thereafter try to determine what 'mental autonomy' might entail. All I can say for now is this: that without such an endowment, machines complex enough to declare their independence, like Clarke and Kubrick's HAL, must remain in the world of fiction.

2

DESIGN OF ANIMALS AND ROBOTS

Suppose that we are going to design a robot, not a toy robot, but an 'intelligent' robot that stands a chance of surviving in the real world. Toy robots include those developed by scientists for research purposes, and those sold on the open market for entertainment. To survive in the real world in the long term, a robot would have to do something useful, so that people would want to buy it. In this chapter we will explore principles of design that apply to both animals and robots, and demonstrate that fairly complex, animal-like, behaviour can be achieved by a robot that has no mental capabilities whatsoever. In other words we are looking for a design that is the most basic design capable of doing the job. Our design is an imaginative fantasy that will help us to understand the parallels between robot design and animal evolution.

Ideally, our robot would cost little, be low maintenance, and be cheap to run. So what could our robot do for a living? One possibility, and one that suits our purposes, is to design a robotic security guard that patrols the grounds of a hotel or hospital, keeps an eye on the car park, etc. Our robot would have to be good enough to compete with human security guards and with guard dogs.

Obviously, a robotic security guard would have to be mobile, and would consume quite a lot of energy. Where is this energy to come from? Solar power is a possibility, but it would probably not be sufficient, except in a very sunny location. Mains electric power would be easy to arrange, but it would be expensive. Hotels and hospitals, on the other hand, the environments in which the robot is designed to live, have one thing in common: they produce a lot of kitchen waste. Neither dogs nor humans can be run on anything as cheap as kitchen waste. A robot able to take its energy from that might not only be effective but cost-effective too. You might think that a better alternative might be to sell the electricity generated from kitchen waste directly to the grid, and to power the robot from the mains. The advantages in having the robot powered directly from kitchen waste are twofold: the robot will not be affected by power cuts, or by changes in policy relating to the supply of electricity to the grid. We want our robot to be independent of such matters.

But first, in order to obtain energy from kitchen waste, our robot would have to be able to digest it. This would require a sizeable digester, kept either on-board the robot or at the robot's 'home'. An on-board digester would mean that the robot would have to collect the kitchen waste from a distribution point, store it somewhere on its body, and gradually feed the food through the digester. Such a robot would be heavy, large, and cumbersome. Like an elephant, it would require a lot of energy. The other alternative would see the waste delivered directly into the robot's home or 'kitchen', where it is fed into the digester. The products of digestion are converted into electricity, and the robot is able to tap this source of energy to charge up its on-board batteries. Such a robot could be smaller, lighter, faster moving, and more economical than the elephant model. The digester requires a certain amount of maintenance (just as ours does), and this could be done by a human maintenance-man. However, there is no reason why the robot should not do the maintenance itself. In other words, the robot would go into its kitchen to do some 'cooking' now and then. The kitchen itself could run on solar power, making the robot energy self-sufficient, apart from the supply of kitchen waste. All is well, good, and practical as far as the domestic life of the robot is concerned.

But the more significant question remains: how would it manage the job? You might think that a robot security guard would be at a disadvantage from vandalism, from bravado, etc. But do not underestimate a robotic security guard; it has certain advantages. It can film any incident and transmit the record via satellite without showing any sign of this communication. It can record what people say and answer back. It can produce a threatening and frightening display, just like a disturbed animal. It can call for help.

Our robot will be somewhat like a domestic animal. It will do useful work for its owner, and it will require low maintenance. Although it relies on humans for food, the management of the hospital or hotel always has to dispose of the kitchen waste somehow; the security robot is not really an extra burden. The designer of the robot on the other hand now must start worrying about details. What senses will the robot require? How will it get around? How will it manage its time? Such design problems are not unique to robots; they have always existed for animals, including ourselves, and looking at how animals are designed might be a useful place to start.

Animals have been designed by the process of natural selection throughout their evolutionary history, by techniques of domestication during the past 10,000 years, and more recently by direct genetic manipulation. In nature design is done by the process of natural selection, as first explained by Charles Darwin, and more recently illuminated by Richard Dawkins.[1] Natural selection acts upon the phenotype (bodily features and behaviour) of an individual. Its effectiveness in changing the nature of a population depends upon the degree to which the phenotypic character is controlled genetically. This, in turn, depends upon the genetic influence that an individual can exert upon the population as a whole. Obviously, an individual that has no offspring during its lifetime will exert no genetic influence upon the population, however great its ability to survive in the natural environment.

So we have two separate concepts to consider—survival value and reproductive success. These two are combined in the concept of fitness, a measure of the ability of genetic material to perpetuate itself during the course of evolution. Fitness thus depends not only on the ability of the individual to survive but also upon the animal's rate of reproduction and the viability of its offspring. The concept of fitness can be applied to individual genes by considering the survival of a particular gene in the gene pool from one generation to another. A gene that can enhance the reproductive success of the animal carrying it will thereby increase its representation in the gene pool. It could do this by influencing the animal's morphology, making it more likely to survive climatic and other hazards, or by influencing its behaviour and making it more successful in mating or in raising young. A gene that influences parental behaviour will probably be represented in some of the offspring, so that by facilitating parental care the gene itself is more likely to appear in other individuals. Indeed a situation could arise in which the gene could have a deleterious effect upon the animal carrying it, but increase its probability of survival in the offspring. An obvious example is a gene that leads the parent to endanger its own life in attempts to preserve the lives of its progeny.

27

William Hamilton was the first to enunciate the general principle that natural selection tends to maximise not individual fitness but inclusive fitness (i.e. an animal's fitness depends not only on its own reproductive success but also that of its kin).[2] The inclusive fitness of an individual depends upon the survival of its descendants and of its collateral relatives. Thus even if an animal has no offspring its inclusive fitness may not be zero, because its genes will be passed on by nieces, nephews, and cousins.

Inclusive fitness is the proper measure of biological success. All that matters is the representation of genes in the gene pool. It does not matter how the success is achieved. It can be achieved by honest toil, by sexual attractiveness, by exploiting other species. For example, one of the most successful North American species of the last century was the turkey. The turkey population grew enormously as a result of genetic changes that enabled turkeys to exploit humans.[3] Turkeys are now white rather than black. They mature much more quickly than they used to, and they are shorter and heavier in the body. The genetic changes that have been responsible for these adaptations have been crucial to the success of the turkey. If white colouration had not been genetically possible, the turkey would not look so attractive when plucked. If shortening of the body had not been genetically possible then a turkey of decent weight would not fit in the normal household oven. Over decades, turkeys have been selectively bred by humans to satisfy market demand.

You may think that this example is not valid because it involves humans as a selective agent. But such relationships between species are commonplace in the animal kingdom. For example, many types of ants farm aphids and milk them for their honeydew. Like turkeys, these aphids have undergone genetic adaptations to this role. Like turkeys, the aphids benefit from protection from predators. Some ants build structures to protect their aphids from the weather. They may move them to new pastures when necessary, and like turkeys, the aphid eggs may be specially cared for. Some ants even collect aphid eggs and bring them into their nest for the winter. From the biologist's point of view, there is no difference of principle between the two cases. Both turkeys and aphids have increased their fitness by genetically adapting to the symbiotic pressures of another species.

Success in animals is measured in terms of fitness. What about robots? In some respects robots already show design analogies with animals. Like other man-made machines, robots develop through a system of trial and error, research and development, and natural selection in the marketplace. In fact, the analogy between the life histories of animals and robots can be developed as a proper analogy in the mathematical sense.[4] Robots are products of human industry, and must be brought to market in the same way as other products. It may seem that the apparent analogy between the life histories of robot and animal is invalidated by the fact that the one is man-made and the other is the result of natural selection. However, what about the turkey? From a biological point of view, the turkey is a very successful species. Turkey genes have achieved a huge net rate of increase over many decades. From the human point of view the turkey is a successful product. Turkey sales have shown a huge net rate of increase over many decades. From the biological point of view, the fact that the turkey is farmed by another species is irrelevant. As shown, similar relationships exist throughout the animal kingdom. From the human point of view, the fact that the turkey is an animal is irrelevant. It is still a product that can be redesigned by careful selective breeding. Similar relationships have existed between man and other animals for centuries.[5]

The criteria for success of animals and robots are similar. Both survive, or not, in a competitive market. Both need to be robust, with reliable bodies and efficient movements. In addition, both need to be energy-efficient and to use their time efficiently. As we shall see, these market pressures lead to similar problems for the designer of the animal, and of the robot. Superficially, there are obvious differences between animals and animal-like robots. Their components and systems have different origins. Those of animals are evolved and grown organically, while those of robots are designed, engineered, and built, inorganically, by humans.[6]

In order to be successful—in life or the marketplace—animals and robots alike must be tailored to fit their ecological niche. There is no such thing as a generalised animal; there will never be successful generalised robots. Robots are always designed with a particular market—or function—in mind. Laboratory and toy robots are unable to provide for themselves, because they need to be under the direct control of their owner. Like animal parasites, they are dependent upon their host for food and for their reproduction. Office robots, on the other hand, are more like domestic animals. They depend upon humans for their energy source, but their reproduction is a function of their own behaviour. They must satisfy their owners through their own behaviour in order to achieve success, and make it worthwhile for the manufacturers to make more of them. Foraging robots are more like wild animals, obtaining energy by their own efforts in the natural environment. Their reproduction, however, is still dependent on pleasing their owners. Solar-powered robots are somewhat like plants. Their success is dependent upon the amount of energy they can gain from sunlight and on their efficiency in converting this into useful work. For example, solar-powered robotic lawn mowers busily cut grass when there is sufficient sunshine. At other times they become dormant, conserving energy. Because the robotic lawn mower lives outside and is always 'on the job', it does not matter that it is sometimes dormant. All that matters, to the owner, is whether the grass gets cut well and sufficiently often.

30

A robot that is self-sufficient must also be economically viable. For example, suppose that a robot is designed to fly in after a nuclear catastrophe and measure the radiation at various locations. This is a task that humans may be reluctant to do. However, it would be no good if the robot came back and reported that it had been so busy refuelling that it had no time to gather any data. As is the case with animals, self-sufficiency is largely a matter of balancing one vital requirement (e.g. foraging/refuelling) against another (e.g. reproductive activities/doing useful work). This balancing act is sometimes called behavioural stability.[7] It involves more than simply balancing one set of priorities against another. The important thing is that the robot (or animal) should not get into a situation of irrecoverable debt. That is, it must not incur any debts of vital resources that it cannot repay through its own behaviour. Such debts may include energy debts (i.e. the robot must not get itself into a position where it cannot replace lost energy) and task debts (i.e. the robot must be able to catch up with those aspects of its behaviour that are designed to please the customer).

So what about our security robot? It too must somehow balance conflicting priorities. On the one hand it must not run out of fuel; on the other hand it must attend to its security duties. To be truly self-sufficient our robot must exhibit both behavioural stability and market viability. Behavioural stability implies that the robot does not succumb to irrecoverable debt of any vital resource. The vital resources are those that enable the robot to carry out its design tasks, and may include energy, time, tools, etc. Our security robot must make sure that it has the time and energy to carry out its duties, and it must have the tools for the job maintained in proper working order. Irrecoverable debt is not simply a question of running out of a vital resource, but may include debts whose repayment engenders other debts. Behavioural instability will occur if the servicing of debts takes so much time and/or energy that our robot is unable to carry out its design tasks. Market viability amounts to pleasing the robot's employer. The employer will be satisfied if the robot is behaviourally stable, provided that the robot is also able to perform the tasks that it is designed to perform and provided also that the running costs are acceptable.

What our robot must do is trade-off between refuelling activities and activities designed to please the employer, which we may call working. To do this our robot must have some internal information (albeit implicit) about its on-board energy supply (lets call it E) and its work progress (this we will call M, because M can stand for memory of the amount of work done, merit points for work done, or money, or market viability). Each time the robot does a certain amount of work (i.e. fulfils part of the task that is useful to its employer) it earns a unit of M. To maintain viability, the robot must perform a basic cycle of activities, a cycle of work—find fuel— refuel. When working M is gained and E lost. In other words, by working, the robot earns units of M, but loses energy E. At some point the robot must break off work and go to find fuel. Foraging for fuel, or in the case of our robot, cooking up fuel in its kitchen, also leads to a reduction of E, but what about M? Should the robot gain or lose M while foraging for fuel? (This is a bit like asking whether a human worker should be paid during the lunch break). The answer to this question depends upon the attitude of the employer of the robot. What M represents is the utility of the robot's work from the point of view of the employer.

There are three basic views that an employer could take:

(a) If the employer is primarily concerned about the robot spending time on activities that are not productive, then M should decline whenever the robot is not working.
(b) If the employer is concerned about energy expenditure on activities that are not productive, then the robot should be designed so that M declines during foraging, but remains static during refuelling.

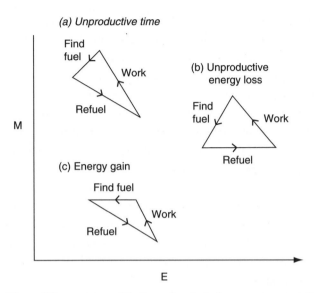

Fig. 1. Three different types of basic cycle, plotted as energy spent E versus material gained M. (a) M declines throughout all unproductive time. (b) M declines only when there is unproductive energy loss. (c) M declines when the robot is refuelling.

(c) If the employer is concerned to minimise energy expenditure across the board, then it makes sense for the robot to pay for its fuel. This means that M is earned during work and spent during refuelling. In other words, M is like money.

These three possibilities can be summarised as three types of basic cycle, as shown in Fig. 1. For the cycles to be stable the triangles must be complete. An unstable cycle spirals out of control. The stability of the basic cycle depends upon two main factors: the nature of the environment, and the decisions made by the robot. Thus the system can become unstable because the environment is just too difficult for the robot to cope with. An animal equivalent

33

might be an environment in which food is very scarce. The system could also become unstable simply because the robot made bad decisions, such as ignoring an opportunity to refuel. Thus behavioural stability and decision-making are closely related.

Our robot must be able to decide for itself when to break off work and seek fuel. Like an animal, the robot must be able to manage its motivational alternatives in a way that makes best use of its time and energy. Somehow it must be able to assess the costs and benefits of the alternative activities open to it. In the long term, the costs and benefits relate to whether the robot is doing the 'right thing', that is, staying alive and pleasing the customer. Similarly, for an animal the right thing amounts to survival and reproductive success. In the short term, however, some index of the long-term costs and benefits is required, in order to guide the animal or robot along the 'right path'.

Doing the Right Thing

You may have read in a magazine, or seen on television, an account of an exercise in which a team of experts compare motor cars of differing makes, in an attempt to decide which is the best buy. Usually, they rate each car (say, on a scale from 1 to 10) separately for various attributes, such as driveability, safety, comfort, and luggage space. For example, car A may score 5 for driveability, 8 for safety, 6 for comfort, and 3 for luggage space. Usually these numbers are then added, giving 22 points to car A, out of a possible 40. They then do the same for car B, and so on. The car with the largest score is the winner.

There is a serious flaw, however, in such a procedure. To give equal weight to driveability, safety, comfort, and luggage space is an entirely arbitrary decision on the part of the experts. Some motorists would think that driveability and safety should be given more weight than comfort and luggage space, whereas others might think that comfort is the most important thing, and so on. Whenever decisions must be made between objects, or courses of action, involving a number of different characteristics (such as safety and comfort), some sensible way of weighting the differing characteristics must be incorporated. For example, an animal might be simultaneously hungry, thirsty, and cold. It must decide whether to forage for food, find water, or find a warm place. How can suitable weights be attached to these three alternatives?

Every animal has limits to its tolerance, its ability to tolerate extreme values of environmental factors, such as temperature and humidity. In the natural environment, the distribution of animals usually reflects their tolerance along environmental gradients of temperature, altitude, etc. Some habitats are too cold for some animals, but not others; some are too dry, and so on. For every type of animal, there are lethal boundaries for bodily conditions, such as cold and dehydration. The weightings given to such priorities as feeding, drinking, and keeping warm are directly related to these lethal boundaries. The same is true of our security robot. In addition to putting in as many hours as possible on security duty, our robot must spend time recharging its on-board batteries, and working in its kitchen servicing its digester. The digestion of human food-waste takes a number of weeks, and the robot must make sure that there is enough material in the pipeline to maintain a steady supply of energy. So our robot must work, prepare food, and recharge. What weights should it attach to these priorities?

It the robot ran out of fuel while working, it would be dead. All the time it is working, it is using up energy from its on-board store. The nearer it gets to 'empty' on its internal energy gauge, the more risk it is taking. To be sure, it has a readily available source of energy at its home, but it could happen that, just when it needed to refuel, it needed to attend to an urgent security issue. It should not quit the work scene at this juncture, but on the other hand it must refuel. Clearly, to avoid this type of situation, the robot should adopt a cautious (risk-averse) refuelling policy. On the other hand, to refuel too often is to take more time off, not a good policy either. What we need, in designing our robot, is some criterion that will enable the robot to achieve the best balance between competing priorities. But what do we mean by the best?

Suppose you wish to hire an administrator. Having decided what kind of administrator you want, you design an advertisement, and following that a selection procedure, likely to obtain you the best possible person for the salary you are offering. Suppose you decide that you want an administrator who can type out passages of text, automatically correcting obvious errors? In that case you must devise a text that has errors of various kinds deliberately incorporated into it. For example, there may be spelling mistakes, punctuation mistakes, and factual mistakes (such as 1851 being described as earlier than 1835). Suppose you introduce ten deliberate mistakes. You then ask each applicant to copy the text as quickly as possible, correcting obvious mistakes as they go along. You then give each applicant a typing score out of ten. Now you also want your administrator to be good on the telephone, so you devise a telephone test along similar lines, and you give each applicant a score out of ten on the telephone test.

Who is the best applicant? Candidate A scores 7 on the typing test and 3 on the telephone test, making a total of 10; B scores 5 and 4 making 9; C scores 2 and 6, making 8; and D scores 2 and 9, making 11. But now we have made the same mistake as the car experts. We have assumed that the typing test and the telephone test should be given the same weight. As things stand, D has the largest score, but if you think that greater weight should be given to the typing test, then A would have the largest score. But we are not out of the woods yet. Why are we adding the scores? What does that imply?

What if one applicant had the highest overall score, but scored zero on the typing test? This would be a possible result of adding the scores. Would you really want an administrator who could not type? One way around this is to multiply the scores from the two tests. The applicants would then have final scores as follows: A = 21, B = 20, C = 12, D = 18. Now A wins and D comes third. The point of this example is that the final choice is made on the basis of a formula, technically called the optimality criterion, that makes it possible to rank the alternatives along a single scale, even though disparate elements (e.g. telephone and typing scores) are involved. The scores are, in fact, the decision variables, the values of which, together with the optimality criterion, will determine the final outcome.[8]

Both design and behaviour involve decisions. In designing a wheel an engineer must decide what weight, radius, and strength the wheel should have. Similarly, in designing a bone (through the process of natural selection) nature 'decides' on the 'best' combination of weight, length, and strength. Such decisions carry no implications of conscious deliberation in either case. In the case of the behaviour of individual animals or robots, the same considerations apply. A person driving a car with a manual gearshift makes decisions (in the normal everyday sense of the word) as to when to change gear. A person driving a car with an automatic gearshift makes no such decisions, but the behaviour of the person–car may be the same. It makes no difference, when talking about the behaviour of the person–car system, whether the decisions to shift are made by the driver or by the automatic device. What matters is the way in which the decision variables (speed, engine rpm, etc.) are deployed. A decision of a person, animal, or robot is simply the

37

process by which changes in the decision variables result in changes in behaviour. This process can be entirely automatic.

Returning now to our security robot: it is a machine that makes decisions about what to do next in an entirely procedural manner. That is, the robot responds to a situation in an entirely automatic manner without prior account of the consequences. Of course, the consequences do impinge upon the robot, but the robot does not guide its behaviour upon the basis of the consequences. Our robot is the simplest robot that can achieve the security task. This does not mean that the robot is not sophisticated. In fact, in both animals and robots, it can be demonstrated that they are adept at trading off competing pressures and arriving at the best outcome. For example, Reto Zach discovered a simple trade-off in the foraging behaviour of crows that feed on shellfish on the west coast of Canada.[9] The crows hunt for whelks at low tide, usually selecting the largest ones. When they find one they hover over a rock and drop the whelk so that it breaks open to expose the edible inside. By dropping whelks of various sizes from different heights, Zach discovered that the number of times a whelk must be dropped in order to break is related to the height from which it is dropped. The crows must expend energy in flying up to drop a whelk, so Zach calculated the total amount of upward flying that a crow would have to do to break a whelk from a given height. He showed that the lowest flying cost is incurred if the whelks are dropped from about 5 metres, which is what the crows usually do. There is a trade-off between the cost in terms of the number of drops required to break the whelk and the height of the drop. Calculations based upon this trade-off reveal that the optimal dropping height is indeed about 5 metres. Thus it appears that the crows have somehow been programmed to exploit this particular feature of the foraging situation.

Animals must spend energy in order to forage and there may be circumstances in which the energy available to spend is limited.

Similarly, the expenditure of a human shopper in a supermarket may be limited by the amount of money available, or by the amount of time available. The shopper with a limited amount of time is constrained by the rate at which items can be selected and paid for. Foraging animals are often constrained by the time required to recognise, capture, and process each food item, usually called the handling time.

Bernd Heinrich studied foraging bumblebees (Bombus), and likened them to a shopper:

A bee starting to forage in a meadow with many different flowers faces a task not unlike that of an illiterate shopper pushing a cart down the aisle of a supermarket. Directly or indirectly, both try to get the most value for their money. Neither knows beforehand the precise contents of the packages on the shelf or in the meadow.[10]

Heinrich's observations showed that time and energy act as constraints upon the bees' foraging efficiency. When the bees must travel some distance to find productive flowers, then time becomes a limiting factor, and it is worthwhile for the bee to expend energy in order to save time. When foraging on relatively unproductive flowers or when foraging at a low temperature, the bees take more time in order to save energy.[11] Similarly, a shopper tends to spend more money (per item) when in a hurry, but to spend more time when short of money.

These examples touch on the subject of animal economics, the application of human economic principles to animal behaviour. The animal is treated as if it were a shopper, obeying the laws of consumer economics. It is spending time and energy in a way that parallels the expenditure of time and money by humans. The animal's budget, or limit to expenditure, of energy or time constrains its behaviour. Thus an animal cannot devote more energy to an activity than it has available. Nor can it devote more time than is available. Experiments with animals show that they exhibit the characteristic features of consumer economics. For example, consider the relationship between the price and the consumption of a commodity. People usually buy less of a commodity when the price rises, a phenomenon called elasticity of demand. However, the extent of the elasticity depends upon the availability of substitutes. For example, if the price of apples rises, then people tend to buy a lot less, because there are plenty of other fruit substitutes. When the price of coffee rises, people buy only a little less, because there are few available substitutes. Demand for apples is said to be elastic, and demand for coffee less so. Now, if an animal expends a certain amount of energy on a particular activity, such as foraging for a particular food, then it usually does less of that activity if the energy requirement is increased, especially when substitutes (other foods) are available. In fact, over the past thirty years it has been shown that many types of animal, when put to the test, obey the laws of consumer economics in very many respects. This is not all that surprising once you realise that the microeconomic laws are basically a way of expressing the logic of choice. Any person, animal, or robot that must expend energy (or money) to obtain necessary resources faces the same kind of situation, and it is not all that surprising that they all home in on the same (logical) laws governing economic behaviour. Thus the elasticity of demand functions in animals gives an indication of the relative importance of the various activities in the animal's repertoire (such as feeding, grooming, and territory defence), and the study of demand functions in animals is an important part of the study of animal welfare.[12]

Bearing all this in mind, we can return to designing our security robot. To incorporate these ideas into our robot we need to know what basic resources will determine its viability. Firstly, we must consider its on-board energy, without which it can do nothing. Our robot must be able to monitor the current state of its battery.

Normally this will be low priority, but if it starts to run down it will be high priority. Secondly, there is the robot's kitchen to design. In the kitchen food waste from the hotel or hospital is provided, and this must be fed into a digester by the robot. This is merely a matter of the robot operating a simple machine, but the robot must be provided with the information to do the job. Moreover, the robot must be provided with a memory of the state of the kitchen when it last visited there. The kitchen resource is not as high priority as the on-board energy supply, but the robot must ensure that there is energy available when it goes to recharge its batteries. The kitchen management will take the robot some time, but recharging its own batteries will probably take more time. Of course, the robot does not have to recharge its batteries fully, and if it has other urgent things to do, it could have a partial recharge. The important thing is for the robot not to get into debt. That could arise if there was not enough energy in the kitchen pipeline to supply current needs. The digester takes about three weeks to turn food waste into electricity, and the robot should not deplete the kitchen store to the point where the digester cannot keep up.

Thirdly, there is the question of the resources required for our robot to do its job. The robot's job it to patrol the premises, monitor any normal arrivals and departures, and detect any anomalies. If there are any undue disturbances, then the robot must be prepared to take some action. The robot uses vision and hearing to detect anyone arriving or leaving, and then moves up to check them out. If it recognises them as people who belong on the premises, it reports their arrival over a wireless network (radio) and takes no further action. If they are strangers it asks them their business, records the reply, and tells them where to report to. None of this requires any but the normal resources. It is when something goes wrong that extra resources are called for. For example, someone may enter in an unauthorised manner, or someone may leave in a suspicious manner.

41

Finally, we need to endow our robot with some defensive behaviour. There are those who might find it amusing to tease the robot, vandalise it, or attempt to kidnap it. You might think it rather difficult to provide our robot with defences, bearing in mind that it would be illegal to supply a machine that could injure a person, or that was a danger to the safety of the public. If we look at the defensive behaviour of animals, however, we can see that there are many that are physically defenceless but nevertheless deter attack. So let us decide that, upon initial provocation, our robot produces a snake-like hiss, a worrying noise to a predator. If the attack escalates, it produces an ear-splitting screech. This serves to paralyze the attacker temporarily, and to alert any employees of the establishment who might be within earshot. Finally, if the attack escalates further, the robot speaks. It tells the attacker that their photograph has been taken and transmitted to the police. It also covers itself with a foul-smelling slimy foam that makes it difficult for an attacker to get to grips with the robot, and also makes the attacker nauseous. A number of animals deploy similar defenses. Kittens and some birds hiss when disturbed, while eider ducks cover their eggs with a truly revolting excretion just before they vacate their nest when disturbed by a predator. Our robot could spray an attacker with foul-smelling liquid, like a skunk, thus simultaneously deterring and identifying them.

Whatever is decided as an effective and legal form of defense will require on-board resources. Everything that the robot does implies resources that must be managed by the robot. Even if it is decided that the robot should have a separate battery for emergency purposes, the robot still must take time off work from time to time to recharge this battery. Any chemicals used also must be replenished. All these decisions must be made at the design stage. Our robot is not able to think up strategies for itself. It is an automaton, involving the simplest design that can do the job. It has no goal-directed behaviour (see Chapter 1). It may appear to be 'intelligent', but it has no mind of its own. In many respects it is like an animal, or at least some types of animal that have no mental faculties.

The point here is that it is possible to design a robot with quite complex behaviour, or to account for quite complex animal behaviour, in terms that require no recourse to mental phenomena. Just how far this behaviourist approach (see Chapter 3) can be taken is a matter of dispute. But there are some fundamentals that apply to all animals (and self-sufficient robots), whether they have mental abilities or not. All animals depend upon certain resources, and all animals must be able to monitor three aspects of these vital resources. Firstly, the state of the resource within the animal's (or robot's) body must be measurable. That is, there must be information about the energy state (hunger for an animal, battery state for a robot) and the state of other vital resources such as water (for land animals) and temperature. Secondly, the animal (or robot) must be able to gauge the availability of the resource in the environment. For example, when you go to pick blackberries, you must be able to tell which bushes have blackberries and which bushes have none. A bush with many blackberries represents high availability, while a bush with few represents low availability. Thirdly, the animal must be able to gauge the accessibility of the resource in the environment. When blackberrying you will find that some blackberries are difficult to reach. These berries may be numerous, but if they require a lot of time and effort to harvest, they have low accessibility. The rate of return for time spent harvesting (i.e. the speed with which you can fill your basket) depends upon both the availability and the accessibility of the blackberries. The berries may be numerous, but if you must spend a lot of time walking between bushes, or climbing to reach the berries, then the rate of return will drop. There is not much one can do about the availability of a resource, but accessibility can often be improved by learning and by the use of tools. An experienced blackberry forager has learnt the skill of quickly picking a handful of berries, before depositing them in the basket. They may also have learned to bring along a walking stick to hook down branches high up with available berries.

The decision as to whether to forage for blackberries or do something else hinges partly on how much you want blackberries (your motivational state with respect to blackberries), and partly on your estimate of their likely availability and accessibility. If the indications are that there are few blackberries around, or that they are very inaccessible because other people have picked the easy ones, then you may well decide not to go on a blackberry expedition. It is these three factors (state, availability, and accessibility) in combination that influence your decision. It is much the same for other things that you might decide to do. It is much the same for animals, and it is much the same for autonomous robots. For example, the slug-eating robot (slugbot) mentioned in the previous chapter does not go foraging for slugs when the sun is shining, because it has been programmed so that sunshine indicates low slug availability. It has been designed this way because the slugs are basically nocturnal, although they will appear on the surface during a very overcast day, especially a wet day. In fact, high humidity is an indicator of high slug availability, and the slugbot must give appropriate weight to the two indicators—light versus humidity.

My dog, Border, comes into the kitchen when hungry, because she has learned that the kitchen is likely to have a higher availability of food than other places. Most of the food is inaccessible, but Border has learned some tricks to improve her chances. Instead of looking up at the person doing the cooking, as most dogs do, she diligently looks down. Border has learned that if someone drops a bit of food, she needs to be quick off the mark to retrieve it before they do. It is not difficult to program a robot to behave like an animal, to react to stimuli, and to learn to improve the accessibility of resources. Much animal behaviour can be explained, to the satisfaction of most scientists, without recourse to mental apparatus. All the robot designer must do is to translate animal strategies into the robot control system, and endow the robot with some animal-like learning ability. As we shall discover, this can be done and has been done. That is not to deny, however, that some animal behaviour remains controversial, and that there are some animals that may have mental abilities, such as the ability to connect beliefs with intentions, or the ability to have a reason for action (see Chapter 3).

Finally, we come to the question of animal and robot intelligence. Studies of animal intelligence over the past century have made it abundantly clear that different species in different ecological circumstances exhibit a wide variety of types of intelligence. This makes intelligence difficult to define, and it emphasises the importance of studying animal intelligence from a design point of view as well as investigating the mechanisms involved. These lessons have been taken over into robotics.[13] Many scientists think that intelligence is not really a matter of what mechanisms an animal (or robot) possesses, but rather a question of whether it can produce the best response to the problem at hand. Let us take as an example some prototypes for a brick-laying robot, illustrated in Fig. 2. The problem is that when robot A picks up a brick it falls over due to the weight of the brick. A possible solution is provided by robot B. By altering the shape of the robot, particularly by broadening its base, the designer can alter its centre of gravity, so that it no longer falls over when it picks up a brick. The disadvantage with this solution is that the robot has increased in weight, has increased its fuel requirements, and may no longer be an economic proposition. A better solution is shown by robot C, which is equipped with a counterweight (either a special limb or another arm capable of holding another brick), which can be

45

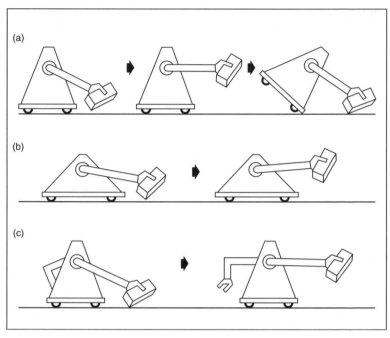

Fig. 2. Design problems associated with a brick-laying robot. (a) The robot is unstable once a brick is grasped. (b) Stability is achieved by altering the body shape at the expense of reduced height and increased weight. (c) Stability is achieved by the intelligent behaviour of using the free arm as a counterweight.

raised at the appropriate time to prevent the robot falling over when it lifts a brick. It may be argued that the intelligence, or lack of it, applied to this problem is a property of the designer rather than the robot. We must be careful here. It is intelligent behaviour of robot C to raise the counterbalance/arm when it picks up a brick. The question of whether the robot thinks up this solution for itself, or does it automatically, is not really relevant to the question of whether this is the best solution to the problem. Robot A has no counterbalance, and cannot attain this solution no matter how much thinking power it has. Similarly, robot B, however big its on-board computer, cannot overcome the fact that it is overweight.

When my dog Border keeps her eye on the floor, she is exhibiting intelligent behaviour for a dog, because she gets more food this way, and she does not annoy the cook. Dogs and cats are domesticated animals and part of their intelligent behaviour involves pleasing their owner. It is important that an animal in the kitchen should not be a nuisance. Border keeps a low profile, quietly moving around like a floor-cleaning robot. Cats operate differently. Their job in the kitchen is to deter mice. The intelligent cat will do this without wrapping itself around the cook's legs. Unfortunately, our current cat has not learned this golden rule. Left to me it would probably end up as an outdoor cat. But since humans have different criteria when rating the viability of one creature or machine against another, and as my partner's criteria with regard to both Border and the cat are very different from mine, she will probably remain indoors.

Finally, what have we learned from our security robot? It carries out a demanding task, one that would appear to require 'intelligence' and even some mental autonomy. In fact, everything it does is entirely procedural, involving no prior consideration of the consequences of its own behaviour, no explicit decision-making (see Chapter 4), and no recourse to the elements of our own folk psychology, such as beliefs and intentions. In these respects the security robot is similar to those animals that also lack these abilities.

3

INTERPRETING BEHAVIOUR

If my dog wanders into my kitchen while I am cooking, I may interpret its behaviour in a number of ways. If I happen to know that my dog has not been fed that day, I may assume that she is hungry, can smell food, and so is performing behaviour appropriate for a hungry dog. If I know that my dog has been fed, I may assume that the dog wants my company. In reality, I know nothing (for sure) about the dog's inner workings, but I am, nevertheless, interpreting the dog's behaviour. I may be interpreting its behaviour in human terms, or I may have learned from experience that, if the dog has not been fed, she behaves in one way in the kitchen, and if she has been fed, she behaves in another way. All dogs are not the same, and I have learned some of the behavioural characteristics of my particular dog.

The assumptions made by the person in interpreting the behaviour of the dog in the kitchen are likely to include the idea that the dog has learned that food is sometimes available in the kitchen. Most animals are capable of learning about the whereabouts of food, and such assumptions seem reasonable. The dog is not being credited with any extraordinary abilities. Indeed, ever since laboratory studies by Pavlov and his successors, scientists have known that dogs, and other animals, are perfectly capable of such *associative learning*.[1] The dog is hungry, and it associates the kitchen with food, because it can smell food in that place, and because it has obtained food in that place in the past. Scientifically, you would be on strong ground if you assumed that your dog comes into the kitchen as a result of learning that rewarding things happen in the kitchen.

It all looks quite simple; hungry dog heads for food source, and gobbles it up. It's what hungry dogs do. But actually the issue is not simple at all. What we must ask is what is in Border's head when she does this? Is she making a simple response to hunger, using previous experience to locate the source of food without any mental image of it? Or does she believe food is to be found in the kitchen and in particular in the cat's dish? Which at once raises the question whether a dog, or any animal, is capable of having a belief. Or come to that, any mental process?

To assume that the dog came into the kitchen because it believed that there might be food is a different kind of explanation from the behaviourist interpretation outlined earlier. It involves crediting the dog with some kind of mental ability, but what does this entail? We can't start to answer the question without first defining what a belief or mental process is. And that can only be done by looking at how philosophers have used such terms. Understanding these concepts is their job and no one else—certainly not scientists—can do it as well. But that is not simple either: philosophers as you might expect disagree on their terminology. And in order to understand the nature of their disagreements and to arrive at some, at least workable, view of our own as to what constitutes having a belief—and thereafter in the light of these theories to estimate the chances of Border having beliefs—we must examine the arguments put forward by various philosophers. In other words we must advance into what my sometimes sceptical—and cat-preferring—partner calls 'philosopher-speak', where terms do not always mean what they appear to mean in common parlance; and where each distinct usage may denote a wholly distinct approach to the problem, let alone the conclusions arrived at.

Mental entities have a property that philosophers call *intentionality*.[2] In its current usage intentionality refers to that property of the mind by which it is directed at, or about, or of, objects and states of affairs in the world. Human intentionality includes such mental phenomena as belief, desire, intention, hope, fear, love, hate, lust, and disgust. Animal intentionality, if it exists, would probably not include the whole panoply of mental states, but it would have to include some aspect of aboutness. So for a dog to have a belief, it would have to believe *that* something was the case. Whether this is possible, we will discuss later. But first, remember, we already have other types of explanation for the dog's behaviour.

Firstly we have the explanation in human terms, treating the dog as if it were human and taking an *anthropomorphic stance*.[3] Secondly, we have an explanation in scientific terms—the dog comes into the kitchen because it associates the kitchen stimuli with food. We may call this the *behaviourist* stance. Now, thirdly, we are suggesting that the dog might really believe that there is food in the kitchen. We may call this a *realist stance*, because it asserts that the dog really does have beliefs.[4] You may think that this stance is very similar to the anthropomorphic stance, but there is an important difference. By explaining the dog's behaviour in anthropomorphic terms we are *attributing* human characteristics to the dog. We know very well that the dog is not a human, but nevertheless, we are thinking about the dog *as if* it were a human. We are treating the dog like a person, and when we think about other people we usually do so in terms of common-sense psychology, or folk psychology, as philosophers often call it. This is a kind of implicit theory that we apply unthinkingly. Thus in embracing the dog in this way, we are applying an implicit theory, whereas when taking a realist stance, we are suggesting that the dog really does have dog-like beliefs, and we are offering this type of explanation as an *explicit* theory, one that is open to falsification.

Let us first look at the behaviourist stance. Behaviourism was launched, as a school of psychology, by J. B. Watson in 1913, following a period of discontent with the current anthropomorphic attitude towards animals. In particular, Conway Lloyd Morgan, in his *Introduction to Comparative Psychology* (1894), was critical of much of contemporary animal psychology on the grounds of its poor methodology and sloppy reasoning. He enunciated his famous canon: 'In no case may we interpret an action as the outcome of the exercise of a higher psychical faculty, if it can be interpreted as the outcome of one which stands lower on the psychological scale.' Later (1900) he added the following rider: 'To this may be added—lest the range of the principle be misunderstood—that the canon by no means excludes the interpretation of a particular act as the outcome of the higher mental processes if we already have independent evidence of their occurrence in the agent.'

Behaviourism was very influential during the first half of the twentieth century. Strict behaviourists would allow only observable stimuli, muscular movements, and glandular secretions to enter into explanations of behaviour. Private events, such as thinking and feeling, were taken (especially by B. F. Skinner, 1953) to be kinds of behaviour subject to the same laws as overt behaviour. The arguments of Watson and Skinner were essentially methodological arguments about the way psychological research should be pursued.[5]

51

Philosophically, behaviourism took a number of forms. In the 1940s some philosophers thought that observation of a person's behaviour could provide a window into their mind. Although this is a behaviourist attitude, it does not necessarily imply that mental concepts should be eliminated from explanations of behaviour.[6] These analytical behaviourists believed that statements containing mental vocabulary can be analysed into statements with purely physical terminology, in contrast to the *eliminative* behaviourists who believed that explanations of behaviour in mental terms will eventually be eliminated by purely physical or physiological explanations.

After the 1950s the influence of behaviourism declined, and it is now regarded as an outmoded approach to the study of human behaviour. However, some of the main principles of behaviourism remain. Accounting for animal behaviour without recourse to cognitive or mental explanations is still regarded by many as the scientifically parsimonious route. Scientists with this viewpoint may be found amongst biologists, economists, psychologists, and roboticists. The fact remains that behaviourism is alive and well, albeit wearing different clothes. However, before going any further, we need to clear up one small issue.

We must agree on what we mean by behaviour. This is especially important, because the term is used differently in different disciplines. In animal behaviour studies, the term behaviour applies to all bodily movement, including reflexes, and to changes in colouration (such as blushing), and to the release of pheromones. In robotics, the term behaviour refers to the activity of behaviour-producing modules. Thus changes in movement patterns produced by external forces, such as gravity, would not count as behaviour. In philosophy, a distinction is often made between physical and agential behaviour. Physical behaviour is a physical change to an agent's body, whereas agential behaviour is something that an agent does.

The relationship between physical behaviour and agential behaviour is controversial. On some views, all *actions* are identical to physical changes in the agents body (however, some kinds of physical behaviour, such as reflexes, are uncontroversially not kinds of agential behaviour). For other philosophers, an agent's action must involve some physical change, but is not identical to it.[7]

The most inclusive usage is that used in animal behaviour studies, and this is the meaning of the term behaviour we will adopt in interpreting Border's behaviour.

Let us now take a walk with the dog, for a breath of fresh air to clear the head. When walking with my dog Border, I know that sooner or later she will be diverted by the sight or scent of something more interesting than walking with me. Something catches her attention and she is off in a world of her own. Some stimulus causes her to change her behaviour. It might be simply investigating a place where something has happened in the past. What stance, or attitude, could I adopt?

Unthinkingly, I might suppose that she believes that there might be a mouse there. I have no reason to suppose this—I do it as part and parcel of my ordinary lazy way of thinking, treating the dog as if it were human. Alternatively, putting on my scientific hat, I might think that my dog, as a result of some past experience with this location, associates some local incidental stimuli with the possible presence of a mouse or rabbit. Such simple associative learning has been well studied in animals. What I am offering here is an explanation of my dog's behaviour in terms of a scientific theory. Like all scientific theory, it could turn out to be incorrect in some respect. On the other hand, I might have philosophical reasons for supposing that my dog really does have beliefs, even though science is not yet able to identify such mental phenomena in animals. In other words, although a behaviourist explanation of my dog's behaviour would be acceptable to most scientists, this does not *prove* that my

53

dog does not have mental abilities, and it would not be irrational of me to take a realist philosophical stance. The behavioural and realist stances can coexist when there is no agreed basis for deciding between them.

What then should we think about the behaviour of an automaton, a robotic dog that can be taken for a walk? Such robotic dogs do exist, and can be purchased on the open market. A behaviourist type of explanation would be entirely appropriate in this case. Numerous robots have been designed with animal-like learning abilities, and there is no reason why a robotic dog should not be able to learn to associate certain place stimuli with some event that was rewarding in the past. Moreover, according to the designer, the robotic dog has no mental abilities. Although the robotic dog may behave *as if* it believed that there might be a rabbit around, any theory that such a dog might really have beliefs can be refuted by the designer. Now, as we shall see later, there are some philosophers who take a non-realist view of beliefs, and for them it is perfectly possible that the robotic dog could have beliefs, even though the designer did not deliberately endow the robot with such abilities.

Obviously, some robots have very simple behaviour that no sensible person would seriously suppose to be the product of mental activity. Other, more sophisticated, robots seem to behave as if they had some mental ability. The security robot we met in the previous chapter is a case in point. It is an automaton, yet it is a fully capable security guard. Its behaviour misleads some people, but not others. So is it possible, on the evidence of behaviour alone, to come to any conclusion? Some behaviourist philosophers have held a behaviour-as-necessary view that anything that has no physical behavioural dispositions of a certain kind and complexity does not have a mental life. A further step is to say that anything that has physical behavioural dispositions of a certain kind and complexity does have a mental life. This behaviour-as-sufficient view is a weak form of behaviourism, because it does not specify what kind and complexity of behavioural dispositions is required. Clearly, there would not be much point in having expensive mental apparatus if it made no difference to the behaviour, but it has proved very difficult to pinpoint exactly what it is that makes the difference. One obvious candidate is language, but the absence of language does not necessarily indicate the absence of mental activity, although there are some philosophers who think that it does, as we shall see in Chapter 4.

All-in-all, the argument that it is possible to diagnose mental activity from observation of behaviour alone has not stood the test of time. The behaviourist view that it is possible to explain the behaviour of some animals and robots in non-mental terms has stood the test of time, and this view is favoured by those who like parsimonious explanations. However, as we have already noted, it is possible for two types of explanation to coexist, if the evidence is insufficient to decide between them.

The extreme behaviourist view, that all mental terminology will eventually be eliminated, has enjoyed a revival in recent decades, as a result of arguments that are not directly to do with behaviour. Many present-day philosophers believe that everything about humans, and about the whole world, is made of matter and energy and will eventually be explained in terms of physics. Thus all physical events in the body, and all bodily movements are, in principle, fully explainable in physico-chemical terms. Moreover, all mental properties of human beings are fully explainable in such terms. This is called a *physicalist stance*. Philosophers who take this attitude are divided about its implications for mental phenomena. Some take the view that mental states can be accounted for in materialist terms (the realists), while others believe that, because all facts about the mental are physical facts, all mental concepts will eventually be reduced to neuroscience concepts, and (presumably) eventually to physics. When that happens, folk psychology, and all mental reference to mental phenomena, will have been eliminated from scientific and philosophical discourse. Those that take this view are called the *eliminative materialists*.

Historically, science has had a profound influence on philosophy. This is not surprising, because science gradually changes our view of the world, and philosophers of past ages lived in a world very different from the present one. One effect of this cultural evolution is that there are now many philosophers who believe in some version of *materialism*: basically, the view that everything is made of matter. This is now a somewhat outmoded view, scientifically, and some philosophers refer to themselves as *physicalists,* implying that there is something fundamental about physics—that everything can, in principle, be reduced to physics. However, as we shall see there are problems with such a *reductionist* view of the world, and some philosophers take a non-reductionist alternative to physicalism, called naturalism.

Naturalism is the view that everything there is belongs to the world of nature, and so can be studied by the appropriate (scientific) empirical methods. Biological naturalism holds that mental phenomena are natural biological phenomena. In particular, all mental phenomena from tickles, and pains, to thought and consciousness are caused by neurobiological processes in the brain. Since mental phenomena are caused by brain processes, any other system that caused mental phenomena would have to have causal powers similar to brains. Although naturalism is sometimes viewed as akin to physicalism and materialism, naturalism does not itself imply anything about reduction. Naturalism simply holds that all the features of a particular realm, and all those events that take place in it, are empirically accessible features of the world. In other words, in taking a naturalist stance, one is not committed to saying that explanations of mental phenomena will eventually be *reduced* to physics.

Eliminative materialism takes the view that the concepts of folk psychology, such as beliefs and intentions, will eventually be explained in purely neurophysiological terms. In other words, our common-sense notions of the mind, including experiences and sensations, are in principle reducible to biochemistry and biophysics.

A problem for such materialist views is the knowledge that we seem to gain by introspection. There is an obvious difference between knowledge of our own mind and knowledge of the outside world, including the minds of other people. A person is said to have *first-person authority* with respect to the content of their own mind, whereas others (third persons) can access this content only indirectly. Some philosophers, notably Descartes, used to think that judgements about ones own mental states were *infallible,* but recent evidence is against this view.[8] Other philosophers claim that first-person authority confers *incorrigibility*; i.e. although your judgements about your mental content might be wrong, you cannot be corrected by others, because you count as the highest authority. Less stringent is the view that first-person authority means that your mental states are transparently available to you, a process known as self-intimation. This does not imply that we are infallible or incorrigible about out mental contents.

Philosophers who claim that mental properties are non-physical cannot also be materialists and hold that mental properties exist. If mental properties are not physical, but everything in the world is physical, then mental properties cannot exist. This is the eliminative materialist argument advanced by the philosopher Richard Rorty in 1979. He argued that since mental states are incorrigible but physical states are not, anyone who claims that their mental states are incorrigible either is a *dualist* or does not actually have any mental states.[9] This argument hinges on the idea that mental states are necessarily incorrigible. If we do not accept that mental states are necessarily incorrigible, then Rorty's argument loses its power.

At one time I used to discuss the question of consciousness with my (more junior) students. I got them to agree that conscious experience is an entirely private matter, and if I said that I had a particular kind of conscious experience, they were in no position to contradict me (i.e. my conscious experience is incorrigible). Then I said that if I was going to teach them, they would have to understand that I have a particular disability for which I hoped they would make allowances. My disability is that I have no consciousness. They did not believe me. Despite previously agreeing that consciousness was a private matter, and that I could not be contradicted about my own experiences, they persisted in contradicting me. What this story suggests is that the idea of mental incorrigibility, despite its intuitive appeal, does not stand up to scrutiny. Not only is there evidence against it, but it lacks credibility, in the sense that some things that one says about oneself are not believed by other people.

However, we must be very careful here, because not all people are the same. Autistic people, for example, are said to be different from non-autistic people, because their minds work differently. They perceive the world differently and react differently to some situations. Temple Grandin is an autistic animal scientist. She claims that 'Autistic people can think the way animals think,'[10] and she claims that this ability gives her a special insight into the minds of animals. Whether this is true is not the point. Other people with long experience of animals may also claim to have special insight, and they may agree or disagree with Temple Grandin on particular issues. The problem, philosophically, is that opinions based upon introspection are basically dogma.[11] Such opinions cannot be contradicted by others, so there can be no argument, or philosophical discourse.

It is this kind of situation that has led some philosophers to claim that folk psychology is deeply flawed. Notably, Paul and Patricia Churchland maintain that common-sense psychology, or folk psychology is not reliable, and that elimination of all such talk about mental states is a fully viable goal for a neuroscientific research programme.[12] This is a kind of crusade, with a vision of the future, arising from the belief that neuroscientific research will eventually make folk psychology obsolete. Indeed, the Churchlands seem to think that it will also make scientific psychology obsolete. But what exactly are the Churchlands trying to eliminate?

Folk psychology is the subject matter of our everyday understanding of one another in psychological or mental terms, such as belief, desire, and intention. In contrast to scientific experimental psychology, folk psychology is usually regarded as a theory that we know implicitly, and which we use to predict the behaviour of others.

The content of folk psychology can be summarised as follows:[13]

(a) *Propositional attitudes*—Our folk psychology involves invoking such conscious mental states as beliefs, desires, and intentions. Such mental attitudes are about things, or refer to things that are describable in propositional terms. For example, my belief that canaries are yellow is identified by the proposition that canaries are yellow. I desire a canary, and I intend to buy a canary. The *content* of my belief, my desire, and my intention is a canary. If I am presented with a bird that is not yellow, even though it be a canary, I will not desire it, or intend to buy it, because I believe (wrongly) that all canaries are yellow.

(b) *Actions and perceptual stimuli*—Folk psychology is also concerned with the impression made upon us by the external world and our beliefs formed on that basis (for example, I believe that all canaries are yellow, because I have seen pictures of yellow canaries, but not of non-yellow canaries). It is also concerned with explaining the connection between our propositional attitudes and how we act (e.g. the connection between beliefs, desires, intentions, and action). Thus I did not buy the bird, even though it was a canary, because it was not yellow.

Taking a realist stance, some philosophers maintain that we really do have beliefs, desires, pains, etc., and that folk psychology correctly (more or less) enables us both to attribute such mental states to other human beings, and to correctly (more or less) identify the roles these states play in governing human behaviour. On the other hand, philosophers taking an anti-realist stance hold that folk psychological language is hopelessly misguided, and that talk about propositional attitudes cannot be scientifically vindicated. They hold that folk psychology will go the way of (the now discredited) folk physics and the anthropocentric view of the universe. There are some philosophers who take an intermediate view, holding that folk psychological language is useful, but it is not the domain of scientific psychology. Thus, folk psychology may be preserved, but all it means is that we have attitudes that can be construed as having propositional content.[14]

Scientifically, there is a consensus about the existence of a shared conceptual framework that people use to try to explain, predict, and manipulate the behaviour of others. There is also general agreement about the content of folk psychology. Research by social psychologists and anthropologists indicates that all adult human beings share some aspects of folk psychology, although there is also considerable variation between individuals according to their gender, age, developmental history, and cultural background.[15] Thus it would seem that it is part of human nature to regard others in terms of their likely propositional attitudes, and it is not surprising that there are considerable individual differences based on experience.

Much of the criticism of folk psychology is based upon the premise that folk psychology is a *theory*, but this is a controversial topic. On the one hand, if folk psychology is a theory, albeit an implicit one, then it may be true or false. If it is true, then the *realists* hold the fort. If it is false, then the eliminativists are on their way. However, many philosophers argue that folk psychology is not a theory, in which case it cannot be true or false.[16] The point here is that the eliminativists want to replace folk psychology with testable scientific theory, but they are not replacing like with like, because intuitive theories are different in kind from empirical theories, in that they are directly given to us (i.e. they are innate), and they are part of practical activities rather than of theoretical discourse. For example, the philosopher Kathy Wilkes notes that folk psychology has countless other things to do besides description and explanation, such as joking, jeering, exhorting, discouraging, blaming, and praising.[17] This means that not only is folk psychology not a theory; it could never become one, because it is part and parcel of human nature, or our normal social practice. So what about the disbelief that I was greeted with when I told my students that I was devoid of consciousness? Their mental attitude to this statement of mine was based upon their natural inborn assumption that other people, like themselves, have consciousness. For them it is not an empirical matter, despite my argument about first-person authority, their folk psychology tells them that I am like them, a fully conscious human being.

Let us summarise this line of argument against eliminative materialism: the claim (made by eliminative materialists) that in talking about other people in terms of folk psychology one is employing a theory that is false is a misguided claim. It is misguided, because folk psychology is not a theory in the ordinary sense, but part of our evolved social behaviour. If it is not a theory, it cannot be a false theory, and there is no point in trying to eliminate it.

On the other hand, if you are a materialist, and believe that everything in the world, including mental phenomena, is subject to the laws of physics, then it is hard to escape the conclusion that, one day, mental phenomena will be explainable in physical terms. Much of the philosophical debate surrounding eliminative materialism is a debate about philosophy of science, concerned with the type of theorising that is appropriate. One criticism of eliminativism centres around the question of whether scientific psychology can ever be *reduced* to neuroscience, or to physics. Some philosophers of science claim that the best scientific explanation will always be that which is reduced to the most fundamental level. In physics the fundamental 'particles' provide this type of explanation. In genetics, the basic chemical components of DNA are seen as offering the best level of explanation. However, the most fundamental level of explanation does not always seem to be the most appropriate. To account for genetics in terms of the fundamental particles of physics would not seem appropriate. To account for sociological movements in terms of the psychology of individuals may, or may not, be appropriate. To account for such movements in chemical terms would certainly not be acceptable to sociologists. The question of whether the most fundamental level of explanation is always the best level remains controversial. It is not surprising, then, to find that some philosophers argue that neuroscience is not the appropriate level at which to discuss psychological matters.[18]

The reductionist view also raises the question of the relation between successive theories within each scientific field. Does one theory completely replace another, or can the old theory be reduced to the new one, in the sense that the former is a deductive consequence of the latter?[19] While some believe that all scientific theories will eventually be reduced to one super-theory (presumably some kind of physics theory), others hold that theory reduction is rarely possible, because the different theories have no values or measures in common. If scientific truth is so mutable, what does it mean to say that folk psychology is false? Some have argued that the eliminativist view of scientific progress requires us to believe not only that all our past scientific theories are false, but also that our present and future theories are falsifiable.[20] We must conclude from this that when a theory is falsified, we are actually discovering that it was really false all along. Thus, if each theory is falsified by its successor, and every theory is succeeded by some other theory, all scientific theories that ever existed or will exist are false.

You can see from all this that eliminative materialism has not met with universal acclaim. Those that take a reductionist line claim that, because all facts about the mental are physical facts, all mental concepts will be reduced to neuroscience concepts, and (presumably) eventually to physics; and when that happens, folk psychology will have been eliminated. The main objection to this view is that the materialist level of explanation is not an appropriate level for psychological theorising. On the other hand, one could hold that although the mind is basically a material mind, the concepts of folk psychology, such as belief and intention, will not disappear as science progresses. This is a form of naturalism.

The Intentional Stance

The philosopher Daniel Dennett notes that in considering the behaviour of a complex system, we can take a number of different stances that are not necessarily contradictory.[21] One is the *design stance*. If we know how a system is designed we can predict its designed response to any particular situation. In ordinary language, we use this stance in predicting what will happen when we manipulate an object with a known function. Thus 'strike a match and it will light.' Another is the *physical stance*, which takes account of the physical state of system and our knowledge of the laws of nature. An example might be: 'If you turn on that switch you will get a nasty shock.' Dennett also advocates an *intentional stance* to the behaviour of complex systems. This stance is appropriate when the system under investigation is what Dennett calls an intentional system: 'Whenever one can successfully adopt the intentional stance towards an object, I call that object an intentional system.'

An intentional system is a system whose behaviour can be ... explained and predicted by relying on ascriptions to the system of *beliefs* and *desires* (and other intentionally characterised features—what I call *intentions* here, meaning to include hopes, fears, intentions, perceptions, expectations, etc.) ... We ascribe beliefs and desires to dogs and fish and thereby predict their behaviour, and we can even use the procedure to predict the behaviour of some machines. ... By *assuming* the [chess playing] computer has certain beliefs (or information) and desires (or preference functions) dealing with the chess game in progress, I can calculate—under auspicious circumstances—the computer's next move, *provided I assume that the computer deals rationally with these beliefs and desires*. The computer is an intentional system in these instances not because it has any particular intrinsic features, and not because it really and truly has beliefs and desires (whatever that would be), but just because it succumbs to a certain stance adopted towards it, namely the intentional stance.[22]

Dennett applies the intentional stance to animal behaviour.[23] He notes that vervet monkeys give different alarm calls to different predators. Recordings of the alarms played back when predators were absent caused the monkeys to run into the trees for leopard alarms, look up for eagle alarms, and look down for snake alarms. Adults call primarily to leopards, martial eagles, and pythons, but infants give leopard alarms to various mammals, eagle alarms to many birds, and snake alarms to various snake-like objects. Predator classification thus improves with age and experience. In adopting the intentional stance towards vervet monkeys, we regard the animal as an intentional system and attribute beliefs, desires, and rationality to it, according to the type or order of intentional system that is appropriate. A zero-order (or nonintentional) account of a particular monkey, called Tom, who gives a leopard alarm call in the presence of another vervet, might be as follows: Tom is prone to three types of anxieties—leopard anxiety, eagle anxiety, and snake anxiety—each producing a characteristic vocalisation that is produced automatically, without taking account of its effect upon other vervet monkeys.

A first-order intentional account might maintain that Tom wants to cause another monkey, Sam, to run into the trees. Tom uses a particular vocalisation to stimulate this response in Sam. A second-order intentional account goes a step further in maintaining that Tom wants Sam to believe that there is a leopard in the vicinity and that he should run into the trees. A third-order account might say that Tom wants Sam to *believe* that Tom wants Sam to run into the trees. Dennett maintains that the question of which order of intentionality is appropriate is an empirical question. Clearly, for a second-order account to be appropriate, Sam would have to be capable of having a belief. So we now come to the question of whether animals can have beliefs.

Daniel Dennett has addressed this question and comes to a surprising conclusion:

A thermostat . . . is one of the simplest, most rudimentary, least interesting systems that should be included in the class of believers—the class of intentional systems, to use my term. Why? Because it has a rudimentary goal or desire (which is set, dictatorially, by the thermostat's owner, of course), which it acts on appropriately whenever it believes (thanks to a sensor of one sort or another) that its desires are unfulfilled. Of course, you don't have to describe a thermostat in these terms. You can describe it in mechanical terms, or even molecular terms. But what is theoretically interesting is that if you want to describe the set of all thermostats (cf. the set of all purchasers) you have to rise to this intentional level.[24]

What Dennett is doing here is taking a type of functionalist stance. *Functionalism* is the view that certain entities, including some mental ones, are best described in terms of the functional role that they play within a system.[25] Thus a word processor is a device that processes words. Physically, word processors have changed greatly over recent decades, but they remain best described in terms of their function. In the natural sciences, it is well known that systems of differing hardware can have behaviour that is mathematically analogous. The components of such systems are often described in terms of their function.

Thus, for Dennett, 'All there is to being a true believer is being a system whose behaviour is reliably predictable via the intentional strategy, and hence *all there* is to really and truly believing that *p* (for any proposition *p*) is being an intentional system for which *p* occurs as a belief in the best (most predictive) interpretation.'[26]

In other words, if an animal, or robot, behaves like a believer, then it is a believer, according to Dennett. If my dog, Border, behaves *as if* she believes that there is a mouse under the cupboard, then a functionalist might say that she does have such a belief, even though her behaviour is readily explainable in behaviourist terms. Other philosophers might argue that my dog does not *really* believe that there is a mouse, she only behaves *as if* she believes it. They are taking a realist stance. For Dennett there is no contradiction between an intentional stance and a realist stance, or a behaviourist stance for that matter, provided they all look like intentional systems.

Let us take a much-discussed example. When an incubating sandpiper is disturbed by a ground predator, such as a fox, it may leave the nest and act as though injured, trailing an apparently broken wing and luring the predator away from the nest. When the predator has been led a safe distance from the nest, the bird suddenly regains its normal behaviour and flies away.[27] We could say, on the one hand, that the bird is behaving *as if* the predator believed that it had a broken wing, but in reality the bird simply reacts in a way that is effective, as a result of either instinct or learning, or both (a behaviourist view). On the other hand, we could say that the bird really does believe that the predator will believe that it is injured if it feigns a broken wing (a realist view). In either case, the bird is communicating with the predator, and to unpack the various possible explanations of its behaviour we need to take a look at communication.

In a simple communication system, a *source* encodes and transmits a signal, which is detected by a *receiver* and decoded into a *message*, defined as an ordered selection from a set of signs designed to communicate information. *Signs* are constructs by which an organism affects the state of another. The *signal* is the physical embodiment of the message.

In the natural environment it is important to distinguish between *transmitted* information and *broadcast* information. An observer measures transmitted information by an increase in the predictability of the receiver's behaviour, following activity by the source. In other words, if an observer notes that one animal (the source) sends a signal and another animal (the receiver) reacts to the signal, then the observer can conclude that information has been transmitted from one to the other.

In the case of broadcast information, the source emits an untargeted signal, by means of which an observer gains information about the source. For example, there are three cockerels on my land; a white one, a black one, and a bantam. I can distinguish one from another by their pattern of crowing. The crowing is not targeted at me, but I still gain information from it. The crowing of a cockerel is a kind of advertisement about the identity of the source. In other words, the crowing cockerel is broadcasting information ('this is me') to the world at large. Thus broadcast information is a measure of the information obtained from a signal by an observer.

Problems with classical communication theory arise in considering the decoding of signals. In decoding, the message is transformed from one mode into another. It is usually assumed that, at this stage, the message becomes meaningful to the recipient. The problem is that much of communication theory applies to ordinary perception, as well as to communication. How can we distinguish between communication proper, by the use of spoken language, or other formalised signs, and other forms of causation? The answer usually given is that the sender intends that the signal should influence the behaviour, or the disposition, of the recipient. However, such an anthropomorphic stance will clearly not do when it comes to animals and other aliens.

In formal terms, information can be said to have passed from one individual to another when the behaviour of the former becomes more predictable to the latter. But not all instances of information transfer should be regarded as communication. For example, just before a dead bough falls from a tree there may be a creaking noise. Anyone standing below the tree is warned of the impending danger and can take evasive action. Similarly, just before a cow defecates it lifts its tail. Anyone standing just behind the cow is warned of the impending danger. We would not want to say that the tree is communicating with the animal or person standing beneath it, because the creaking noise is a fortuitous by-product of the breaking process. It is not designed by natural selection as a warning signal. We would not want to say that the cow is communicating with the person standing behind it, because the function of raising the tail in these circumstances is not to provide a warning signal but to promote cleanliness. To count as communication, the behaviour must be designed to influence the behaviour of another animal. This means that natural selection must have acted on the sender to fashion the signal, and on the receiver to detect and decode the signal.

In other words, to count as communication, either a series of events (or putative signal) must have been designed as such by natural selection, or by some other designing agent, or it must be intentional.[28] Human communication involves all three of these. Some, such as facial expression, has been designed by natural selection; some, such as speech, is intentional; and some, such as electronic communication, has been designed by engineers. All three are formally equivalent, in that they are all intentional systems, interpretable in terms of the intentional stance.

Returning, now, to the injury-feigning bird, we could say, on the one hand, that the distraction display has been designed by natural selection to lure the predator away from the nest, either by invoking an innate reaction on the part of the predator or by inducing the predator to believe that the bird is injured. From the evolutionary point of view, it does not matter how the bird deceives the predator, provided that its communication is effective. From the point of view of the intentional stance, it does not matter whether the predator believes (in the realist sense) that the bird is injured. All that matters is that the predator behaves as if it were part of an intentional system. In other words, if whatever is going on in the predator's head serves the function of a belief in an intentional system, then the predator does have a belief.

On the other hand, we could say (taking a realist stance) that the bird intends to fool the predator by feigning injury. The bird may believe that the predator will be deceived because it automatically pursues an apparently injured prey, or the bird may believe that the predator will be deceived because it believes that the bird is injured. In either case, the bird really does have a belief that is in principle identifiable outside the role that it plays in the system. As we shall discover, there are many philosophers who take the view that beliefs are mental states that take up space in the brain, and are in principle (physically) identifiable. Taking this view, it is possible that either the bird or the predator (or both) may act automatically, but it is also possible that one, or both, of them may have a real mental state (belief) that plays a role in the system.

At the beginning of this chapter we noted that if your dog walked into the kitchen you could interpret its behaviour in a number of ways. You could take an anthropomorphic stance (treating the dog as if it were human) and suppose that it came into the kitchen because it believed there might be food available. But you know that the dog is not a human, so you might want to take a more scientific behaviourist stance. The dog comes into the kitchen because it is hungry and it associates the kitchen with food. This is a viable explanation of the dog's behaviour, but this does not mean that it is necessarily correct. It might be that the dog does believe (in the realist sense) that there is food available in the kitchen. If you take this view, you are taking a realist stance. On the other hand, it might be that the dog does believe (in the functional sense) that there is food available in the kitchen (i.e. it has a mechanism that functions like a belief, but this mechanism is not physically identifiable in the brain).

In taking a realist stance you are assuming that the dog is capable of true beliefs, just as we are. You are not treating the dog as if it were human—you are simply supposing that dogs can have beliefs, as we do. After all, dogs have legs as we do. They are not exactly the same as ours, but they are legs nevertheless. So why can't dogs have beliefs, even if they are not exactly the same as ours?

Some eliminative materialists would say that dogs cannot have beliefs like ours, because we don't have beliefs, we only think we do. We think we do as part of our folk psychology, but we are mistaken, because folk psychology is a theory that is false. As we have seen, other philosophers counter the eliminative stance by saying that folk psychology is not a theory, and so it cannot be a false theory. So what about the dog?

The problem is that you cannot tell simply by looking at the dog's behaviour whether it is capable of belief. A realist would claim that whether dogs can have beliefs is an empirical matter, because beliefs are mental states residing (and taking up space) in the brain, and one day it might be possible to identify beliefs in the brain of a human or a dog. Such identification would settle the matter.

But wait a minute—surely we can tell something by interpreting behaviour. After all, stones do not have beliefs, because their behaviour is entirely the result of outside forces. A clockwork mouse does not have beliefs, because its behaviour is very simple. So what aspect of behaviour is required for us to attribute beliefs to the behaving agent, whether it be an animal or a robot? The answer, according to the philosopher Daniel Dennett, is that if the behaving agent is part of an *intentional system,* then the agent behaves as if it has beliefs. As far as Dennett is concerned, if the agent behaves as if it has beliefs—then it has beliefs, because he defines beliefs from a functional stance. For Dennett, the stone and the clockwork mouse are not part of any intentional system, so they do not have beliefs. The dog is part of an intentional system, so it can have beliefs. For Dennett it is not necessary for the dog to have beliefs in the realist sense (if it does, then well and good), all that is necessary is that it has something that functions like a belief. When it comes to humans, Dennett does not commit himself to realism, and he does not really tackle the question of what human beliefs entail. As we see in the next chapter, other philosophers are not satisfied with this situation. They want to know what beliefs entail in the realist sense.

To sum up, when I see Border entering the kitchen, and heading for the cat's food, I may assume (taking an anthropomorphic stance) that she thinks like a human, and approaches the food with the preformed intent of eating it. If I dismiss this idea as unscientific, I can adopt a behaviourist stance that accounts for the dog's behaviour in terms of associative learning—the cat's dish is associated with food, the kitchen is associated with the cat's dish, etc.—and so there is a chain of stimulus and response that leads the dog to the cat's food. Putting on my philosophical hat, I can

71

suppose that the dog is part of an intentional system and, therefore, has a belief about the cat's food in the sense that the dog has something that functions like a belief. I am now adopting a type of functionalist stance. On the other hand, taking a realist stance, I can suppose that the dog might have brain states that are (in principle) identifiable as beliefs.

4

BEYOND AUTOMATA

The previous chapter ended with a realist supposition. The supposition is this. My dog Border comes into the kitchen because she is hungry and believes that there will be food available. What would be necessary for this supposition to be true? For most philosophers, it would be necessary for Border to have a desire for food, to believe that food is available in the kitchen, and to be able to connect these two mental states to form the intention to go into the kitchen. (e.g. I am hungry, I believe that there will be food in the kitchen, therefore I should go to the kitchen). Traditionally, philosophers regard a belief as a mental state, representational in character, taking a proposition (either true or false) as its content. So the content of Border's belief would be 'there is food in the kitchen.' But this might be true or false. Border's voluntary behaviour (going to the kitchen) is instigated both by her desire and by her belief.

What we are suggesting here is what is called by philosophers the orthodox realist view. This says that for a person or an animal to have a belief there must be some kind of representation in the brain that corresponds to that belief. As we have seen, some philosophers, such as Daniel Dennett, seem to take the view that, provided there is evidence for the functional equivalent of a belief (e.g. the system seems to be an intentional system), there does not have to be a one-to-one correspondence between a belief and its representation in the brain.

But what do we mean by representation in the brain? What kind of representation in the brain would be necessary for an animal to have a belief in the realist sense? In this chapter we explore various kinds of representation, and we ask how these relate to the idea that animals might be capable of belief, cognition, feelings, and related phenomena.

Information and Its Representation

Knowledge is a form of stored information. Our knowledge is stored in our brains, our bodies, and our environment (diaries, books, etc.) We usually think of knowledge as information in memory to which we have access, but much of our knowledge is inaccessible and guides our behaviour in hidden ways. The information stored in our brains, bodies, and environment can be put to a variety of uses.

Tree rings contain information about the age of a tree. In a sense, they naturally represent the age of the tree. Information is an objective commodity, and in itself it is inert. Trees do not make any use of the fact that their rings indicate their age. To make a difference to the course of events, information somehow must be accessed, picked up, and used. A prospective user of information must develop or acquire devices for picking up the information and for putting it to some use.

Suppose I cut down a tree and count 50 tree rings. The tree bears information that it is 50 years old, but what if the tree were 50 years old yet there were only 49 rings due to lack of growth in a particular year. The fact that the tree is 50 years old is not the cause of there being 49 rings (so the 49 rings do not contain information about the exact age of the tree). It is the combination of the true age of the tree and the missing growth during one year that causes the 49 rings. It would be incorrect to conclude that the 49 rings bear misinformation about the age of the tree. Rather, the 49 rings may prompt a human observer to misinterpret the true age of the tree.

To take another example, normally, a car petrol gauge indicates 'empty' when the tank is empty. It indicates a state that is, from the point of view of the designer, the state that it was intended to indicate. Therefore, the petrol gauge cannot (correctly) indicate that the tank is empty if the tank is not empty. If something goes wrong, then the pointer on the petrol gauge can point to the 'empty' sign without the tank being empty. In this case the petrol state is not properly indicated. What the pointer on the 'empty' sign does indicate, when the tank is not empty, is the fact that there is something wrong with the device. To say that the petrol gauge misinforms the driver simply means that it induces the driver to misinterpret the state of the tank, because the driver assumes that all is well. Thus we can conclude that information is always objectively there, but the system that makes use of the information must rely on some assumptions about reliability, and about the absence of 'counteracting causes'.

A device used to provide information, to a prospective user of the information, must represent the information in some way. The representation must have content and satisfaction conditions.

By content we mean that a representation refers to or denotes something. It is about something and states something about that which it denotes. For example, a road sign that indicates a school (usually depictions of children) denotes that a school is in the vicinity and states that the driver of an automobile should be cautious. Representations also must be satisfactory, that is, provide certain satisfaction conditions. They can be evaluated as accurate, as reliable, as correct, as well founded, etc. For example, if you came across a school sign in the middle of the desert, far away from any habitation, you might be sceptical about its veracity.

There are many types of representation. Natural representation is more or less interchangeable with information. Thus smoke represents fire, footprints indicate animals, etc. This type of representation means little more than registration, or indication. Another type, namely implicit representation, is the same as information available for use by a competent user. For example, a DVD displays information about top–underside, which is important if the user is to insert it the correct way up. If the designer of the DVD is satisfied that every user will recognise the topside by signs inevitably present on all diskettes—it is always grooved on one side and not the other—then he may decide to add no further information. If he decides otherwise, then he may add a symbol, or explicit representation, of the topside. In the former case, the required information is already implicit in the design of the diskette, and we may say that 'topside' is implicitly represented. In the latter case, topside is explicitly represented, because the designer decided that this was necessary.

Implicit representation is a form of true representation, because the state of affairs may be misrepresented. For example, it may be that the DVD reader is installed in the computer in an unconventional orientation, so that the normal topside is now not the side that should be on top when the DVD is inserted. Representation can be implicit in more than one way:

(1) The information is somehow there, but must be inferred. One can infer from the structure of a diskette that one side is the topside.

(2) The information is structurally 'embedded'. For example, a person's body temperature is measured by sensors calibrated so that the outcome is in tune with other bodily processes. Implicit in the calibrated information is a conversion process not accessible to, or appreciated by, the person, but is nevertheless embedded in the structure.

(3) The design of a particular process is based upon an 'assumption' that there are certain relevant reliabilities about the world. For example, our visual perception is based upon the design assumption that light comes from above. Now, concave objects cast a shadow in the region nearest to the light source, while convex objects cast a shadow in the region furthest from the light source. In nature the light source (the sun) is above the animal, so to discriminate between concave and convex objects it is necessary only to look at the direction of the shadow. Many animals, including humans, use this cue in object recognition. Here the implicitness rests upon a 'presupposition' by the designer. The presupposition is that the environment in which the device is designed to work has certain properties. In other words, the representation makes sense only in the context of its normal usage, a property that philosophers call normative.

We now come to explicit representations. By 'explicit' it is meant that the information is made obvious in a physical manner, and is not simply part of a procedure. If a representation is to be explicit, then there has to be a physically identifiable bearer of the information (the token) and, additionally, something, most likely someone, who can be identified as the user of the information. For example, many motor cars have icons on the dashboard that light up when there is a certain kind of fault. Such icons provide information, but if we are considering only the car as the system, they cannot be said to be explicit representations. If, however, we count both the car and the driver as the system, then the icons explicitly represent some fault in the system. Thus explicitness is not a local property, but a systemic property. A system involving an explicit representation must be defined in such a way as to include the user. In the case of implicit representations, there is no such requirement. For example, the designer of a DVD player could provide a symbol representing topside, but this would not be necessary if all DVD readers were mounted in a particular orientation, because inserting the diskette the correct way up would be a simple procedural matter. But if some DVD readers are mounted in a different orientation, then it might be prudent for the designer to provide an explicit representation of the orientation of the DVD. Moreover, this explicit representation would have to be readily understood by the user. The designer would have to take the user's abilities into account in designing the symbol.

Where explicit representation is a proxy for an object, property or event, it is usually called a sign. In some cases, there is a straightforward one-to-one relationship between a sign and its referent. Thus icons are signs that resemble the things that they represent (e.g. a thermometer icon represents temperature). Indices are signs that causally relate to what they represent (e.g. smoke is a sign of fire). Finally symbols are not straightforward proxies for objects, they are arbitrary labels. When an explicit representation takes the form of a symbol, it leads the agent to conceive of the object, in the sense of putting it into a mental context. What a symbol signifies is an act of conception. It is an act which is reactivated anew in the agent's mind each time he, she, or it encounters the symbol.

Knowledge and Belief

We have seen that external representations can be implicit or explicit. Now we come to the question of internal representations. We have eyes and ears that receive information from the external world, and we have numerous other senses that obtain information from inside our own bodies. It is the same for animals and robots. Our security robot monitors the external world for the possibility of intruders via cameras and microphones, and at the same time has internal monitors for temperature, fuel level, etc. Our slugbot looks for slugs, and according to assessments made by its internal monitors on its need for energy, it shifts its activity to refuelling (taking the slugs to the digester).

The information that we receive from outside we traditionally think of as adding to our knowledge. Some of this incoming information is stored in memory, and provided we can recall it, we tend to think of it as our store of knowledge. This tradition tends to equate all knowledge, and all forms of intellectual behaviour, such as reasoning, with knowledge of facts and knowledge of rules. The philosopher Gilbert Ryle attacked this picture as 'the intellectualist legend' and pointed out that intelligence is not only manifested in behaviour guided by knowledge that (i.e. knowledge of facts and knowledge of rules), but also in behaviour guided by knowledge how.[1] His main argument was the following: if behaviour is intelligent only when it is guided by reasoning and if reasoning itself can either be done intelligently or not, then reasoning is intelligent when it is guided by reasoning, and you are trapped into an infinite regress. We often believe and do the right things without having previously consulted all relevant reasons and rules. Practice and know-how precede articulated knowledge that. This know-how is fundamental to the rest of our mental lives.

79

What do we normally mean by know-how? We mean knowing how to do something, like how to ride a bicycle or how to swim. It is not possible to articulate such knowledge. We cannot tell someone how to ride a bicycle, or how to swim. We cannot use such knowledge for purposes other than the task in hand. It is irrelevant to give reasons for such knowledge. We can summarise this by saying that knowledge how is (somehow) in the system, in contrast to knowledge that which is available for the system.

What do we normally mean by knowledge that? We mean knowing as a matter of having accessible, in different ways, explicit information about a person, object, place: as in 'I know he is a philosopher'; 'I know this car is a sports car'; 'I believe that building houses a dog's home' (or a robotics laboratory). It is possible to articulate such knowledge. We can tell someone about an object, person, place, etc., and they can act on the information. We can use such knowledge for more than one purpose. We can give reasons for believing such knowledge to be true, or correct.

Knowledge requires some kind of representation. Know-how depends upon implicit representations. To know how to touch my nose with my eyes closed, I have to know, amongst other things, the length of my forearm. This information is represented implicitly in my kinesthetic system. The representation changes as I grow, and can be changed by learning—must be changed in fact. 'I can't play football any more,' complained a boy I knew during a period of rapid growth. 'I've stopped knowing where my feet are.' Since he took up playing football again very soon, he must have learned to relocate his feet. Similarly, to ride a bicycle, I must learn to coordinate numerous kinaesthetic systems to do with steering and balance. I can then say that I know how to ride a bicycle, but this type of knowledge is tied to the procedure of riding a bicycle. For this reason, it is sometimes called procedural knowledge.

This type of knowledge has to do with accomplishing tasks. For example, the question 'Do you know how to breath?' seems pointless, simply because the recipient is already demonstrating the answer. However, doing x does not always imply knowing how to do x. It is possible to do x by chance (e.g. unlocking a safe by fooling around). Moreover, in some cases the agent could not do otherwise as a result of natural laws. If a robot starts moving around, it does not make sense to say that the robot knows how to displace molecules in the surrounding air. Displacing molecules of air is not a task relevant to the robot. It is an inevitable consequence of moving, by virtue of natural laws. Robots can be said to have know-how when they exhibit behaviour relevant to some task that the designer intended the robot to accomplish. Similarly, animals have numerous procedures that enable them to engage with the natural world. These include searching (e.g. for food), navigation by the sun and stars, and many other tasks that the designer (nature) has selected.

Now we come to the explicit type of representation involved in knowing that. As we have seen, explicit representations require a token, also an interpreter and user of the representational system. In the case of mental representations, the token lies in the memory system of the brain. The interpreter lies in the memory retrieval system. The user is the cognitive system (see below). Some philosophers believe that the only evidence that someone has this or that explicit knowledge comes from their utterances. Others accept other types of evidence.[2] Most philosophers agree that all explicit representations can be articulated (we can talk about our explicit knowledge in a way that we cannot talk about our implicit knowledge), and for this reason the term declarative knowledge is applied.

Philosophers usually distinguish between knowledge and belief (propositions involving knowledge are true, whereas beliefs may be false), but this distinction is not important here. What is important is that declarative knowledge (the kind that people declare) is available only to language-using agents. This means that it is not available to animals (assuming that no non-human animals have language). But it does not follow that animals are incapable of using knowledge. To be open-minded, we should regard declarative knowledge as a variety of explicit knowledge that pertains to humans. This leaves us free to recognise that there may be some animals, or robots, that can make use of explicit knowledge.

The question is: do animals have explicit knowledge? When my hungry dog, Border, comes into the kitchen, does she know that there is likely to be food there, or does she simply use her know-how (this is what to do when hungry)? A behaviourist would have no difficulty in explaining how Border gained her know-how through associative learning.

Suppose we train a rat to push a lever to obtain a reward. With repetition the rat comes to associate the situation with reward, and it learns that it can obtain rewards by responding to the situation in a certain way. This kind of animal learning can readily be explained from a behaviourist stance, without invoking any supposed mental abilities on the part of the rat.

Suppose now that we have two groups of rats trained to press a lever to obtain one type of reward (one group gets food pellets, the other sucrose solution), and two other groups that are trained to pull a chain to obtain the same types of reward. After training, half of all the rats (i.e. half of each group) are removed to another apparatus, in another room, where they are given the following treatment. They are allowed free access to their previous reward (pellets or sucrose) either when already pre-fed on the food (i.e. satiated), or when injected with lithium chloride (LiCl), which makes them sick for a day or two (a procedure called food-aversion conditioning). In the first case the rats are not hungry, so offering them food somewhat devalues the rewards that they have previously been receiving. In the second case, the food was devalued by being associated with sickness. The remaining rats act as controls, being placed in the new situation without any special treatment.

Next, all the rats are tested back in the original situation under the original conditions. The rats that received no special treatment behave just as before, but the rats placed in the new situation when not hungry, and those dosed with lithium chloride, behave very differently. They are not prepared to work as hard as previously for a reward that had been devalued by their experience in the second situation, either by pre-feeding or by the lithium chloride treatment.

It is difficult to explain these results from a behaviourist stance, because the rat associates the training situation with normal reward, and it has never experienced devalued reward in this situation. It has only experienced devalued reward in another situation.

It is not difficult to account for these results from Daniel Dennett's intentional stance. These results, and similar results from numerous other experiments, suggest that the rats are behaving rationally, in the sense that they are not prepared to work so hard for an outcome that has lost some of its value (for whatever reason). The situation can be interpreted as an intentional system; thus 'the rat believes that if it presses the lever it will obtain food (which it believes to be of a certain value)'. In other words, the rat behaves as if it believes that the outcome of the work is of little value.

Anthony Dickinson, the scientist responsible for many such experiments, takes a realist stance, claiming that the rat's behaviour is mediated by explicit knowledge of the contingency between the action and its outcome.[3] The fact that the rats learned to work to obtain R in situation A, then experienced R (devalued) in situation B, and then declined to work for R in situation A, strongly suggests that the rats are making use of their knowledge that R has been devalued. In other words, the rats really do believe that R is of little value.

Does this mean that a procedural explanation of the rats behaviour is not possible? Suppose we could design a robot that could learn to obtain R in situation A, and could experience R (devalued) in situation B. What would happen when the robot found itself back in situation A? Obviously, much would depend on what went on in the robot's 'brain'. A knowledge-based process, similar to that postulated for rats would not be difficult to engineer. But what about a purely procedural process? Could the outcome-devaluation effect be demonstrated by a robot using purely procedural learning? The answer is—yes it can.[4]

Our robotic rat is placed in an instrumental learning experiment, involving both lever press and chain pull, just like the real rats. The robotic rat can learn, and produces learning curves typical of real rats. The robotic rat is now trained. It is then subjected to reward-devaluation experiments with both satiation and aversive types of devaluation, as were the real rats. The results are illustrated in Fig. 3. They demonstrate that the typical outcome-devaluation effect occurs in the robot rats, and the data are very similar to those from real rats.

Here we have a situation in which a robot, programmed in a purely procedural way, involving no symbolic or explicit representations, is behaving in the same way as a rat in a typical outcome-devaluation experiment. This shows that a purely procedural account of the outcome-devaluation effect is possible, and that an explicit knowledge-based account is not necessary to explain the observed behaviour. Of course, this does not mean that the rat is not in fact using explicit representations in solving the problem. Indeed, there have been many experiments that suggest that they do.[5] What the robot study shows is that the results of such experiments are open to alternative interpretation, what we might call cognitive versus procedural explanations of the various findings.

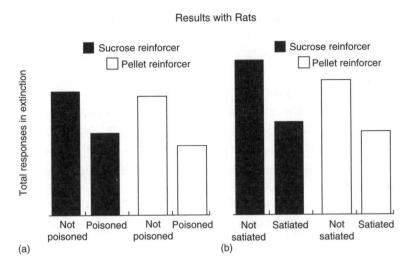

Results with Rats

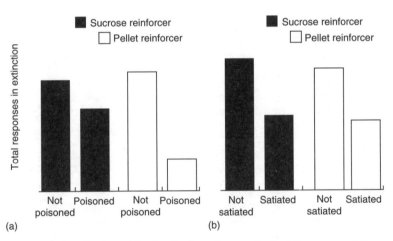

Results with Robots

Fig. 3. Results of outcome devaluation experiments obtained from rats and from robots. A high column indicates a willingness to continue to work when no reward is available (extinction), and a low column indicates unwillingness to work (caused by devaluation of the expected outcome in a different situation, as explained in the text).

Let us now look at another example of scientific investigation of explicit representations in animals. Many species of ants and bees can navigate over long distances using cues from the sun, etc. However, when they come near to their home destination they use landmarks to guide them over the final stages. For many years, a popular theory has been the 'snapshot' theory. According to this theory, an insect records a panoramic 'snapshot' image of the surroundings at the target position, and this snapshot is stored in memory. When it must return to this location, the insect compares this snapshot with its current visual image in order to determine a home direction. The snapshot is an explicit representation of the landmarks near the target.[6]

To test this, and other, theories of insect navigation, robotic 'ants' have been devised and tested in the real (desert) environment. Overall, these experiments showed that some of the theories about navigation do work well when tested in the real world environment. However, the robotic studies also showed that a stored snapshot image was not really necessary to achieve navigation by landmarks. Once again, the possibility of a purely procedural explanation arises.

Now what? Taking a realist stance, the question is whether the animals (rats or ants) have explicit representations that function as beliefs (i.e. the rat really believes that the outcome of a certain behaviour will be such-and-such, and the ant really believes that this (the snapshot) is what home looks like). The numerous experiments on these animals show that a realist account is certainly plausible in that the animals behave as if they had such beliefs. By the same count, the robotic experiments show that a procedural account is also plausible. In other words the realist must admit that the robotic rat and the robotic ant do not really have beliefs, even though they behave in the same way as the real rats and ants.

Taking a functionalist stance, both the real animals and the robotic animals behave as if they had the requisite beliefs. Whatever the responsible mechanism is in the brain, it plays the role of a belief; therefore it is a belief. Whether the real animals and the robotic animals have the same type of mechanism is an empirical question on which the jury is still out.

So are Anthony Dickinson's rats capable of cognition? The answer to this question depends partly upon our view of cognition. Is cognition primarily a matter of ability, or of mechanism? There is no question that many animals can do apparently clever things. An obvious example is tool-using—the use of an external object as a functional extension of the body in attaining an immediate goal. Tool use has been studied in animals for many decades, but whether tool-using requires cognition remains controversial. Part of the problem is that many people, including some scientists, tend to attribute cognition to an animal when it does something that would require cognition in a human. This is to characterise cognition functionally, i.e. in terms of what is achieved by the animal. But, as we saw in Chapter 2, we already have a term for that kind of thing, namely intelligent behaviour. It would be better to think of cognition in terms of mechanism, that is to say, cognitive processes involve a certain kind of mechanism—one that requires manipulation of explicit representations, and making them available for use by other processes.

If I drive along a familiar route, and discover that the road is blocked at some point, I make a diversion. Knowing that the road is blocked at a particular point, I can use this knowledge in a number of ways: I can alter my route, warn other drivers, complain to the authorities, and so on. This ability to use knowledge in various ways (and not restrict it to a particular procedure) is necessary for cognition. As mentioned earlier, explicit knowledge (knowledge that) is available for the system, whereas procedural knowledge

(knowledge how) is embedded in the system and not available for use outside the procedure to which it is tied. The ability to manipulate explicit representations is an important aspect of mental activity, but it is only part of the story. After all many modern machines can manipulate explicit representations, but this does not imply that they have minds. Mental activity is also characterised by a certain degree of rationality, and by certain types of feelings.

Rationality

We have seen that to adopt the intentional stance towards something is to ascribe beliefs, desires, and rationality towards it in order to explain or predict its behaviour. For example, in discussing the removal of dead bees from the hive, Dennett writes 'when a bee dies its sisters recognise that it is dead, and, believing that dead bees are a health hazard and wanting, rationally enough, to avoid health hazards, they decide they must remove the dead bee immediately.'[7] In fact experiments show that bees remove anything on which they smell oleic acid. If oleic acid is daubed on a live bee it is carried off. The bees follow a simple rule. It is Mother Nature that appreciates the adaptive nature of the behaviour pattern and chooses it for this reason.

What does Dennett mean by rationality? According to Dennett, the intentional stance is—and here I opt for the accuracy of what non-philosophers might term philosopher speak—the tactic of interpreting an entity by adopting the presupposition that it is an approximation of the ideal of an optimally designed (i.e. rational) self-regarding agent. For most philosophers, on the other hand, rationality is a feature of cognitive agents that they exhibit when they adopt beliefs on the basis of appropriate reasons. Rationality can be contrasted with non-rationality and irrationality. A stone is non-rational because it is not capable of carrying out rational assessments. A being capable of being rational, but who nevertheless violates the principles of rational assessment, is being irrational.

A rational agent capable of rational thought must, at least, be coherent, responsive, and self-critical. Thus a person holds beliefs irrationally if any one belief conflicts with any another, if their beliefs are not adapted in the face of contrary evidence, or if their assumptions are not open to question. In everyday life, a rational person does not have to subject each and every belief to constant or conscious deliberation. He or she may hold beliefs intuitively, through habit, or on some authority. However, a rational person must be able to muster a good defence of a belief when the occasion demands. A belief contrary to the dictates of reason is irrational. Some beliefs, however, are non-rational because they are matters of taste and no reasons are required. (I prefer the colour blue, say; many small girls prefer pink.) Similarly, some beliefs are non-rational because they are necessarily matters of faith, or of ingrained emotional response, e.g. certain phobias. (My partner is terrified of cockroaches even though, rationally, she knows they cannot harm her.)

However, Dennett is not referring to the type of rationality outlined above and it may seem that he is stretching a point when he claims that bees believe that dead bees are a health hazard and want (rationally enough) to remove them. What he means is that 'Mother Nature appreciates the adaptive nature of the behaviour pattern and chooses it for this reason.'[8] But is Mother Nature a rational agent capable of rational thought? Can Mother Nature have reasons?

The problem is that the notion of rationality arises in a variety of disciplines.[9] For example, philosophers and psychologists regard a rational process as one where beliefs, actions, etc., are adopted for appropriate reasons. This type of rationality has been dubbed philosophical or psychological-rationality (P-rationality).[10] Economists regard behaviour as rational when it maximises a quantity (usually some kind of utility), no matter what process produces the behaviour. This may be called economic-rationality (E-rationality). Biologists are interested in principles of maximisation that relate to fitness (see Chapter 1), and this may be called behavioural-rationality (B-rationality). Whereas P-rationality refers to a process, E-rationality and B-rationality relate to behavioural outcome. Thus I see my dog, Border, catching and eating a lizard, I can ask whether a rational process is involved (P-rationality), whether she is behaving efficiently and economically (E-rationality), and whether she is improving her genetic fitness (B-rationality). If she catches the lizard in an unthinking reflex manner, then the first answer is no. If she catches it with speed, skill, and little energy expenditure, then the second answer might be yes. If she eats a lizard that is poisonous, then the third answer might be no.

Rational processes do not necessarily imply reasoning processes. Philosopher Fred Dretske distinguishes between minimal rationality, doing something for reasons, and normative rationality, doing something for good reasons.[11] The drunken man looking for his keys under a lamp post—not because he left them there, but because the light is better there—is demonstrating minimal rationality.

Dretske points out that animals and/or machines may have minimal rationality, in the sense that their behaviour is governed by some thought-like process, even though their reasons for action are not what we would regard as good reasons.

Rational thought does not always result in rational behaviour. A person may know what behaviour is rational, but may be compelled, or may choose, to opt for one that is not. Normally, we think of a rational person as being capable of performing a number of actions at any one time, knowing the consequences of each, and having a complete and consistent order of preference among them. We also expect a rational person to be able to solve certain types of problem, such as a transitive inference problem. Suppose we tell a person that A is bigger than B and that B is bigger than C, and then ask whether C is smaller than A. We would expect them to be able to infer, from the information provided, that C is smaller than A. If a person was unable to deal with such a problem, or was inconsistent in answering such questions, we would conclude that they were being non-rational (e.g. not paying attention), or being irrational.

At one time it was thought that a capability for rational thought was necessary to be able to solve transitive inference problems, but it is now known that young children, squirrel monkeys, and even pigeons can master such problems.[12] The evidence suggests that some non-cognitive, seat-of-the pants ability to order things transitively can be revealed in a variety of animals, by well-designed experiments. In other words, a rational decision-maker is one that consistently makes the same choice when in the same state and when given the same set of options. This implies that the options can be ordered with respect to one another, and that the first option in the ranking is always the one chosen, and that multiple choices are transitive. Moreover, the choices are made in accordance to some maximisation principle (always choose the top option in the ranking). In other words, the E-rational decision-maker maximises a quantity, usually called *utility*.

Theories of rational behaviour are commonly used in the disciplines of economics and psychology. These theories have nothing to say about the psychological processes that generate rational action. They merely state what would be rational in certain circumstances. There are various microeconomic laws logically derived from rationality assumptions, and there is considerable evidence that a wide variety of animal species obey these laws.[13] These studies provide another line of evidence supporting the view that animals exhibit E-rational behaviour that may, or may not, be the outcome of a thought process. In other words, scientific evidence that supports the view that animals are E-rational, or B-rational, does not imply that they have minimal rationality in Dretske's sense.

In an uncertain world, it makes sense to behave consistently and rationally (i.e. to maximise utility), and this is probably what Dennett (above) had in mind when he said that the intentional stance involves 'the ideal of an optimally designed (i.e. rational) self-regarding agent'. He did not mean that Mother Nature literally 'appreciates the adaptive nature of the behaviour pattern and chooses it for this reason'. He meant that natural selection is a process that can have the same results as the series of choices made by a rational person. As we saw in Chapter 1, natural selection is a type of design process that can often have the same results as well-informed rational human design. Animals are designed to behave rationally in the circumstances that they would normally meet in nature. The bees (above) remove their dead comrades, because this is the rational thing to do in the circumstances. They are exhibiting B-rationality.

Rational behaviour is not necessarily an indication of mental activity. On the other hand, normative rationality—the way that beliefs, desires, and actions fit together as a coherent whole—is regarded by most philosophers as an essential component of a mind.

Feelings

There is more to having a mind than having explicit knowledge and making rational decisions. After all, a chess-playing computer has an explicit representation of the state of play, and can makes rational decisions in accordance with the rules of chess. But we do not think of a chess-playing computer as having a mind. It may be that the computer is capable of minimal rationality, but does this imply that it has a mind? Many philosophers would take the view that, while minimal rationality is necessary for a mind, it is not sufficient.

Suppose our security robot has an on-board map of the premises that it is supposed to patrol. Such a map would be an explicit representation of the premises, and it would not be difficult to endow a robot with such a map. Moreover the robot can decide (rationally) how to use the map in a number of different ways to suit the occasion. Thus it could use the map to find its way around. It could use the map to report the location of disturbances. It could even print out a copy of the map and give it to someone upon request. There is no question that such a map would be an explicit representation that could be put to various uses, and there is no question that the robot could be programmed to make rational use of the map. However, we would not think of such a robot as having a mind.

What then is missing from the robot? Suppose the robot caused an accident by making a mistake. Rational beings can make mistakes. Our security robot would (sometimes) know when it had made a mistake, and it could easily be programmed to say sorry on such occasions. However, such an apology would not cut much ice with the injured party, because the robot would not feel guilty. It would not feel guilty, because it has no feelings. The injured party would regard the mistake as being due to a fault in the robot, not a fault of the robot. What is the difference here? We cannot attempt to answer this question now, but it is clear that part of the difference is due to the fact that this particular robot has no feeling, and does not feel guilty.

Does my dog Border feely guilty when she is caught lying on the sofa? She certainly looks guilty to my anthropomorphic eye, but then I know that anthropomorphism is not a good guide to reality. Does my dog have feelings? What are feelings anyway?

Have you ever wondered what it is like to be the Queen of England? Of course, in a material sense you know what it is like

93

(more or less), but that is not what is meant by the question. What is meant is—what does it feel like to be the Queen? After all, the Queen had an upbringing very different from yours; she has responsibilities very different from yours, etc. So have you ever wondered what it feels like to be the Queen?

Have you ever wondered what it feels like to be a clockwork mouse? No you have not, because you know that a clockwork mouse is not an appropriate subject for this type of question. A clockwork mouse cannot have feelings, so there cannot be anything that it is like to be a clockwork mouse.

Many philosophers regard the kind of agent, for which it is possible that there is 'something-to-be-like', to be the kind of agent that could have a mind.[14] For them, our security robot could not have a mind, because there is not something that is something-to-be-like that robot. The security robot was deliberately designed to be an automaton, a mindless machine with no feelings.

Philosophically, the issue here is subjectivity. Every person is a subject of experience, and every person experiences the world (somewhat) differently. If animals and robots are capable of subjectivity (i.e. are subjects of experience) then they are likely to see the world very differently from us. By subject of experience we don't simply mean that the agent is subjected to some stimuli, as in the notion that a building was subject to damage. What is meant is that the agent is the recipient of experience, and knows it. Thus a person has self-knowledge about their own experiences. For example, I can say that I had a dream, meaning that I know (believe or remember) that I had a dream. If my spouse has nightmares and I don't have nightmares, then it makes sense for me to wonder what it is like to be a person who has nightmares. It makes sense, because I believe that other people have the mentality to have nightmares. When my dog, Border, is asleep, she sometimes appears to be dreaming. Does it make sense for me to ask what is it like to dream like a dog? It makes sense only if I believe that my dog has the mentality to be the subject of dream-like experiences. When my dog dreams she exhibits dream-like behaviour (vocalisations and rapid-eye-movement), but this does not necessarily mean that she is subject to dream experiences. To have the requisite mentality, my dog must not only have the experiences, but she must know that she has them.

The purpose of this discussion is not to establish whether certain animals do, or do not, have subjective experiences. The purpose is to outline (only outline) what is minimally necessary for mental activity. Most philosophers agree that the mark of the mental is intentionality,[15] and the most fundamental kind of mental state is belief. To have a belief in the realist sense there must be an explicit representation of the content of that belief. In the non-realist sense, there must be something that functions like a belief (e.g. in an intentional system). In either case, the belief must interact with other mental states in a normative or P-rational way. Finally, for an agent to have a mind, there must be something that it is like to be that agent. In other words the agent must be capable of being the subject of mental experiences. So, as a rule of thumb, for an animal or robot to have a mind it must have intentionality (including rationality) and subjectivity. Not all philosophers will agree with this rule of thumb, but we must start somewhere.

5

MENTAL POSSIBILITIES

Is it possible for a non-human alien, an animal, or robot, to have a mind? Some scientists and philosophers think that some animals have some mental abilities, others disagree. Some scientists and philosophers think that, one day, some robots will have minds of their own, other disagree. Why do we want to know anyway?

We want to know about animal minds because animals are important in our lives. We hunt them, we husband them, and we eat them. Some people think that animals are given to us by nature (or by god) to treat as we like and do with as we will. Other people worry about animal welfare to the extent that their opinions dictate their diet, their lifestyle, and sometimes their hostilities. There is no question that our prejudices about animal minds influence the lives we lead, our laws, and our politics.

We want to know about robot minds, because robots are becoming increasingly important in our lives, and we want to know how to manage them. As robots become more sophisticated, should we aim to control them or trust them? Should we regard them as extensions of our own bodies, extending our control over the environment, or as responsible beings in their own right? Our future policies towards robots and animals will depend largely upon our attitude towards their mentality.

So far we have seen that a prima facie case for alien mentality can be based on two basic questions. Firstly, is the alien behaviour part and parcel of a rational or intentional system? Secondly, is there something that it could be like to be that alien? (Let us call this property *subjectivity*.) These two starting points result from the work of two philosophers, Daniel Dennett and Tomas Nagel.[1] They do not get us very far, but at least we can say that agents that are not intentional systems, or agents that cannot conceivably have subjectivity, do not even get to the starting point for consideration as candidates for agents with a mind. An example might be a clockwork mouse. In this chapter we will look at animals and robots that might get to the starting point. We will look at various interesting behavioural situations suggestive of mental activity, maintaining a neutral stance for the time being.

If I want my dog, Border, to desist from busily digging up the flower bed while hunting for vermin, I can use a carrot or a stick. I can order her out (stick), or I can pick up her lead (carrot). The latter move is a form of deceit, because I have no intention of taking her for a walk. Deceit is a term used by scientists for a form of communication in which the signaler benefits at the expense of the receiver. For example, a young chimpanzee, seeing some food not noticed by others, gives an alarm call to divert the attention of seniors, and then takes the opportunity to secretly grab and eat the food. Some theorists, taking a behaviourist stance, assume that this is a matter of ordinary learning, and that the young chimp had simply learned the alarm trick to obtain food secretly, just as I use the lead trick to get my dog moving. Others claim that the chimpanzee has theory of mind. This is a claim that some animals are capable of mental state attribution (i.e. one animal attributes a particular mental state to another). In other words, the young chimp induces the others to believe that there is a predator in the vicinity. A belief is a mental state, and in this case it is attributed by the young chimp to other chimps. In other words he believes that by giving an alarm they will believe there is a predator in the vicinity. Theory of mind implies that the animal is capable of cognition, and exhibits true intention. Theory of mind is deployed by some scientists in investigating apparent deceit, teaching, and self-awareness in animals. Note, however, that the scientific definitions of deceit, teaching, etc., are neutral with respect to the mechanism responsible.

An underlying assumption here is that we (humans) assume that other individuals, just like ourselves, have minds, and we treat them as having mental states, such as beliefs, feelings, and intentions. Moreover, this attribute is biologically useful, in that it enables us to predict (to some extent) the consequences of our social actions. Some biologists like to ask 'whether animals, like us, treat other individuals as if they have mental states, because if they do, it would make an observable difference to their behaviour. Any animal that did act as if other individuals have mental states would then be said to have a *theory of mind*.'[2] 'When I assume you have particular thoughts and fears, I am using my theory of mind.'

We need to distinguish, here, between 'weak' and 'strong' theory of mind. If an animal simply acts as if other individuals had mental states it has a weak theory of mind, in the sense that it is simply (unthinkingly) attributing properties to another animal. As we have seen, people often interpret the behaviour of animals and robots from an anthropomorphic stance, as if they were like us, when they know perfectly well that this is not the case. They do not actually believe that an animal, such as an ant, has a mind. Nor do they believe that a simple 'ant-like' robot (see Chapter 1) has a mind. They take an anthropomorphic stance, because it is part of human nature to do so.[3] Moreover, they do not really have a theory about the mind of the animal or robot. They may behave as if they had a theory, but they do not have a theory that is in principle falsifiable.

A strong theory of mind implies that the agent who attributes mental states to another actually believes that those states exist. In other words, the agent attributing mental states to another has a mind capable of such attribution. Strong theory of mind also implies that the agent is prepared to have their belief falsified. In other words the agent has a theory. For example, if I truly believed that a particular robot really did have mental states that influenced its behaviour, I would have a theory about the mind of the robot. If the designer of the robot then convinced me otherwise, by providing evidence that I was not previously aware of, then I would see that I was mistaken, and I would revise my belief in the face of the new evidence.

From the point of view of the scientist who sees an agent behaving as if it had theory of mind, it is reasonable to conclude that the animal might have a mind capable of mental-state attribution, but it is also possible that the animal concerned has no such mental abilities, but is merely behaving as if it had them. Obviously, if a young chimpanzee can really believe that another chimp believes something, then the young chimpanzee is capable of mental activity. Chimpanzees are closely related to humans, and this raises the question of how we know about our own beliefs.

This topic is philosophically controversial.[4] Some hold that such self-knowledge is intuitive, others that it is inferential. As we shall see, the evidence from developmental psychology is that, between the ages of 3 and 4 and a half, children develop the capacity to

99

distinguish their own beliefs from those of others. The older children are capable of, and can make use of, theory of mind. So we might expect that some chimpanzees are too young to have theory of mind, whereas older chimps are capable of it. However, we are not able to investigate young chimp behaviour in the same way that we can investigate theory of mind in human children (i.e. using language). So, when applied to aliens, strong theory of mind is in danger of begging the question of when it assumes that the agent who attributes mental states to another really believes that those states exist. In other words the agent has the mental ability to make a truly cognitive attribution, the very ability that we are trying to investigate.

Weak theory of mind is also not entirely straightforward. You will have seen the way that people talk to babies. Mothers speak to their babies in a manner that differs considerably from normal human speech, and this trait seems to be culturally universal.[5] The mother expects (and often receives) some response from the baby, so this seems like a case of natural communication (see Chapter 3). What other people may think varies. Some think it perfectly normal, even though the mother is using baby talk that does not make grammatical sense, or have any real (linguistic) meaning. Others think that it would be better (for the baby) if the mother spoke properly to it (presumably the assumption here is that the baby is mentally capable of being influenced by normal speech). Others may think that talking to babies is a waste of time and effort (presumably because they think that the baby is not mentally capable of being influenced in this way).

It appears that four-month-old infants prefer to listen to baby talk than to normal human speech.[6] So it may be that baby talk is the best way to communicate with a baby. Whether this is so does not provide a reason for mothers to behave in this way, because most mothers are unaware of this evidence. What the evidence does suggest is a functional justification for baby talk (i.e. that it is good for the baby in some way).

What is the mother doing? She is communicating with her baby. Is this a case of strong theory of mind? Probably not, because this would imply that the mother really believes that she is doing the right thing, in the sense that she has a reason for talking in a particular way, or a theory about what is good for the baby (i.e. she would have to be in a position to say 'I do it because I believe that the consequences will be such and such'). Some mothers may behave in this way, but most simply (unthinkingly) talk to babies in a natural (and culturally universal) way. In other words baby talk is an aspect of communication by design, like most of animal communication. Thus mothers naturally respond to babies in this way, and this behaviour is somehow beneficial for the baby (and the baby's response reinforces the behaviour of the mother). However, much baby talk is delivered in the language that the baby will later grow up to understand, and it would seem that the mothers behave as if the baby has some mentality. In other words, the mother has weak theory of mind with respect to her baby. This is not to say that the mother is not capable of strong theory of mind, simple that she does not usually exercise this capability in these circumstances.

Some people talk to plants. Do such people have theory of mind? First we should ask whether there is any communication here. If talking to a plant alters the physiology or behaviour of the plant, then in the biological sense, there is communication. Thus if the plant grows more quickly, blooms earlier, or reacts in any way, as a result of being talked to, communication exists between the person and the plant. Whether there is good evidence that such communication exists is another matter.

It might be that the person has simply developed a habit of talking to plants, and does not know or care whether the plant responds. This would be behaving like a zero-order intentional system (see Chapter 3). On the other hand, it might be that the person wants to influence the plant in some way and talks to it for that reason. In other words, such a person really believes that by talking to the plant they can influence it in some way. This would be a first-order intentional system (note that the belief that the plant is influenced by being talked to might be incorrect, in which case communication would not have taken place). Finally, it might be that the person talks to the plant because they believe that the plant is capable of responding mentally.

If the person simply behaves (e.g. like baby-talk) as if the plant was registering the message, the person would have weak theory of mind. If the person intends or believes that the plant will respond mentally to his or her speech, then the person would have strong theory of mind. The person may be mistaken in their belief, but the belief may be rational in the absence of evidence to the contrary. Talking to plants may be confusing to other people who do not believe that plants are capable of responding, but this is a matter for debate, and the issue hinges on an empirical question.

We now come back to the question of whether animals can have theory of mind. Let us go back to a previous example. When an incubating sandpiper is disturbed by a ground predator, it may leave the nest and act as though injured, trailing an apparently broken wing and luring the predator away from the nest. When the predator has been led a safe distance from the nest, the bird suddenly regains its normal behaviour and flies away. We could say (weak theory of mind) that the bird is behaving as if the predator believed that it had a broken wing, but in reality the bird has no theory about the predator, it just reacts in a way that is effective, as a result of either instinct or learning, or both. From the evolutionary point of view, it does not matter how the bird deceives the predator, provided that its communication is effective.

On the other hand, we could say (strong theory of mind) that the bird intends to fool the predator by feigning injury. The bird may believe that the predator will be deceived because it automatically pursues an apparently injured prey (just as I believe that my dog will react automatically when I pick up her lead), or the bird may believe that the predator will be deceived because it believes that the bird is injured. In all these cases the bird would have to have the mental ability to harbour such beliefs about the predator. The last of the above possibilities is a second-order intentional system. According to Dennett,

An intentional system S would be a second-order intentional system if among the ascriptions we make to it are such as S believes that T desires that p, S hopes that T fears that q, and reflexive cases like S believes that S desires that p.

The difference between animals and humans, according to Dennett, is that

it is hard to think of a case where an animal's behaviour is so sophisticated that we would need to ascribe second-order intentions to it in order to predict or explain its behaviour.[7]

After a quarter of a century of intensive work on the possibility of second-order intentions in animals, it appears that Dennett may have been right on this point. Richard Byrne has reviewed the evidence for intentions in animals involved in imitation, tactical deception, teaching, and communication. The best case for second-order intentions seems to come from studies of teaching. According to Byrne,

The techniques of demonstration, moulding, and scaffolding imply teaching in the intentional as well as the functional sense: an understanding of the specific lack of knowledge of the young animals which are being taught. The finding of (second-order) intentional teaching in a great ape, the chimpanzee, is consistent with what we have already seen of the species ability to attribute mental states in several other areas.[8]

Let us examine this claim. To count as teaching an animal must 'modify its behaviour, to no immediate benefit to itself, only in the presence of a naïve observer, and with the result that the observer gains knowledge or learns a skill with greater efficiency than otherwise.'[9] This definition rules out cases of learning aided by social facilitation, enhancement, or imitation, where the animal whose behaviour is copied takes no account of whether it is watched. (Note that this definition also covers teaching in ants.)[10] Borderline cases occur in many species. Thus cats allow prey to escape in the presence of their young; raptorial birds release prey that are less and less disabled as their young grow older; many primates pull their youngsters away from novel objects.

Richard Bryne claims only two cases where teaching proper has been observed, both involving chimpanzees. He reports that

After the death of her own baby, Washoe, a chimpanzee taught to sign American Sign Language, was given an infant chimp, which she adopted. The human caretakers did not teach the infant Loulis to sign, and indeed they stopped signing at all in her presence. Washoe used both demonstration (with careful attention to Loulis' gaze direction) and moulding of Loulis' hands to teach her to sign. Washoe herself had been taught by humans, who sometimes mould her hands into the correct configuration and put the hands through the necessary movement: this is what she did several times with the infant Loulis. The direct effect of Washoe's demonstration and moulding is hard to measure, but certainly Loulis learnt many signs during the years in which she saw no human sign and got no human encouragement for doing so: after 5 years she reliably used 51 signs, often in two-sign combinations like 'person come'.[11]

Chimpanzees have also been observed teaching their infants in the wild. Christopher Boesch observed mothers demonstrating nut-breaking skills to their young.[12] The technique is to crack the nut using one stone as a hammer and another as an anvil. The mother demonstrates the skill slowly and in full view, paying close attention to the eye-gaze of the youngster and continuing only when it is watching. Mothers have also been seen setting up the situation so that the youngster can achieve something itself. A process called 'scaffolding'. For example, when a juvenile puts a nut on the anvil, the mother removed it and replaced it in a more favourable orientation. A mother may also reorient the hammer for a youngster, so that it could crack the nut itself.[13] It is not our purpose here to attempt to evaluate this evidence scientifically. No doubt there will be other studies, and the scientific community will eventually draw its own conclusions. What is of interest now is some kind of philosophical evaluation of the situation.

If one animal (the 'teacher') manipulates the behaviour of another (the 'pupil') by demonstration, moulding, scaffolding, or whatever, does this imply second-order intention on the part of the teacher? Certainly, we can say that the teacher behaves as if it wants, hopes, or desires the pupil to behave in a certain way. Whether it really wants, hopes, or desires in the true mental sense is another matter. Even if we grant that the teacher wants, hopes, or desires in the strong intentional sense, we still only have a first-order intentional system.

To have a second-order system the teacher would have to want, desire, or hope that the pupil not only learns a skill (e.g. learns how to crack a nut), but has a mental experience such as understanding or knowing that something (e.g. about cracking nuts). It is not clear that this has been achieved in the cases outlined above.

This situation is rather like that of a parent helping a child to learn to swim or ride a bicycle. The parent is not actually teaching the child in the sense that the parent believes that the child will come to believe something. What the parent is doing is putting the child in a situation (e.g. of confidence) where it can learn how to swim or ride a bicycle.

But even granting this, there remains the question of whether:

(a) the teacher believes that the pupil has the mental capacity to understand what it is being taught (as would have to be the case for a second-order intention to be relevant);

(b) the teacher believes that the pupil will learn by association (i.e. without any real mental processing), giving a first-order intentional system; or

(c) the teacher simply goes through the teaching routine, like baby talk and teacher ants, without any true intention, in which case we would have a zero-order intentional system.[14]

In cases (a) and (b) the teacher would have to have the mental ability to hold the relevant beliefs, but in case (c) no mental ability would be required. The evidence (reviewed above) suggests that the teacher attributes mental abilities to the pupil. Whether this attribution is explicit or implicit is unclear. Even if it is explicit (i.e. the teacher really believes that the pupil will learn), it remains unclear as to whether the attribution is correct (i.e. the teacher could have strong theory of mind about the pupil, but the theory might be wrong). To sum up, observations of animal behaviour have, in some well-documented cases, provided evidence of some aspects of mental activity in animals. However, there remain problems of interpretation that we will have to leave to the scientists to sort out.

The ability to copy the actions of another person, to imitate them vocally, etc., would seem to involve a certain amount of mental activity. After all, to imitate someone you must observe them, remember the movements you wish to copy, and translate this memory onto movements of your own body. Studies of imitation in humans are very much tied up with notions of the self. 'By imitating the other we come to know how he feels and thinks simply because we know how we ourselves thought and felt when we made similar movements or held similar postures in the past. Empathy [in the sense of objective motor mimicry] would seem to be a case of kinesthetic inference.'[15] As we shall see (Chapter 6) developmental studies suggest that the 'machine self' (which includes the ability to distinguish between self-made movements and other movements, the ability to imitate others, and to respond to oneself in a mirror) develops before awareness of the objective self (i.e. knowing about oneself as an object in the world).[16]

Studies of imitation in animals offer some hope of penetrating the question of whether there are any non-human animals that are aware of themselves objectively. However, studies of animal imitation must be undertaken with care, because much of the apparent imitation seen in animals is not true imitation. Apparent imitation may occur as a result of social facilitation (e.g. eating the type of food that others are eating), emulation (achieving the same goal as another animal, but by different behaviour), and a tendency to pay attention to the behaviour of other animals, and then seeing the opportunity that they have seen (stimulus enhancement). However, there are cases where true imitation does seem to occur in animals. For example, in one study quail were allowed to watch other quail, either pecking a treadle to obtain reward or stepping on a treadle to obtain reward. Birds that watched others receiving food for operating the treadle in a particular way were more likely to adopt the same behaviour when it came to their turn to operate the treadle. If they did not see their comrades being rewarded, then they did not copy them.[17]

There have also been numerous demonstrations of robots imitating people, or other robots.[18] Robot researchers are inspired by imitation and social learning in animals and humans to create controllers for their autonomous robots. Autonomous robots? Well, not autonomous in every respect (see Chapter 8), but nevertheless impressive. To get a robot to imitate another body requires that the robot has information about its own body and the body that it is trying to imitate. This information does not have to be designed in, but can be learned. The robot perceives its own body primarily through propriocention (just like us), and perceives other agents through external senses. So there must be a cross-modal matching mechanism that perceives equivalences between the two modalities. It is a short step from here to a robotic 'machine self' (see above) and a further step to a robotic 'objective self'.

So when I see a robot imitating a human, I am likely to attribute mental qualities to the robot, but should I ascribe such qualities? Attribution and ascription are almost synonymous, but it is useful for us to make a distinction here. By attribute we mean to intuitively endow an agent with certain qualities, as a mother does to her baby. By ascribe we mean that we have reason to endow such qualities.

For the philosopher Peter Strawson the way we ascribe properties to an agent is central to the concept of a person.[19] For example, we may say 'he is tall', denoting physical characteristics, and we also ascribe mental characteristics. Thus we may say, 'he is clever', 'he is in pain', or 'he is writing a letter'. These relate to assessment of character, of feelings, and of behaviour. For Strawson, a person is a being to which such properties must be ascribed.

Strawson insisted that our nature makes it impossible for us not to hold that normal people ought to behave in certain ways. Consequently, we are disposed to have certain feelings (e.g. resentment, indignation) towards them if they behave badly. If we believe that they ought to behave in certain ways, then we must also believe that they can behave in those ways. If it is revealed to us that they cannot so behave, then we alter our views, because we no longer regard them as normal people. In other words we ascribe certain properties to other people on the basis of our belief that they are normal people like us.

Strawson's account of people is important, because it focuses our attention on what it is about an agent (person, animal, or robot) that would make us suspect that it had mental abilities? In particular, to what extent is that other person/animal/robot like me? When we have a case of a robot imitating a person, we have a primitive sort of reciprocity. If we ask the question—can machines have intentional stances applied to them?—the answer is obviously yes, when the machine in question is one that can imitate our actions.[20] Would we ascribe mental qualities to it? Maybe so, maybe not, but note that if we do not ascribe such qualities on the basis of imitation by a robot, it is difficult to argue that we should ascribe such qualities on the basis of imitation by an animal.

Reciprocity enters into Dennett's intentional stance at the level of a second-order system. As we saw earlier in considering an example of teaching in chimpanzees, to achieve a second-order intentional system, the teacher would have to desire or hope that the pupil not only learns a skill (e.g. learns how to crack a nut), but has a mental experience such as understanding or knowing something about cracking nuts. Both teacher and pupil are chimpanzees, and to demonstrate reciprocity there must be evidence of mental process in both animals. Another way of putting this reciprocity idea is that 'There is only something that it is like to be, say, a dog, if there is something that it is like for the dog to be you.' Strawson himself writes that 'There would be no question of ascribing one's own states of consciousness, or experience, to anything, unless one also were ready to ascribe, states of consciousness, or experience, to other individuals of the same logical type as that thing to which one ascribes one's own states of consciousness.'[21]

Another possible indicator of mentality is false belief. Suppose that I am playing dominoes against a robot. If I am unable to play (match one of the two numbers) then I must draw a piece from the boneyard (stock of unused pieces). However, suppose I draw from the boneyard even though I do have a matching piece. I am then deceiving my opponent into believing that I cannot match either of the required numbers. This ploy could be to my advantage. This strategy would work only if my opponent was capable of believing that I could not play a certain number. Of course, a clever opponent could detect that I was cheating, not immediately, but in the long run. Suppose now, that I begin to suspect that my robot opponent is using this ploy against me. My robot opponent is inducing me to have the false belief that it does not hold the two particular numbers required. By careful observation, and by remembering all the numbers played, I could probably verify that this was happening. What should I conclude? If the robot was a person, I would conclude that my opponent had a belief about my (false) belief that my opponent did not hold certain numbers.

Demonstrating false belief is a way of investigating the development of theory of mind in children. A typical scenario is as follows: The child subject watches a scene in which a man (the experimenter) and a boy are in a room together. The man hides a piece of chocolate under a box in front of the boy. The boy then leaves the room, and while he is absent the man moves the chocolate to another hiding place, say a cupboard. The subject is then asked where the boy will look for the chocolate upon his return. Three-year-old subjects invariably say that the boy will look in the cupboard. They are unable to distinguish between the current state of the world (chocolate in the cupboard) and the absent boy's mental state (his belief that the chocolate is in the box). By the age of four and a half, most children can consistently make this distinction.

An important point about this type of work is that we, as humans, have no difficulty in coming to the conclusion that, by the age of four and a half, most children are capable of correct belief ascription. The evidence is convincing partly because we know that the children are going to grow up to be mentally competent adults like us (this is part of Strawson's point about being prepared to ascribe to others what we ascribe to ourselves), and partly because both investigator and subject have the benefit of language. There comes a point when the child can understand the question, and can provide an answer that is convincing to the investigator.

Another possible candidate for behaviour of an animal or machine that would make us suspect that it had mental abilities is cooperative behaviour. Cooperative behaviour takes many forms, ranging from cooperation among ants (usually termed collective behaviour, because there is no direct communication between the participants as explained in Chapter 1) to human behaviour that requires cooperation at the mental level. There are numerous studies of cooperation among robots designed to fulfil particular tasks, such as security surveillance, reconnaissance, bomb disposal, and even playing soccer. Some of these cooperate by sharing both knowledge and know-how. However, this does not mean that these robots have any mental abilities. For computer scientists, there is no problem in endowing a robot with explicit representations. It is the other aspects of mentality that is a problem for them.

Let us now do a thought experiment. Suppose that you are cooperating with a sheepdog robot (such robots have been made). The robot is perfectly capable of rounding up sheep without minute-to-minute guidance from you. In fact the only influence that you have over the robot is to urge it to go faster or slower.

The robot (type-I) is perfectly capable of rounding up sheep, or ducks, provided that they are of the domestic type that flock. In fact the robot's overriding priority is to keep the flock together. It must adjust its speed of manoeuvre to the state of the flock. If it moves too quickly the flock will tend to break up, because not all the individuals can go at the same speed. If the robot moves too slowly, the flock momentum is lost, and they may head off in a new direction. The type-I robot is an automaton and carries out all these manoeuvres automatically. It can do no other.

One day you and the robot are rounding up a few sheep, and you notice that one of them is lame. The robot has adjusted to the slow speed of this animal and the flock is moving rather slowly. Even so, the lame sheep is finding it hard to keep up. You would prefer that the robot leave the lame sheep out of the flock—but how to do it? The thing is to get the robot to speed up so that the lame sheep is left behind, but the robot is programmed to keep the flock together at all costs. Give it a try anyway.

You order the robot to speed up. It speeds up very slightly then slows down again. It is keeping the flock together and must adjust is pace to the slowest sheep. You order it to speed up again—no response. As expected, the robot will not speed up and break up the flock. Then suddenly it does speed up dramatically, leaves the lame sheep behind, and rounds up the others. You are surprised.

Later you ask the robot designer why the robot broke the overriding rule of keeping the flock together. 'Oh, I forgot to tell you that was a type-II robot. It is the same as type-I but a bit more intelligent.' What does this mean? Surely a more intelligent sheepdog robot is one that is better at rounding up sheep. Now here's a thought—did the type-II robot realise that you wanted to separate the lame sheep, and so it acted accordingly? In other words, by requesting the robot to speed up, even though it was against the normal 'rules', you were in effect asking for the robot's cooperation.

My dog, Border, has a special yip, accompanied by a fixed stare at me, that indicates that she is requesting something (water, food. cuddle, or to be let out). If she is in the house and hears a commotion outside (someone arriving, or another dog vocalising), she wants to join in the fun, but does not go to the door and attempt to get out, she comes to me and requests to be let out. She is, in effect, asking for my cooperation. I realise, from the context, what she wants. Similarly (somehow), the robot realises what you want (to separate the lame sheep). We are tempted to say that the robot believes that you want it to speed up and that the consequences will be that the lame sheep is left out of the flock, and the robot believes that this is what you want. Similarly, it is tempting to endow Border with some cognitive ability in seeking my cooperation. There are many situations where the behaviour of an animal prompts us to think that the animal must have some mental ability. Unfortunately, in such cases we cannot ask the designer, as is the case with robots, and we cannot rely on language, as is the case with children.

Let us now examine one more possible candidate that would make us suspect that an animal had mental abilities: tool-using is usually defined as the use of an external object as a functional extension of the body in attaining an immediate goal. A crow that drops a mussel from a height onto rocks to smash it open is not using a tool; but an Egyptian vulture that throws a stone at an ostrich egg to break it is using the stone as an extension of the body. There have been many studies of tool-using in animals, notably those of Wolfgang Kohler, who was interned on the island of Tenerife during World War I. He devoted his energies to studying chimpanzees at the Anthropoid Station there, and reported on his work in *The Mentality of Apes* (1925). Kohler's experiments required chimpanzees to use tools to obtain food rewards. For example, in one experiment the chimpanzee is required to use a stick from outside its cage. All the ingredients necessary for the solution to the problem were visible to the chimpanzee.

One of the chimpanzees was given two bamboo poles, neither of which was long enough to reach the fruit placed outside the cage. However, the poles could be fitted together to make a longer pole. After many unsuccessful attempts to reach the fruit with one of the short poles, the chimpanzee gave up, started playing with the poles, and accidentally joined them together. The chimpanzee jumped up and immediately ran to the bars of the cage to retrieve the fruit with the long pole. Kohler interpreted this, and other instances of problem solving, as 'insight' on the part of the chimpanzee. Although Kohler's results were initially accepted, they came under fire from the behaviourists, who were able to provide behaviourist explanations, primarily based on the discovery that chimpanzees that were allowed to play with poles, etc., prior to any experiments, did much better at problem solving.[22] In other words, they were able to provide procedural explanations based upon ordinary associative learning.

Now let us look at a modern version of this type of experiment. Zoologist Alex Kacelnik and his colleagues have studied New Caledonian crows.[23] These birds have been observed to make and use tools in the wild to obtain food. Wild-caught birds, kept in captivity, were able to select tools of the appropriate size for a novel task, without trial and error learning. In another study, juvenile crows were raised in captivity, and never allowed to observe an adult crow. Two of them, a male and a female, were housed together and were given regular demonstrations by their human foster parents of how to use twig tools to obtain food. Another two were housed individually, and never witnessed tool use. All four crows developed the ability to use twig tools. One crow, called Betty, was of special interest.

Basically, we were interested in a problem which is a classic in animal cognition, and this is the ability of an animal to choose between tools which are appropriate for a task or inappropriate for a task. So we gave the crows a problem and we supplied two tools. And the appropriate tool, the hook, was stolen by this bird's partner. So this bird was faced with a tool that did not work to solve the task. At that point, we would have expected to conclude the trial. But we didn't, because we saw this animal picking up the straight wire, which could not be used to get food out of a vertical pipe, and bend it, in a very determined action, and use it to solve the problem.

To see that led us to say, come on, this is a very striking ability. We were not expecting it. Can she do it again? And then we designed a new experiment, in which we only supplied the straight wire. The animal, every time, or nearly every time, picked it up, and using different parts of its environment, shaped the wire to the appropriate final shape. This completely suggested a new kind of ability that we hadn't thought about before.

What we saw in this case that was the really surprising stuff, was an animal facing a new task and new material and concocting a new tool that was appropriate in a process that could not have been imitated immediately from someone else.[24]

A video clip of Betty making a hook can be seen on the Internet.[25]

This type of study usually comes under the heading of 'animal cognition', but what is actually observed is problem-solving behaviour. As we have noted, it is better to reserve the term 'cognition' for the mechanism involved; otherwise, there is a danger of assuming that a particular mechanism is implied by the observed behaviour.

In this chapter we have reviewed some mental possibilities—in particular the possibility of mental activity in animals and robots involved in apparent reciprocity, false belief, mental cooperation, and tool-using. These examples do not, of themselves, enable us to conclude that the agent responsible has true mentality, but they require explanation, and they provide a platform for further investigation. In order to conduct further investigation, we need to have some idea about the kind of mental mechanism that might be responsible. We make a start on this in the next chapter.

6

THE FEELING OF BEING

Although some of the apparently clever things that animals do induce us to *attribute* cognitive abilities to the animals concerned, these do not permit us to *ascribe* such abilities. In Chapter 5 we made a distinction between attribution and ascription. Although attribution and ascription are almost synonymous, it is useful for us to make a distinction. By *attribute* we mean to intuitively endow an agent with certain qualities by saying, for example, the animal behaves *as if* it had certain mental capacities. By *ascribe* we mean that we have *reason* to endow such capacities. Certainly, in some of the examples outlined in Chapter 5, the animals behaved as if they had cognitive abilities, but the scientists concerned rarely have *good reason* for such attribution. As we saw in Chapter 4, in some cases where it seemed obvious that cognitive abilities were involved, other non-cognitive explanations were subsequently suggested. Remember that (to distinguish cognition from intelligence) we are regarding cognition as a *mechanism* involving manipulation of explicit representations (Chapter 4). So when we ask, 'What kind of explanation are we looking for?', the answer is that we are looking for an explanation in terms of a mechanism that embodies mental phenomena. Whether such explanations are possible, we will discuss in Chapter 7.

In this chapter we will be concerned with that other major component of the mind, namely *subjectivity*. Are animals capable of subjectivity or, in other words, is there *something that it feels like* to be another animal? Those concerned with animal welfare often refer to animal *sentience*, and this term appears in much animal welfare legislation. Unfortunately, it is not entirely clear what the term *sentience* means. To some it means consciousness, to others it means 'capable of sensation', but these are very different matters. All animals are capable of sensation, in the sense that they have sensory apparatus that provides them with information, but this is not what is usually meant by animal welfare scientists. Their most usual argument goes like this—logically we cannot tell whether animals are sentient, just as we cannot logically prove that other people are sentient, therefore we should give animals the benefit of the doubt, and treat them as if they are sentient. But this is a *moral* or *ethical* argument, not a type of argument usually found in science or philosophy (of mind). In other words, we are all happy for those concerned with animal welfare to attribute sentience to animals, but this is not the same as ascribing sentience. In this chapter we are looking at the possibility of ascribing subjectivity to animals. We are looking for a *reason* to suppose that there is *something* that it is like to be that animal. This does not mean something that it is like *to us*. It does not make sense to ask what it would be like (to a human) to be a bat, because a human has a human brain. No film-maker, or virtual reality expert, could convey to us what it is like to be a bat, no matter how much they knew about bats. All that we are being asked is—is there *something* that it is like to be a bat?

Qualia

Qualia is the philosophical term given to subjective qualities, such as the way coffee smells, the way a cat's purr sounds, the way coriander tastes, and the way it feels to receive an electric shock. Philosophers disagree on the definition of *qualia*, some even doubting their existence. But an ordinary person knows what you mean if you say, 'this wine tastes the way chocolate tastes.' However, a person who has never tasted chocolate might know what you mean, but would not be able to imagine the taste. A person who has never had an electric shock cannot bring to mind what it is like to have an electric shock. On the whole, people who have experienced the same qualia as you can bring the experience to mind when you describe your experience, and people who have not had this experience cannot do this. This is not to say that all people are the same. Some people like the taste of coriander, while others dislike it, because it tastes 'soapy' to them. It turns out that people to whom coriander tastes soapy have a known genetic difference from ordinary people. Nevertheless, you know what they mean when they say that coriander tastes soapy, and you can imagine what coriander is like for them, because you know from experience what soapiness is like.

Many qualia, such as tastes and smells, seem very distinct to us, and stick in our memory. The same appears to be true for animals. The psychologist Paul Rozin has investigated specific hungers in rats. Most animals are unable to detect many essential vitamins and minerals either by taste or by their levels in the blood. Nevertheless, animals deficient in certain vitamins or minerals do develop strong preferences for foods containing the missing substances. For many years such specific hungers posed something of a problem for scientists trying to explain how animals knew which food contained the beneficial ingredients.

Paul Rozin and his co-workers showed that rats deficient in thiamine develop an immediate marked preference for a novel food, even when the new food is thiamine deficient and when the old food has a thiamine supplement (which of course they cannot detect). If the deficiency persists, the preference is short-lived. On the other hand, if consumption of novel food is followed by recovery from dietary deficiency, then the rat rapidly learns to prefer the novel food. Such rapid learning on the basis of the physiological consequences of ingestion enables the rat to exploit new sources of food and thus find out which contains the required ingredients. Rozin realised that a vitamin-deficient diet is like a slow-acting poison. He noted that an aversion to a familiar but deficient food persists even after the rat had recovered from the deficiency. Rats (and other animals) that become sick after eating a poisoned food also show an aversion to such food and show a more than normal interest in novel food.[1]

Two points arise from this work that are of interest to us. Firstly, the evidence suggests that animals learn to avoid dangerous foods and to consume beneficial food on the basis of *general sensations* of sickness or health, rather than on the detection of specific chemicals. This theory is important to us, because it implies that animals are capable of experiencing general sensations of sickness or health (though not necessarily in the something-that-it-is-like sense). Secondly, the research shows that animals, having *only once* experienced the taste or smell (or sight in the case of pigeons) of a novel food that subsequently made them sick, never touch that food again, indicating that the distinctive novel taste or smell sticks in the memory, just as distinctive taste and smell *qualia* do in humans.

These discoveries do not prove that animals experience *qualia* but they are suggestive of it, in the sense that having and remembering such experiences is necessary for qualia.

In Chapter 2 we saw how animals are adept at trading off competing pressures and arriving at the best outcome.[2] One scientist who has been in the forefront of this kind of research is Michel Cabanac. In one study he kept rats at a comfortable temperature (25°C), with *ad libitum* food, but with restricted water availability.[3] To obtain water when thirsty, the rats had to venture into a run housed in a climatic chamber and stay there for 2 hours. The rats were tested over a range of temperatures, and were allowed to drink tap water, or water containing saccharin in a range of concentrations. The amount of water drunk under these various conditions was measured. The amount of water drunk during a session reflected the animal's thirst (which was the same for all sessions, i.e. 22 hours of water deprivation), the palatability of the water, and the ambient temperature that the animal had to endure to obtain water.

The results of these experiments showed that the rats drank more water the greater the concentration of saccharin, but at the same time they drank less water the colder the environment. The total amount drunk per session was therefore the result of three influences: the animal's water need, the palatability of the water, and cold discomfort. These results are in line with other research showing that many animals, including a variety of reptiles, birds, and mammals, trade off among competing motivational priorities. What is interesting about this particular experiment is that saccharin has no nutritional value for a rat and does not suppress appetite. It seems that rats simply like the sweet taste. On the basis of this and other experiments, Cabanac suggests that the animals make their behavioural choices so as to maximise their sensory pleasure.

As long ago as the 1940s the famous psycho-biologist Kurt Richter indicated that there is a kind of harmony amongst the animals' physiological and behavioural responses, and his insight has been vindicated. There have been numerous demonstrations of trade-offs in animals. These include trade-off between feeding and risk of predation in stickleback fish, trade-off between feeding and drinking in pigeons, and trade-off between food and territorial defence in pied wagtails.[4]

These, and other, studies (especially those of animal economics see Chapter 2) show that some quantity is maximised in animal decisions between one activity and another. This quantity has different names in different disciplines. When these principles are applied to robots (as we saw in Chapter 2) the term *utility* is often used, without implying anything about the mechanisms involved. However, in his animal studies when Cabanac calls it *pleasure*, he is deliberately implying something about the mechanisms involved. He is claiming that there is an explicit quantity that he calls pleasure, that acts as the common currency of decision-making in animals. You may think that this is going a bit far, on the basis of the evidence. However, Michel Cabanac and his colleagues extended their research to humans.[5]

In one study they asked young male volunteers to report to the laboratory once a week to walk on a treadmill, housed in a climatically controlled chamber.[6] In some sessions the slope of the treadmill was set by the experimenter at a specific gradient, and the subjects were asked to climb 300 m. The speed of the treadmill was under the control of the subject. In other sessions, the speed of the treadmill was set by the experimenter and the slope of the treadmill was under the control of the subject. The duration of all sessions was the time taken to climb 300 m. The stride rate and heart rate of subjects was monitored, and each subject was also asked to rate the 'pleasure or displeasure aroused in his chest and in his legs'.

In a separate set of experiments, both the slope and speed of the treadmill was set by the experimenter for a period of 16 minutes. At minute 14, and again at minute 16, each subject was asked to rate the 'pleasure or displeasure' of their perception in their legs and chest. The experiment covered a range of combinations of slope and speed.

The results of the first set of experiments showed that after an adjustment period of about 7 minutes, each subject made a rather constant choice of speed or slope, whichever was under his control at the time. The outcome was that the subjects adjusted speed and slope reciprocally, with the result that the duration of sessions was constant. In other words, the subjects adjusted treadmill speed and slope to produce an approximately constant ascending speed and physical power. Analysis of the pleasure/displeasure ratings, in both sets of experiments, showed that the ratings followed the same pattern as the subject's choice of slope or speed, when this was allowed. The data were consistent with the view that the choices made by subjects were determined by the discomfort aroused in the lower limbs and chest.

In a similar set of experiments Cabanac found that subjects asked to trade off treadmill slope and ambient temperature adjusted their behaviour to maintain approximately deep body temperature and to limit their heart rate below 120 beats per minute.[7] Again, their ratings of pleasure/displeasure were consistent with the view that the choices made by subjects (they could make alterations to the slope or the temperature) were determined by the discomfort arising from the cold temperature and/or the high work rate.

It is well established that a person's preferred walking gait is that with the highest mechanical efficiency and least oxygen cost. Just as in animals, people are capable of optimising their behaviour to suit their physiological circumstances. Amongst scientists, there are two basic views as to what is going on here. One is that the behavioural and physiological adjustments are automatic, and that the system is attuned to produce the best compromise among the competing demands. We may call this the *automaton view*, since it implies that the body is a kind of self-adjusting machine. The other view is that the feelings of pleasure and displeasure that arise from various parts of the body in situations of motivational compromise are combined in some way, and behavioural adjustments are made so as to maximise pleasure and minimise displeasure. We may call this the *hedonic* view, since it implies that pleasure is the common currency of decision-making.

Both views imply that, in compromise situations, the system strives for the best (or least harmful) solution. As we have seen (above) there is considerable evidence to support this conclusion from animal studies. The fundamental difference between the two views is that in the automaton view the quantity maximised is *implicit*, while in the hedonic view it is *explicit*.

Michel Cabanac, being in the hedonic camp, interprets the pleasure/displeasure ratings given by human subjects as an indication that the pleasure/displeasure is the *cause* of the behavioural and physiological adjustments. The automaton view would be that the pleasure/displeasure ratings are the *consequence* of these adjustments (i.e. the subject is simply reporting on what it feels like to make the adjustments). One of the problems in discussing the automaton and hedonic views of behavioural and physiological adjustment to compromise situations is that these types of adjustment are common to all animals, including humans. Animals cannot report on their feeling, and humans can, but this difference is not sufficient to enable us to distinguish between the implicit and explicit views of the common currency. Michel Cabanac addresses this question by involving humans in choices that he regards as unequivocally explicit.

In one set of experiments, ten young males were invited 'to have lunch in the laboratory at their own usual time for lunch, and receive $12'.[8] Each came on four different days, one preliminary session and three experimental sessions. In the first session they were asked to eat one small (one mouthful) sandwich from each of ten plates, and to give a magnitude-estimate verbal rating of the pleasantness (positive rating) or unpleasantness (negative rating) of each item. The rating was to be a number of their own choice. After first eating ten different sandwiches, the subject ate another one from each plate to modify, if necessary, the rating they had given to each type of sandwich. The subject was then told that he could eat whatever sandwiches were left, because he had been promised a meal. The total number of sandwiches eaten in this preliminary session by each subject was recorded.

In the experimental sessions, the price of each type of sandwich was set according to each subject's rating in the preliminary session. The subjects had to pay for sandwiches that they had rated positive, and were paid for eating sandwiches that they had rated negative. The rates of pay varied from one session to another, there being little difference between sandwich types in the first experimental session, medium differences in the second session, and large differences in the third session. Subjects were told to eat the same number of sandwiches that they had eaten in the preliminary session. The subjects paid for their food out of the $12 that they were given for attending each session.

The results showed that not all subjects preferred the same sandwiches. However, the price rank-order of the ten types of sandwich presented to each subject was based upon their preferences as revealed in the preliminary session. The results of the first experimental session showed that the subjects ate mostly medium and high-palatability sandwiches, but no low-palatability sandwiches, although they could have received a small amount of money for eating the latter. In the second experimental session the subjects ate sandwiches from all the plates. In the third session, they ate sandwiches from all the plates, but the majority were taken from the low-palatability plates.

These results were entirely consistent with the mathematical predictions made on the basis of the pricing of the sandwiches in the three experimental sessions. The hypothesis underlying these predictions was that the subjects should eat more sandwiches whose palatability outweighed the price than sandwiches whose palatability was not worth the price. Cleverly, the relative weighting given the palatability and price indices was different in the three experimental sessions.[9] In other words the subjects could trade off palatability versus money in the same way that they could trade off purely physiological variables in other experiments. In similar experiments Cabanac has shown that people can trade off money versus pain, and money versus cold discomfort.[10]

In another set of experiments, Cabanac pitted thermal discomfort against the pleasure of playing a video game.[11] In the first part of the experiment, the subject played a video game for 1 hour, and every 5 minutes was requested to rate, on a magnitude-estimation scale, the pleasure of playing the video game. In the second session, the subject (without playing the video game) was subjected to a progressively declining temperature (from 25 to 7°C) over 1 hour, and every 5 minutes was requested to rate the pleasure-displeasure aroused by the ambient temperature. 'No anchor (landmark) was given for the ratings; the only instruction received by the subjects was to use positive figures for pleasure and negative figures for displeasure.'[12] In the third session, both video game and falling ambient temperature were presented simultaneously, and the only instruction received by the subjects was that they could terminate the session whenever they wanted to. The pertinent result of the experiment was the duration of the subject's stay in this situation. The hypothesis under test is that

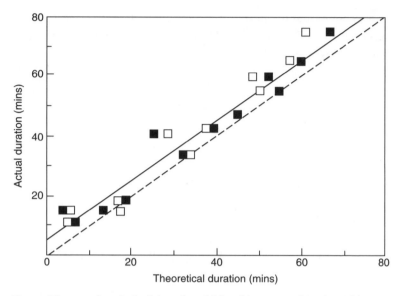

Fig. 4. The actual period of time for which subjects stayed in the cold room playing a video game, plotted against the duration calculated from theory. The dotted line shows the expected result and the solid line shows the result obtained from the experiment. The black and white squares show the results of two different theoretical measures.

at each instant the subject will tend to maximise the algebraic sum of his pleasures. It can therefore be expected that a subject would end the session when the sum of the ratings obtained in the first two sessions equalled zero. It is thus possible for the experimenter to compare the theoretical and actual durations endured by each subject. The results are illustrated in Fig. 4. These results initially disappointed Cabanac, because the data fall systematically to one side of his predicted line. He later learned that, from a theoretical point of view, this is exactly what one would expect. Cabanac had initially overlooked the fact of cost of changing. (When changing from one activity to another no benefits are gained during the actual act of changing. Theoretically, the cost of changing is always carried by the current activity, thus postponing the change.) When this is taken into account, Cabanac's results are exactly as predicted.

Michel Cabanac favours maximisation of an *explicit* quantity, which he calls *pleasure*, because not only do people's pleasure/displeasure ratings agree *quantitatively* with their behaviour in a number of different tasks, but also some of these tasks seem to have distinctly *mental* components. The benefits that the subject gains from money or from watching a video game would seem to be mental benefits. However, there is one experiment that casts doubt on the view that the subject is necessarily trading off *personal* comfort/discomfort. In one of his earlier experiments, Cabanac asked subjects to adopt a certain posture and to hold this posture for as long as they could.[13] It was a sitting posture, back against a wall, but with nothing to sit on. After a short while, holding this posture becomes painful. In a different experiment Cabanac paid subjects a different amount (per second) for the time that the posture was held. He found that, within limits, the greater the rate of pay the longer the subject would hold the painful posture. In subsequent years this experiment has been repeated a number of times by other scientists with the same results. However, in some of these experiments the money went, not to the subject, but to a named relative of the subject. The experiments were carried out on UK students, and on South African Zulus from both urban and rural environments (the rural Zulus, and their relatives, were paid with food). In all cases it was found that the subjects would hold the posture for longer the more closely related they were to the recipient of the money/food. In other words, the subjects were putting up with pain, not for their own benefit, but for that of a relative. In the case of the UK students, the amounts of money sent out to relatives were rather small (in the region of £1 or £2), and it is hard to imagine that the subjects really believed that their relative

127

would benefit greatly from such sums. These experiments are the first unequivocal evidence that humans abide by Hamilton's Rule (see Chapter 1), and they have important biological implications. However, from our point of view, the results suggest that the subjects, while conforming to some ultimate (evolutionary) principle, are also following some proximate urge (to help a relative) that is not a conscious motive, but deep-seated subliminal process. Therefore, it is not clear that Michel Cabanac is correct in assuming that trade-offs involving money necessarily involve a conscious mental component. On the other hand (and possibly in support of Dickinson's view) it might be that the value of the outcome (of sitting in a painful position) is altered by association with the knowledge that the money (or food) is going to a particular relative.[14] That is, the subject believes that the reward is going to a particular relative, and this explicit knowledge influences their behaviour.

Cabanac's experiments, and other work on animal trade-offs, taken together with the work on animal economics, strongly suggest that animals have an internal coherence (of their behaviour and physiology), and that this is also true of humans. In fact, the finding that people behave as they do in very animal-like situations (e.g. the treadmill experiments) supports his view that animals and humans operate in the same way. If Cabanac is correct in thinking that animals maximise explicit pleasure, the implication is that animals experience *qualia*, are capable of *subjectivity*, and have a *self*.

Can animals have a self? When my dog, Border, starts to limp, I pick her up and examine her paws. A little squeeze on each paw tells me where the trouble lies, because she makes a reflex withdrawal of her paw and gives a little yelp. *Does Border experience pain?* In 1945 a Colorado farmer was sent out by his wife into the yard to procure a chicken for supper. He chose a cockerel and decapitated it. Unfortunately he did not aim very well, and although the cockerel lost its head, part of the brainstem remained intact. The animal did not die. In fact it lived a further 18 months. The farmer fed it with an eye-dropper directly into the esophagus, and the bird increased in weight from 2.5 pounds to 8 pounds. It could walk, get up onto a high perch, and even attempted to preen and crow. Now suppose I picked up the headless chicken and pinched its foot, so that it made a foot-withdrawal movement. *Would it experience pain?*

You, the reader, probably answered yes to the first (dog) question, and no to the second (chicken) question. If asked, you would probably say that because the chicken has no brain it cannot experience pain. In other words, because you *believe* that a chicken requires a brain to experience pain, you are not willing to *ascribe* pain to a headless chicken, even though its behaviour is the same as that of the dog. (We will call this the *argument from anatomy*, because we will be returning to it later.) There are two points to make now. Firstly, your *belief* about headless chickens gives you a *reason* for not ascribing pain in this case. Secondly, the question—does *it* (the chicken) experience pain?—raises another question, namely what is the *it*? Is *it* the chickens' body, or is *it* the head? The common-sense answer would be that the head can experience nothing, because it is dead, and the body can experience nothing because it has no head. But neither of these answers really grasp the nettle, because neither refer to the *self* of the chicken.

The Animal Self

As far as other humans are concerned, we *ascribe* mental properties to them, and we expect them to take responsibility for their actions. We have seen (Chapter 4) that for an animal to have *feelings* there must be *something that it is like* to be that animal. An animal capable of feelings must be a *subject* of experience. For an animal to have even the rudiments of self-consciousness (which we will call *self-awareness*, so as to avoid confusion with human self-consciousness), it must have some kind of *subjectivity*. But, you may ask, what is the alternative? The alternative is that the animal is an automaton (see Chapter 1). An automaton can have sensors and can receive information (see Chapter 4). It can be a user of implicit information (and it could even handle explicit information, if it was a knowledge-based automaton). Such automata can be very sophisticated, like our security robot (Chapter 2). An automaton acts on information in a procedural manner, and to do this it must gain the information from the sensors by which it monitors both the external world and its internal state. It is much the same for animals, except that the animal does not always have direct information from sensors. A rat that responds to the absence of thiamine in its diet, without being able to detect the presence or absence of thiamine, is relying on a general experience of sickness or well being. Of course, the information must get through somehow. The *feeling* of being well or unwell must be based on some kind of information. This is a problem that those interested in animal welfare are well aware of. Captive animals seem to suffer from boredom, but what is boredom if not a mental experience?[15] It may seem anthropomorphic, but there is no doubt that animals change their behaviour and demeanor when they have too little to do. The name given by scientists to this change is boredom, without implying anything like human boredom. Nevertheless, there is a problem here. Animals do not have boredom detectors that become activated when they are in captivity. The fact that animals seem to respond to general states of well being, sickness, and boredom do not prove that animals have *subjectivity*, but they are suggestive in the sense mentioned above.

In 1970 Gordon Gallop reported that chimpanzees could recognize themselves in a mirror, and did not simply regard their image as a conspecific (member of the same species), which is the case with most animals. Since then there has been a large amount of work on self-awareness in animals.[16] This work has provided evidence that apes, dolphins, and possibly some monkeys can recognize themselves in a mirror. Some workers are of the opinion that animals that cannot do this do not have *self-awareness*, because to think otherwise would imply that the self is not *unitary* (see below). Others take the view that there can be multiple kinds of self, and that species that do not pass the mirror test may, nevertheless, have selves of a different nature. Just because we tend to think of our own selves as unitary does not imply that this must be true of other species. Phenomena such as possessiveness of objects (this is mine), object keep-away (I am hiding this for myself), and jealousy occur in many species and are suggestive of some sort of self-interest. What then is the minimum concept of *self* that we can imagine?

Philosophers usually distinguish among three different aspects of the self:

(1) awareness of oneself as a material body;
(2) awareness of oneself as the author of actions; and
(3) awareness of one's own thoughts.

(1) Some kind of awareness of one's own body occurs in all animals in the sense of *self-reference*. The most basic type of self-reference is egocentric orientation, by which people and animals determine the positions of external objects in relation to themselves. This orientation is achieved through complex mechanisms of vision, gravity sensing, and kinaesthesis (body-image).[17] However, these mechanisms are entirely procedural, involving knowledge how, but not knowledge that. For example, if a tiny object is placed upon a frog's back, it can move its 'hand' onto its back with great accuracy and remove the offending object. This manoeuvre is entirely automatic, the reflexes responsible being confined to the spinal cord.

131

Animals also exhibit *self-reference* in avoiding obstacles, jumping between gaps, etc. A dog can easily judge whether it can pass through an opening or gap, but when it is carrying a stick, it does not adjust to the necessary extra width, and is liable to become stuck. Such self-reference is entirely procedural, a matter of know-how, whereas self-awareness, even in its most basic form, implies knowing *that* something is true, or believing *that* something is true, about your own body.

One avenue of research in this direction is the ability of animals to copy or imitate others. In child development studies this ability is called *kinaesthetic-visual matching*. Once a child has this ability, it knows what it looks like when it acts, such that it can recognise the identity between its kinaesthetically experienced actions and the visual appearances of these actions. Kinaesthetic-visual matching allows an organism to recognise itself in a mirror. If an organism has this ability, it looks in a mirror and recognises that the visual display in the mirror matches its kinaesthetic experience.

Human children recognise their own mirror images and concurrent video images at about 15–18 months. This is long before they pass the false-belief test (see Chapter 5). Thus imitating others, and recognising that one is being imitated, is an ability separate from understanding that other people can have beliefs. This kind of discovery reinforces the view that the *self* is not a *unitary* phenomenon in humans. It also opens up the possibility that different species of animal or robot can have different kinds of self. Those animals that can recognise themselves in a mirror may well be aware of themselves as material bodies, but this does not necessarily mean that they have the other aspects of self that we ascribe to humans.

(2) To be aware of oneself as the author of actions is a controversial topic even when applied to humans, never mind animals. An *action*,

in philosophical terminology, is behaviour that a person does voluntarily, as opposed to something like snoring, which is involuntary. People are taken to be morally responsible for their actions if they are the cause of the action and could have done otherwise. Traditionally, a certain sort of causal history distinguishes actions from other behaviour. According to this view, a person doing something *intentionally* (or on purpose) results from that person *desiring* something and *believing* something, and therefore having a *reason* for doing something (the action). Thus *action* results from the nexus of *desire*, *belief*, and *intent*, all of which are mental states. Moreover, a *rational person* is expected to be able to give a *reason* for their action. A reason is a kind of explanation in terms of desire and belief. For example, the *reason* that I bought this bird is that I *desired* a singing bird, and I *believed* that this bird was a canary, and that a canary is a kind of singing bird.

Needless to say, philosophers vary considerably in their attitude to *action*. Some hold that all actions are performed as a result of the person having a reason (i.e. they hold that reasons can be causes). Others maintain that actions are movements that we are aware of making, but others claim that (for example) picking up a glass and drinking water whilst engrossed in a conversation is an action of which we are not aware. Some philosophers insist that actions are, at least, aspects of behaviour that involve some *explicit* representation of the goal-to-be-achieved (i.e. they are goal-directed, see Chapter 1). Others see it as a means to an end.

Let us take a specific example,

There are few physical activities that are a necessary part of performing the action of turning on a light. Depending on the context, vastly different patterns of behaviour can be classified as the same action. For example, turning on a light usually involves flipping a light switch, but in some circumstances it may involve tightening the light bulb (in the basement) or hitting the wall (in an old house). Although we have knowledge about how

133

the action can be performed, this does not define what the action is. The key defining characteristic of turning on the light seems to be that the agent is performing some activity, which will cause the light, which was off when the action started, to become on when the action ends. An important side effect of this definition is that we could recognise an observed pattern of activity as 'turning on the light' even if we had never seen or thought about that pattern previously.[18]

In this scenario, there is a task to be done (turning on the light) that is explicitly represented in the mind of the actor, who then sets about accomplishing the task. In other words, the actor has in mind an intended effect (or goal) that is instrumental in guiding the behaviour. The actor *believes* that flipping the light switch will turn on the light, and this is the *reason* for the action. The implication here is that flipping the light switch is a means to an end, and is *functionally equivalent* to other ways of making the light come on, such as tightening the bulb. A criticism of this view is that the alternative ways of achieving an end, or outcome, are never functional equivalents. Thus writing a sentence by hand is not the functional equivalent of typing it on a typewriter or on a word processor. These three ways of writing the sentence have differing results, and involve differing costs in their prosecution That is why the writer chooses to write the sentence one way and not another.[19]

Now let us consider another scenario. Our security robot enters the kitchen and recognises that things would be better if the light were on. In other words, the state 'light on' is a desirable state of affairs (but so are many other states). Having entered the room, the robot reviews the behavioural options. Let us say these are (a) turn on the light, (b) pick up a bottle of cleaning fluid, (c) exit the room. The consequences of these are then evaluated and the option with the most beneficial consequences is chosen. Let us suppose that this is option (a). The robot then starts to move towards the light switch, but at the same time is reevaluating the options, which now include (d) avoid a box in the middle of the room. This type of reevaluation is a frequent occurrence and the robot automatically chooses the most beneficial option each time. This may or may not result in the robot turning on the light. If the robot does turn on the light, we may say that the task has been accomplished, but at no point does the goal (turning on the light) control the behaviour of the robot. In fact the robot is not capable of any explicit representation. It has no cognitive ability and it has no mentality. All its evaluations and decisions are made in an entirely procedural manner, as described in Chapter 2.

Clearly, the philosophical notion of *action* is not a necessary type of explanation in all cases. Some hold that there are alternative explanations that apply in all cases, even those where a person states their intention and then proceeds accordingly.[20] On the other hand, the concept of action is central to our notions of *responsibility* and an integral part of our folk psychology. However, this is a problem of understanding the *human* mind, and when we come to consider *animals* we have little to go on. There have been a few reports of apes attributing *intention* to others, but the evidence is very flimsy.[21] Then there is the work of Anthony Dickinson and his colleagues (see Chapter 4), which provides a good experimental case for the view that rats are capable of goal-directed action, which is regarded by them as the most fundamental behavioural marker of cognition.[22] By goal-directed action, they mean those actions that are mediated by *explicit knowledge* of the causal relationship between the action and its outcome. However, this body of work is not complete, because it has not yet arrived at an explicit model (or explanation) of what is supposed to be going on.

(3) Finally, we come to the aspect of self that involves introspection or self-reflection, involving awareness of one's own thoughts. Can

135

animals introspect? When you ask someone if they know something, such as 'Do you know the way to the station?', you are asking
about their *metacognition*. You are testing their ability to report on
the state of their own knowledge. Numerous tests for metacognition have been carried out on animals. These often take the form of
a 'delayed matching-to-sample test'. In such tests the animal is
shown a sample stimulus (say a square) for a short period. Then,
after a variable but experimentally controlled *retention interval*, they
are given a choice between the stimulus (square) and another
stimulus (circle). For the correct choice they obtain a large reward,
while for the incorrect choice they obtain no reward. After a small
retention interval, an animal is more likely to make a correct choice
than it is after a long retention interval. In other words the animal is
more likely to *remember* what the stimulus was like after a short
retention interval. In the type of trial just described the animal is
forced to make a choice after the retention interval, but in other
trials the animal may be given the option of 'saying I don't know'—
it can press an escape button that terminates the trial, and for which
it gets a small reward. If the animal does know the answer, it can
gain a large reward by making the correct choice, but if it is
uncertain it can gain a small reward by opting out instead of risking
no reward by giving an incorrect answer. Provided rigorously
controlled tests are employed, this type (and other types) of test
for *metacognition* in animals can provide valuable evidence about
whether animals know what they know. Reviewing this evidence, it
appears that, at the time of writing, there is positive evidence for
metacognition in some primates and dolphins, but negative evidence for birds.[23] However, it is fair to say that not many species
have been tested in this way.

To sum up: to *attribute* subjectivity to an animal, you (the reader)
may do so on the basis of *anthropomorphism*. For example, 'My dog

missed me while I was away.' You did not observe your dog while you were away. You suppose that your dog missed you, because that is what you would do in the circumstances. You may also attribute feelings on the basis of *observation of behaviour*. For example, when you return after being away your dog greets you more than usual, but this does not necessarily mean that it has missed you, just that it remembers you in a positive manner. Suppose you observe that 'The dog is behaving as if it feels pain, when it walks.' You may be correct in supposing that the dog has an injured paw, but you cannot see that it is in pain. Vetenarians often attribute pain to animals that limp when injured. They call the behaviour *pain guarding*, but it would be better to call it *injury guarding*.[24] They attribute the *feeling* of pain to the animal, because they suppose that the animal is somewhat like a human, but they do not know whether it is sufficiently like a human to merit the *ascription* of pain.

Similarly, if my dog, Border, comes into the kitchen and eats the cat's food, I may attribute *intent* to my dog, implying that she came into the kitchen meaning to steal the cat's food. If she really did voluntarily, and with intent, steal the cat's food, then I could justifiably blame her and hold her *responsible*. The problem is that in attributing intent to my dog, I am merely *attributing* on some flimsy basis or other. I have no real reason to *ascribe* the crime to my dog. Moreover, there are perfectly good *behaviourist* explanations of my dog's behaviour, and I could justifiably scold my dog in the hope that this punishment might deter her in the future (some hope), but this is not the same as holding her responsible. To blame my dog and hold her responsible, I would have to have *good reason* to believe that my dog's behaviour (eating the cat's food) was a voluntary action, and that in holding her responsible she has the necessary *self* to which responsibility can be attached. The question is, what good reason could I have?

137

Our security robot (Chapter 2) is designed along good *behaviourist* principles. It is fairly sophisticated, compares well with my dog in terms of intelligence, but I would not blame it for doing something wrong. I would not blame it, because I have *good reason* to believe that it does not have a *self*, it does not have *subjectivity*, and it is not capable of *actions*. I have good reason to believe these things, because the robot designer asserts that they are true, and his testimony is verifiable. (Note that for the designer to be mistaken, the robot would have to have mental autonomy.) On the other hand, if a *person* stole the cat's food (unlikely, but possible), then I would *ascribe* intent to that person and I would hold them responsible. I would have *good reason* to believe that the person acted with intent, because a person is unlikely to steal the cat's food and put it in her handbag, unless she knew what she was doing. Most of all, I would have *good reason* to believe that the person acted with intent, because she is a *person* (like me), and I *believe* that people are capable of acting with *intent*. In the case of my dog, I am not so sure. I do not have assurance from her designer that she is an automaton, nor do I have any assurance about her personhood (or the animal equivalent). But to *ascribe* intentions to my dog, I must have good reason to do so.

Michele Cabanac has good reasons to *ascribe* the subjective experience of *pleasure* to animals. He *believes* that pleasure is an explicit mental phenomenon that some animals posses. His *reasons* are (1) that pleasure, the necessary common currency of decision-making, is *explicit*, and physically identifiable in principle (i.e. he is taking a *realist* philosophical stance) and (2) his experimental evidence points in the direction of *psychological continuity* among animals, implying that what humans identify as pleasure/displeasure, animals would also so identify, if they had language. (Psychological continuity is the view that there is continuity across species with respect to mental abilities.)[25] Anthony Dickinson, also, has good reason to *ascribe actions* to rats on the basis of his realist philosophical stance, and of experiments pertinent to the issue in hand. This is not to imply that Michel Cabanac and Anthony Dickinson have got it right. Indeed, as we shall see, there are severe philosophical problems with their views.

7

THE MATERIAL MIND

We have seen that animals and robots can, on occasion, produce behaviour that makes us sit up and wonder whether these aliens really do have minds, maybe like ours, maybe different from ours. These phenomena, especially those involving apparent intentionality and subjectivity, require explanation at a scientific level, and at a philosophical level. The question is, what kind of explanation are we looking for?

At this point, you (the reader) need to decide where you stand on certain issues. Historically, a distinction has been made between material substances of the physical world and spiritual or mental substances of the non-material world. *Monism* claims that reality is made up of only one kind of substance, whereas *pluralism* claims that reality is made up of more than one kind of substance. The most famous form of pluralism is *dualism*, the doctrine that mind and matter are two distinct things, and that the one cannot be accounted for in terms of the other. Dualism gives rise to the question of how the mind is attached to the body, often called the *mind–body problem*. The main problem is to explain how, if immaterial mind is distinct from material body, how the two interact causally, as they evidently must. Other forms of pluralism exist, particularly as part of religious doctrine. Some religions envisage parallel worlds (e.g. heaven, earth, and hell), some a spiritual afterlife, etc. The main issue here, however, is that we are enquiring into the alien mind, not the human mind. It is difficult to see how any form of pluralism could be relevant to our enquiry, unless we adhere to some kind of spiritual doctrine concerning animal spirits, etc. This is not a path we can go down in this book.

There are two main types of monism, *idealism* and some kind of *materialism*. Idealists claim that reality is confined to the contents of our own minds. Whatever exists is mental in the sense that it has a certain character known to us by introspection. There is no access to reality apart from what the mind provides us with. Once again, this kind of philosophical stance is not really relevant to the questions about the alien mind. So we are left with some kind of materialism, the idea that everything in the universe is made of one kind of 'substance' that we conveniently refer to as matter (although some scientists might prefer to think of it as energy).

So far, in this book, we have rejected the idea that we can tell, solely by observing behaviour, what processes are responsible for the behaviour we observe. We have also noted that the *behaviourist* and *eliminative* stances, disavowing all mental processes, are not really adequate for the task in hand. If you, the reader, agree with this view, then you are, in effect, rejecting *eliminavism* (for reasons outlined in Chapter 3). In this view you are in the company of the majority of present-day philosophers of mind.

You, the reader, also have another issue to confront—prejudice. We humans tend to judge the behaviour of an agent (human, animal, or robot) differently, according to our perceptions of that agent. Thus we ascribe mental properties to other people (including children) largely upon the basis that they are like ourselves We are more inclined to attribute mental states to a chimpanzee than to an ant, even though the behaviour in question (e.g. teaching) is basically the same. As we shall see, some scientists base their arguments on the concept of *psychological continuity*, the idea that there is a mental continuum between humans (at the top) to some other animal below. However, it is unclear what this other animal is (a mammal, a bird, an octopus?) The layman, also, makes intuitive attributions of the basis of prejudice (e.g. is likely to consider that a dog is more intelligent than a sheep). One prejudice that many people have, including some philosophers and scientists, has to do with language. Some philosophers hold that language is necessary for thought, and that, therefore, agents (e.g. animals and robots) without language cannot have thoughts, and cannot have minds. Other philosophers go to the other extreme:

Finally, there is the old question of whether, or to what extent, a creature who does not understand a natural language, can have thoughts. Now it seems pretty compelling that higher mammals and humans raised without language have their behaviour controlled by mental states that are sufficiently like our beliefs, desires and intentions, to share those labels.[1]

(It would seem that the author Stephen Schiffer knows something that we don't.)

What we need is a way of proceeding with our enquiry, without prejudice, and without entangling ourselves in the language-based approach to the philosophy of mind. For, as Schiffer says, 'It is somewhat surprising how little we know about thought's dependence on language.'[2]

So, what we are looking for is some kind of materialist account of mind that does not imply eliminativism, and does not exclude beings that have no language. However, there is a problem.

The Problem of Mental Causation

In ordinary common-sense psychology (folk psychology) we explain other people's behaviour in mental terms. For example, John *desires* a canary to keep in a cage, because he likes to hear canaries singing. John *believes* that a canary, if kept in a cage, will sing, so John *intends* to buy a canary. A friend of John has a canary that he is willing to sell to John, so John goes to his friend's house to see the canary. Now John believes that all canaries are yellow, but when he sees his friend's bird, he is looking at a bird that is not yellow. The bird is a (wild-type) canary, and it is not yellow. It is brownish with a green-yellow breast. John believes (wrongly) that all canaries are yellow, so he does not buy the canary.

John's *reason* for not buying the canary is that it is not yellow. To get John to buy the canary he would have to be persuaded that not all canaries are yellow. In other words he would have to alter his *belief*. On the face of it, it looks as though John's *intention* to buy a canary stems from his *desire* to have a singing bird. His *action* (refusing to buy a particular canary) is due to his (mistaken) *belief* that all canaries are yellow. This nexus of *intentional* states (desire, belief, intention, action) is the essence of our normal explanation of behaviour. It is not entirely clear, however, as to what *causes* the behaviour. Certainly, John's *belief* about canaries provides a *reason* for his action, but can a reason be a cause?

For the philosopher Donald Davidson, reason-giving explanations perform two different tasks: firstly, showing that an action (or belief) is *rational*, and secondly, pointing to its *cause*.[3] John justifies his refusal to buy the bird by pointing to his belief about canaries, and his action is rational in the light of his belief. Why does John do this? Presumably, because he thinks that some explanation is expected. We all give such explanations to other people when asked, and we expect such explanations from them. It is part of our normal social intercourse. Should I expect reasons from my dog, Border? Probably not, because it would not benefit her in any way to give reasons for her behaviour, even if she was capable of saying what they were. Reasons (of this type) only have a role in certain kinds of social situation, in which reasons are expected, given, and responded to.

Donald Davidson also maintains that reasons can be *causes* of actions. His argument is, basically, that there can be no empirical causal laws employing concepts of *intentionaliy*. In other words, intentional states cannot be causes; therefore mental states must cause actions by virtue of their *material* characteristics. Davidson holds a view that, although everything in the world (objects, changes, and processes) is material, and explainable in physical terms, there can be no full *reduction* of the mental to the physical. Thus although we may come to know all about the brain in physical, or physiological, terms, we would not thereby have knowledge of such things as belief, intention, and other mental phenomena. This view is called *anomalous monism*.

Davidson holds that the irreducibility of mental concepts results from the *holism* of the mental. The entities by which mental events are characterised cannot exist in isolation. 'Individual beliefs, intentions, doubts and desires owe their identities in part to their position in a large network of other' entities.[4] Davidson also emphasises the coherence of rationality, 'fitting one thought to another'. Now, while I am doubtful that my dog, Border, has *reasons* (because reasons are for giving to others, which she cannot do), does this necessarily mean that she could not have beliefs, desires, and intentions? For an animal (or robot) to have a mind, is it necessary to have the whole panoply of human mental processes? Indeed, they could not, because they lack language. So is Davidson's idea of mental holism as irreducible as he claims? Some philosophers argue that acting for reasons does not have to presuppose the fully fledged rational system envisaged by Davidson. Thus Susan Hurley argues, 'Often we can make patchy sense of animal action at the animal level and correctly attribute reasons for action to animals, even if these reasons are specific to certain domains.'[5] Thus animals could have practical reasons for doing things, which of course remain private, because they are unable to communicate them to others.

Davidson also notes that

'mental characteristics are in some sense dependent, or supervenient, on physical characteristics. Such dependence—or *supervenience*—means that there cannot be two events alike in all physical respects but differing in some mental respect, or that 'an object cannot alter in some mental respect without altering in some physical respect.' Thus *supervenience* is closely associated with the notion of *dependence* (supervenient properties are dependent upon, or determined by, their subvenient bases), and with the notion of *property covariation* (if two things are indiscernible in base properties, they must be indiscernible in supervenient properties); and with *non-reducability* (the two notions (above) involved in supervenience can obtain even if the supervenient properties are not reducible to their base properties).[6]

In other words, the supervenient (mental) properties go hand-in-hand with the base (physical) properties, without being reducible to them.

Let us take an everyday example. Some paintings consist of a very large number of small dots. From a distance the painting seems coherent and representational. The picture may be straightforward, or it may generate particular illusions. However, in reality, the picture is nothing more that a collection of tiny dots of pigment.

The picture reduces to the dots, because the picture supervenes on the arrangement of dots. If the arrangement changes, then the picture changes accordingly.

The idea of *supervenience*, as a theory of the mind–body relationship, has lasted more than thirty years, and is seen by many as the solution to the problem of mental causation. However, this line of thinking comes at a price. Supervenience holds that the mental depends upon the physical, but it says nothing about what kind of dependence is involved. In other words, the idea of supervenience does not really do any work. It is a kind of symbol of the idea that it is OK to be a materialist. What we are looking for is an *explanation* of mental phenomena in material terms.

Realism

Many scientists and philosophers are realists in the sense that they believe that mental entities, such as belief and intent, really do exist in a material sense. For example, for many decades scientists believed that animals must have some kind of internal (endogenous) biological clock. Evidence from the study of a wide variety of animals shows that there are rhythms in their behaviour and physiology attuned to the annual cycle (circannual rhythms), the daily cycle (circadian rhythms), and even the tidal cycle (lunar rhythms). Moreover, these rhythms persist when the animal is isolated from all external influences in the laboratory. For example, North American ground squirrels and woodchucks have a marked annual rhythm of activities related to hibernation (fat storage, etc.) that can persist under isolated laboratory conditions for two or more years. Recently it has been discovered that proteins, called cryptochromes, located throughout the body, are involved in setting the body's clock. Genes that code for the clock protein have been identified in fruit flies. Interaction of four regulatory proteins, entrained by light, creates the daily rhythm of the fruit fly's clock.[7] Recently, variations have been found in the human clock gene, which may predispose people to be 'early birds' or 'night owls'.[8]

Clearly, our endogenous biological clock is something that is real. It can be identified in the brain and takes up space in the brain. It also influences our behaviour, albeit in a subliminal way. But it is not entirely unrealistic to suppose that, sometime in the future, mental states of which we are aware will be identified in the brain. The theory that mental states are no more or less than physical states of the brain is called *identity theory*, first suggested by the philosopher John Smart in 1962. But what does *identical* mean? Suppose that when I sign a cheque, my *intention* (a mental state) to validate the cheque is identical to a certain physical state of my brain. Does this mean that when I next sign a cheque, my brain state must be identical with the brain state on the occasion that I previously signed one? Obviously, this cannot be the case, because the circumstances are different, my mood is different, I am older, etc. However, it could be that every mental-state type is identical with a physical-state type (this is called *type identity*), so that my brain must be in the same type of state each time I sign a cheque. Many species possess an internal clock, but it is probable that the exact chemical nature of the clock varies from species to species. The clock is a *type* of mechanism that serves a particular time-keeping role.

A problem with this idea is that some types of mental state (e.g. pain) may be common to different species of animal, even though their anatomical and physiological differences are so great that they could not possibly share the same types of bodily state. For example, suppose I am interested in whether an octopus feels pain. The nervous system of an octopus is completely different from that of vertebrates, and there is no way that an octopus brain state could

147

be of similar type to a vertebrate brain state. According to type identity theory, an octopus could not, therefore, feel pain because it does not have the vertebrate type of pain mechanism. To argue this way would be to introduce a kind of zoological chauvinism—an octopus cannot feel pain because it is not a vertebrate. But it may be that an octopus can feel pain, as a result of having a non-vertebrate, octopus type of pain mechanism.

The obvious way out of this problem is to type brain mechanisms according to the role that they play in the system. For example, the philosopher David Lewis holds that the whole of mental truth supervenes upon the physical truth.[9] Lewis notes that *folk psychology* associates with each mental state a typical causal role. Lewis calls this the M-role. When we describe mental state M as the occupant of the M-role, we imply nothing about what sort of state it is that occupies that role. For Lewis it does not matter what kind of state occupies the M-role, so long as it is a physical state, identifiable (in principle) in the normal scientific manner. Thus it might be a neural state, a chemical state, or a state of a silicon chip. Thus, in theory, an invertebrate, a vertebrate, or a robot could have a mental state M, so long as it occupied the M-role. In other words, the same mental states could be caused in different ways in different agents. The possibility that mental states can be caused in different ways is called *multiple realisability of mental states*, and this kind of approach is a kind of *functionalism*. Be that as it may, the *realist* can still insist that every instance of a mental state is identical with the corresponding instance of a physical state (this is called *token identity*). Indeed, it is hard to see how one could be a materialist without believing this to be true.

Realism has another problem to contend with, namely content. In terms of folk psychology, many of our mental states have *content*, in the sense that they are about something, or refer to something. They involve reference to objects, properties, or relations. For example, I believe the door (an object) is locked; I believe that he is clever (a property); I believe that the reciprocal of 7 is 0.1428 (a relation). When we attribute the mental states of a person as having content, we assume that their states are somehow organised in a *rational* way. Thus my perception of a yellow singing bird makes rational my *belief* that yellow birds can sing. My *desire* for a singing bird, together with my *belief* about yellow birds, makes rational my *intention* to buy a yellow bird, and leads to the *action* of buying a canary. So not only do some mental states have content, they seem to be bound together by some set of rules. A person who does not follow the rules is deemed to be irrational. Thus a person who said that they did not like singing birds, and who believed that all yellow birds were singing birds, would be acting irrationally to buy a yellow bird.

The problem is how do the rules work in a material way and how is the content made manifest? Philosophers differ in their approaches to this problem. The philosopher Jerry Foder sees it in terms of a *language of thought*. Thoughts have contents carried by mental *representations,* and Fodor argues that thought is a form of *symbol manipulation*, and in this it is similar to language.[10] The philosopher Fred Dretske takes a different view: 'reasons explain behaviour not by causing it, but, rather, by having their content—what one believes and desires—explain the causing.'[11] For Dretske, 'beliefs are maps by means of which we steer,' and they become incorporated into the apparatus, or circuitry, that controls our behaviour. The philosopher John Searle claims that 'There isn't any gap between the level of intentionalistic explanations and the level of neurophysiological explanations.' Moreover, 'it is even possible that mental states could be biological phenomena within the brain. . . . pains and other mental phenomena are features of the brain.' Thus Searle is not only a realist, he is invoking an *argument from anatomy*. 'Mental phenomena are as much a result of electrochemical processes in the brain as digestion is

149

a result of chemical processes going on in the stomach and the rest of the digestive tract.'[12]

Such arguments from anatomy have a long history, but they do not get us very far. Saying that certain processes occur in a certain place does not tell us how those processes work. When we do know how certain processes work, as is the case with digestion, we can recognise them outside their familiar context. Thus in many invertebrate animals digestion takes place outside the body (the products of digestion are then ingested). Searle claims that 'if the events outside the brain occurred but caused nothing in the brain, there would be no mental events, whereas if the events in the brain occurred the mental events would occur even if there were no outside stimulus.'[13] Here he is falling into the anatomy trap. While it may be true that mental events can occur in the brain when there is no outside stimulus, it does not follow that when there is nothing in the brain there are no mental events. The mental events could be occurring elsewhere, unrecognised by Searle, because he does not know what to look for. We can recognise digestive processes outside the body, because we do know what to look for. As we shall see, many philosophers and scientists have no problem with the idea that mental events can take place outside the brain.

The acid test for those materialist philosophers who think that they know how the mind works is to produce a model that works. The model could be instantiated in a computer, or in some other way. Attempts to do this have been going on for the past fifty years. With the advent of the digital computer, it became possible, for those with an open outlook, to envisage machines with minds. This general area of investigation is often called *computational theory of mind*. Needless to say those working in this area don't all sing from the same hymn sheet. For some, such as Jerry Fodor, the essential issue is *symbol manipulation* in which a computer program follows a series of instructions that effectively specify the information processing to be carried out by the machine.[14] By manipulating various symbolic representations, the programmers hope to arrive at the kind of process that occurs in the human mind. John Searle objects to this approach because 'Instantiating the right program is never sufficient for having a mind. There is something more to having a mind than just instantiating a computer program. And the reason is obvious. Minds have mental contents. They have semantic contents as well as just levels of description.'[15] Searle claims that as a consequence of the view that mental activities can be instantiated in a computer program,

any system whatever, could have thoughts and feelings—indeed it not only could have, but must have, thoughts and feelings—in exactly the same sense that we do, provided only that it is having the right program. That is, if you have the right program with the right inputs and the right outputs, then any system running that program, regardless of its chemical structure (whether it is made of old beer cans or silicon chips or any other sub-stance) must have thoughts and feelings in exactly the same way you and I do. And this is because that is all there is to having a mind: having the right program.[16]

In support of his argument, Searle set out a famous thought experiment called the Chinese room. Imagine that you are unfamil-iar with Chinese writing, and you are locked in a room, and given a batch of Chinese script, together with a set of rules (in English) for relating the one set of writing to another. Upon receipt of a new set of Chinese symbols, written on a card, you can check each symbol against those on the first batch and, using the rules provided, compose a Chinese text of your own. In fact, you are answering questions without knowing it.

Suppose that after a while, [you] got so good at following the instructions for manipulating the Chinese symbols ... that from an external point of view—that is, from the point of view of somebody outside the room in which [you are] locked—[your] answers are indistinguishable from those of native Chinese speakers.[17]

According to Searle, you do not really understand Chinese, even though you become adept at manipulating Chinese symbols, because you are manipulating 'uninterpreted' symbols. You are 'behaving like a computer', and Searle claims that a computer could never 'understand' Chinese, because all a computer can do is run programs. So you do not understand Chinese, in the sense that we normally mean by 'understanding': 'Minds cannot be identical with computer programs, because programs are defined syntactically in terms of the manipulation of formal symbols . . . , whereas minds have mental or semantic contents; they have more than syntax, they have a semantics.'[18]

Needless to say, there have been numerous attempts to wriggle out of this argument on the part of those wedded to symbol manipulation and the computational model of mind. We need not be concerned with such arguments here, but it is worth noting that the appeal of Searle's argument is an appeal to our subjective experience—what it feels like to understand a foreign language. We like Searle's argument because it appeals to our intuition, but we do not in fact have any direct verifiable knowledge about the true nature of our understanding of a language. Such understanding might in reality take the form of a sophisticated look-up table, while seeming to us to involve semantics. Philosopher Andy Clark makes a similar point very nicely.[19] Searle is invoking an argument from intuition, and like his argument from anatomy, this involves a certain amount of dogmatism. Statements like 'the mind is entirely a property of the brain', or 'computers can never understand language', although intuitively appealing, are not statements that can be refuted, when they are presented as axioms or givens.

Ironically, many computer scientists have embraced the idea that all there is to having a mind is having the right program, especially those working in artificial intelligence. In its early days *artificial intelligence* was described as 'the science of making machines do things that would require intelligence if done by men'.[20] Clearly, it was expected that artificial intelligence would enable robots to do useful things. The approach taken by what is now known as the GOFAI (good old-fashioned artificial intelligence) view of classical artificial intelligence is that mental processes involve two things: (1) there must be internal (mental) representation of the world (including aspects of the agents themselves), and (2) there must be operations, or computations, over these representations to yield new beliefs, such as beliefs about the necessary means to accomplish some goal. The representations are articulated in some sort of *symbol system* and, together, they make up the knowledge base from which an agent is supposed to reason and decide what to do next. Thus, within the world of classical artificial intelligence, intelligent behaviour is seen in terms of *sense–think–act* cycles. The relevant internal processing is seen in terms of *symbol manipulation*.

So we can see that those working in classical artificial intelligence have no problem with *explicit representations*. Symbol manipulation is their bread and butter. However, when it comes to robots, classical artificial intelligence does not have a good track record. It has been argued that the early robots were overdependent upon representational systems. The successful real (as opposed to simulated) robots have been *reactive* and *situated* (see Chapter 1) while their predecessors were 'all thought and no action'. In the words of philosopher Andy Clark

The New Robotics revolution rejects a fundamental part of the classical image of mind. It rejects the image of a *central planner* that is privy to all the information available anywhere in the system and dedicated to the

153

discovery of possible behavioral sequences that will satisfy particular goals. The trouble with the central planner is that it is profoundly impractical. It introduces what Rodney Brooks aptly termed a 'representational bottle-neck' blocking fast real-time responses.[21]

It has also been claimed that, from a design stance, the *sense-think-act* cycles of classical AI are not well suited to mobile multi-tasking robots.[22]

It is widely recognised that there is no need for symbolic repre-sentation in the control of *situated* activities, such as walking, running, and avoiding obstacles.

In fact representations often *get in the way* of behaviour control. (In the interests of efficiency and parsimony it is better to design action control systems that are representation-free).... Moreover, unless we *first* under-stand the 97 per cent of behaviour that is non-representational ... we will never correctly understand the remainder.[23]

However, many robot designers do recognise the value of sym-bolic representation, and symbol manipulation, for certain types of task, including activities that involve responses beyond the current sensory limits, such as navigation; activities that require a degree of problem solving, such as wrapping a parcel (how much paper to allow); and activities that involve other agents, where these require predictions about the behaviour of others. For example, a map on paper is an explicit representation of a particular area of land. A robot could store a copy of such a map in memory and use it for many purposes. It could use it to navigate. It could produce a copy on request. It could refer to the map to produce a series of instructions and pass these (either verbally or physically) to another robot. We recognise that these tasks would require a degree of cognition, if performed by a person. Yet these are all tasks that could be performed by a modern robot, and to endow the robot with the necessary explicit representations would be no problem. Would such a robot embody mental states? It would certainly embody the minimal requirements for cognition, outlined in Chapter 4, but would it have a mind?

Classical artificial intelligence, with its reliance on symbol systems, failed to address some fundamental problems, and nowadays many philosophers and cognitive scientists are doubtful about the scope and limits of purely symbolic models of mind. In 1959 John McCarthy drew attention to a problem to do with the application of classical artificial intelligence to robotics, which became known as the *frame problem*.[24] Daniel Dennet has provided an illuminating example:

Once upon a time there was a robot, named R1 by its creators. Its only task was to fend for itself. One day its designers arranged for it to learn that its spare battery, its precious energy supply, was locked in a room with a time bomb set to go off soon. R1 located the room, and the key to the door, and formulated a plan to rescue its battery. There was a wagon in the room, and the battery was on the wagon, and R1 hypothesized that a certain action which it called PULLOUT (WAGON, ROOM) would result in the battery being removed from the room. Straightaway it acted, and did succeed in getting the wagon out of the room before the bomb went off. Unfortunately, however, the bomb was also on the wagon. R1 *knew* the bomb was on the wagon in the room, but didn't realize that pulling the wagon would bring the bomb out along with the battery. Poor R1 had missed the obvious implication of its planned act.

Back to the drawing board. 'The solution is obvious', said the designers. 'Our next robot must be made to recognize not just the intended implications of its acts, but also the implications about their side effects, by deducing these implications from the descriptions it uses in formulating its plans.' They called their next model, the robot-deducer, R1D1. They placed R1D1 in much the same predicament that R1 had succumbed to, and as it too hit upon the idea of PULLOUT (WAGON, ROOM) it began, as designed, to consider the implications of such a course of action. It had just finished deducing that pulling the wagon out of the room would not change the colour of the room's walls, and was embarking on a proof of the further implication that pulling the wagon out would cause its wheels to turn more revolutions than there were wheels on the wagon—when the bomb exploded.

Back to the drawing board. 'We must teach it the difference between relevant implications and irrelevant implications', said the designers, 'and teach it to ignore the irrelevant ones.' So they developed a method of tagging the implications as either relevant or irrelevant to the project in hand, and installed the method in their next model, the robot relevant-deducer, or R2D1 for short. When they subjected R2D1 to the test that has so unequivocally selected its ancestors for extinction, they were surprised to see it sitting, Hamlet-like, outside the room containing the ticking bomb...'Do something!' they yelled at it. 'I am' it retorted. 'I'm busily ignoring some thousands of implications I have determined to be irrelevant. Just as soon as I find an irrelevant implication, I put it on the list of those I must ignore....' The bomb went off.[25]

These robots suffer from the *frame problem,* a problem that arises because many of the possible consequences of a planned action are not really relevant to the decision whether to perform the action. The frame problem remains a problem for classical AI, and its strictly means–end approach. It is worth noting that animals do not suffer from the frame problem, and this may be because they have a *value system* (see Chapter 8), the costs and risks involved in their decision-making acting as constraints on their behaviour.[26]

As we saw in Chapter 4 *symbols* are explicit representations that lead the agent to conceive of the object that the symbol represents. What a symbol signifies is an act of conception. It is an act which is reactivated anew in the agent's mind each time he, she, or it encounters it. In philosopher-speak the symbol requires *semantic* interpretation, so that it means something to the agent. In attempting to implement such a system in a computer, we face a problem. 'How can the semantic interpretation of a formal symbol system be made intrinsic to the system, rather than just parasitic on the meanings in our heads? How can the meanings of the meaningless symbol tokens, manipulated solely on the basis of their (arbitrary) shapes, be grounded in anything but other meaningless symbols?' This is the *symbol grounding problem,* posed by psychologist Steven Harnad.[27] Despite numerous efforts to solve the problem, it persists to this day, and it is beginning to look as though a purely symbolic *computational theory of mind* will not work.[28] This is not to say that symbol manipulation does not have its place in the alien mind. While there are many who hold that humans are the only animals capable of symbol manipulation, it still has a place in robotics.[29] Many roboticists are *realists* in the sense that the systems that they employ in their attempts to get robots to think and act intelligently can be materially identified within the robot, but herein lies another problem.

Many of the theories put forward to account for mental causation suffer from the *exclusion problem.* It is called the exclusion problem because it looks as if the physical properties that realise mental properties exclude the latter from causal relevance. For example, in discussing *pleasure* in Chapter 6, we noted that Michel Cabanac's experimental results could be accounted for *either* that the pleasure / displeasure is the *cause* of the behavioural and physiological adjustments *or* that the pleasure / displeasure ratings are the *consequence* of these adjustments (i.e. the subject is simply reporting on what it feels like to make the adjustments). In the first case, we could imagine (taking a *realist* view) that some brain chemical (for example) causes the adjustments and also gives rise to the feelings of pleasure reported by the subjects. In the second case, taking an *automaton* view, the adjustments are entirely automatic and there is no obvious role for the mental entity *pleasure* (except, perhaps, something to do with communication). The automaton view does not deny that the subjects experienced the pleasure / displeasure that they reported; it simply claims that this mental entity was not the cause of the behaviour. So, by this account, the mental entity *pleasure* is *excluded* from any causal efficacy. However, it may be that both views are correct: i.e. the behaviour is caused in an automatic way *and* the pleasure generated *also* plays a causal role. For example, if someone goes surf-boarding for the first time they make automatic bodily adjustments in the course of learning the skill, and they enjoy the experience. The next time they go out, they push themselves harder in their attempts to master the waves, because of the extra pleasure generated thereby. So the pleasure now plays a causal role in addition to the automatic component of their behaviour. In other words by explicitly maximising the pleasure they obtain, the surf-boarder becomes more expert. Many philosophers would claim that the dual role of mental and non-mental is a case of *overdetermination*, meaning that some of the properties are causally irrelevant. Be that as it may, there is psychological evidence in favour of simultaneous multiple causation. However, these issues are equally apparent if we take a *functionalist* stance, and to this we now turn.

Functionalism

Do not get the idea that functionalism is a substitute for realism. Obviously, for any materialist, some things must be real. We remember things, so the information that we recall must be stored somewhere. It must be real. The biological clock is real, but this does not mean that every mental entity is real in the sense that it is (in principle) physically identifiable.

As we have seen, functionalism[30] is the view that certain entities, including some mental ones, are best described in terms of the functional role that they play within a system. Thus a word processor is a device that processes words. Physically, word processors have changed greatly over recent decades, but they remain best described in terms of their function, and not in material terms. The functionalist argument against *type identity* (see above) is that if pain is determined (only) by a particular *type* of brain state, then animals or robots that do not have that type of state cannot experience pain. Many philosophers argue that what is important is not being in a particular type of state, but what that state does—its role within the system.[31] They accept that *token identity* pertains—that is, in any particular instance of pain there is an identity between the pain and the state responsible—but for pain as a type of mental experience, there needs to be a more abstract concept.

The philosopher Hilary Putman compares mental states with functional states of a computer. Just as a computer program can be realised by a number of different hardware configurations, so we can imagine that mental 'programs' might be realisable in different physical ways, such as a human brain, an octopus brain, or a robot 'brain'. This kind of functionalism has come to be known as *machine functionalism*, and it has become popular amongst those working on *artificial intelligence* and *computer models of the mind*. Machine functionalism holds that a physical brain-state can be described (a) physically (or biophysically), (b) functionally (in terms of its role in the system), and (c) in everyday mental terms. Now a merit of this approach is that 'the mental' remains distinct from 'the physical' and cannot be *reduced* to it. The property of being in a particular mental state is not the property of being in a particular physical state, because many physical states can give rise to the same mental state. *Multiple realisability of mental states* is achieved. States of mind that are multiply realisable can be seen as 'higher level' properties that arise as a result of appropriate realisers. The state of mind called *pain*, for example, could result from realisers such as injury, disease, or poison in a human, but a different set of realisers in an animal or a robot. Pain is seen as a functional state

159

that plays a particular role in the system. Thus in humans it serves to activate avoidance, aversion (to the external circumstances), communication to others, etc. But one could argue that it is the realisers that cause these effects, and that pain is simply an *epiphenomenon*.[32] In other words, this scenario brings us back to the *exclusion problem* (see above). The exclusion problem demands that we explain how mental properties could be causally relevant given that they appear to be screened off by their physical realisers.[33] Well, we have already encountered one suggestion (see Chapter 6) as to how pleasure and pain could be causally relevant—they act as the common currency of decision-making, and therefore have a role in the inevitable trade-offs that occur in the process of physiological and behavioural adjustments. For example, Michael Cabanac would argue that pleasure/pain (opposite sides of the same coin) have a particular *biological function* in animals, including humans. Does this make Cabanac a functionalist? Not really, because even a realist, who believes that every mental state is, in principle, physically (or physiologically) inentifiable, is also likely to believe that such states serve some kind of function.

Traditional philosophical *functionalism* emphasises the role played by mental entities, but tends to avoid the issue of what a *role* is. It is all very well to say that the role of, say, a belief is to provide a reason for action, but why is a reason for action necessary? Machine functionalism, especially as practised in *artificial intelligence* (AI) and by those making *computer models of mind*, has been accused of being 'agenda-driven'. That is, the programmer endows the machine with those *roles* that the designer thinks desirable. In other words, it can be argued that whatever comes out of the machine has already been put in, or its precursors have been put in. The danger is that we end up not with an explanation, but a re-description of the situation. This is why some philosophers have accused machine functionalists of *liberalism*, obtaining results that are far too easy to come by from the initial starting assumptions.[34] In other words, if functionalism ends up ascribing minds to things that don't have them, it is liberal. Other philosophers have sought to remedy this defect by imposing a teleological requirement, such that the functional explanations relate more to biological function. (*Teleology* is a philosopher's word for what we (Chapters 1 and 2) would call purpose, design, or biological function.) Those philosophers who espouse *teleological functionalism*, such as Jerry Fodor, Robert Cummins, and Daniel Dennett, seek to place their functional explanations in a biological or behavioural context, rather than the logical or mathematical context favoured by machine functionalists. This approach is in danger of the opposite fault, namely *chauvinism*, because it is all too easy to relate the functional roles of mental events in humans to their biological utility, but these may not be applicable to animals and robots. This chauvinism/liberalism problem is one that we must keep in mind in thinking about the mental abilities of aliens.

According to teleological theories of mental content, what a representation represents depends on the functions of the systems that make use of the representation. The relevant notion of function is the one used in biology in attributing functions to components of organisms (e.g. the function of the internal clock is to entrain certain physiological processes, such as sleep, to the clock-driven rhythm). Philosophers generally understand this notion of function to be what something was selected for, either by ordinary natural selection or by some other design process. Thus the internal clock of some species of crab causes the animal to become dormant during certain phases of the tide cycle, such as low tide (when they may become stranded on the beach), and crabs that do this have a better chance of survival than crabs that remain active at low tide. Similarly, the function of the internal clock of the slug-catching robot is to induce periods of dormancy during the day when slugs are scarce. Robots that do this

161

do not catch more slugs, but they save more energy, and so they do better on the open market (see Chapter 1). As we have seen, the teleological function of communication is to influence the behaviour of others. In fact communication is distinguished from other forms of causation, because it is designed (by nature or by man), or intended, to influence the behaviour of others.

Teleological functions are often seen as distinct from the causal-role functions involved in what is called 'functionalism' in philosophy of mind. Causal-role functions are those mental states that play a particular role in the system. They can be seen as causal *dispositions*, whereas teleological functions are seen as selected *effects*. However, it is fairly obvious that selected effects must depend partly upon selected dispositions (i.e. dispositions of traits for which the traits were selected). For example, an animal that becomes sick after eating poisoned food quickly learns the disposition to avoid that food in the future (see Chapter 6). Natural selection has seen to it that the animal learns to *avoid* the food and not to prefer it. So the disposition to avoid a certain type of food is a disposition that (through learning) is selected. Such selected dispositions are not overriding because they exist within a complex activity-selection system. Thus, if extremely hungry, the animal might sample the poisoned food again.

Let us take this example a little further. A pigeon is fed, once a day, on multicoloured wheat grains. The grains have been dyed a variety of colours, with the exception of red, and the pigeon is allowed to become familiar with this food. One day, the pigeon is given its normal food, but including some grains dyed red, which it eats. After feeding, the pigeon is injected with lithium chloride (LiCl) that makes it sick. Two days later it has recovered, and for the following week it is fed on its normal food (excluding red grains). Then, on the eighth day, it is given normal food, but including red grains. The pigeon immediately vomits at the sight of the food.

Clearly, the pigeon has developed an aversion to red grains. The *realist* interpretation of this phenomenon would be something like this—having been made sick after eating red grains for the first time, the pigeon now *believes* that the red grains are poisonous. That is, the pigeon has a belief with the *content* 'red grains are poisonous'. This belief takes the form of an *explicit representation* in the pigeon's brain, just like the explicit representation of M in our security robot (see above). The *reason* that the pigeon vomits at the sight of the food is that the pigeon sees the red grains, the very grains that it believes to be poisonous. The vomiting is an *action* (called a disgust reaction, triggered by the sight of anything that the pigeon believes to be poisonous.[35]

Now wait a minute, can a pigeon have reasons? If a pigeon can have beliefs, desires, and intentions, then by the same logic, it would seem that pigeons can have reasons. In humans, reasons are given to others as an explanation of something, and pigeons cannot do this. But now we are making a functional point, that the *role* of reasons has to do with communication. But this role is not one that would make functional sense for pigeons. Therefore, if pigeons have reasons, they must play some other role. To say that pigeons need reasons to play a particular role (i.e. practical reasons for use in the process of reasoning) is *liberal*, because what pigeons could achieve by reasoning (the effect) could possibly be achieved in another way. On the other hand, to say that pigeons cannot have reasons (like ours) that can play a role in explanations, because they cannot give explanations, does not imply that they cannot have any reasons. Suppose we say that the reason the pigeon vomits is such and such, meaning that *our explanation* of the pigeons behaviour is such and such, then we are offering an explanation in teleological terms: i.e. as a result of natural selection, pigeons quickly learn aversive reactions to food that *indicates* deleterious consequences. Note, however, that we have not yet come up with a reason for vomiting at the *sight* of food. The role of vomiting is to eject food that has been eaten, but in this case no food has been eaten. So why does the pigeon vomit?

Scientifically, the pigeon's vomiting response is a *disgust* reaction, part of the animal's normal defence against pollution.[36] In humans, disgust reactions often result from *phobias* (acute anxiety), which can be innate (e.g. fear of spiders) or learned (aversion to specific food items). The biologist Desmond Morris demonstrated that a chimpanzee, born and reared in captivity showed disgust reactions to mushrooms, snakes, and spiders when presented with them for the first time. Although the chimp had never seen them previously, it nevertheless showed strong aversive reactions to these stimuli, brushing them away with the hand, and grimacing. In humans, phobia is a type of *mental state* that gives rise to disgust, or other aversive reactions. Pigeons and chimps have the same types of reaction, but of course this does not prove that they have the corresponding type of mental state. But why do the pigeons and chimps express their disgust behaviourally? Why do the pigeons vomit when they have no food to bring up? Why don't the chimps simply ignore the mushrooms and spiders?

One possibility is that the aversive behaviour is reflex; there is no mental state corresponding to disgust, or if there is, it plays no causal role (*the automaton view*). Implications of this view are that the disgust (if it exists as a mental state) is an *epiphenomenon* that has no functional role, and the reflex behaviour has no obvious biological function, because there is no real danger. From a *behaviourist stance*, the pigeon's reaction to the sight of the red food is the result of Pavlovian conditioning. Such conditioning does have an important biological function, and the unnecessary vomiting is simply the price that must be paid for possessing such a mechanism. From a *realist stance* the animal has a *feeling* of disgust/aversion (a mental state), and that this feeling is the *cause* of the behaviour. From a *functionalist stance* the disgust behaviour is caused by whatever plays the necessary *role*. A machine functionalist who simply invents some entity to play the role is open to the accusation of *liberalism*. Teleological functionalism recognises that the behaviour is rational (one can adopt the *intentional stance* towards it), but is agnostic about the cause of the behaviour. The animals behave *as if* they believed that objects were dangerous/disgusting, but the mechanism may be different in the different cases (e.g. a conditioned reflex in the case of the pigeon, and a mental phenomenon (disgust) in the case of the chimp). There may be other reasons for supposing that the two cases are different, but there is also a danger of *chauvinism*.

The teleological functionalist can argue, however, that the design criteria of an agent (animal or robot) in a particular environment are subject to constraints. The design criteria may be those laid down by the process of natural selection, or (in the case of robots) those employed by human designers where these are basically dictated by the market (see Chapter 1).

Constraints upon design criteria arise because, in the real world, there are costs to consider. In the biological sciences, this kind of consideration is called *life-history strategy*. Species of animal that live in unstable or unpredictable environments usually reproduce quickly (i.e. have a short generation period). There is little advantage in adaptations that permit competition with other organisms, since the environment is likely to change. They tend to invest in numerous (inexpensive offspring) that disperse widely. For species that inhabit stable and predictable environments, competition with other species is an important factor. Such species tend to have a long generation period and few offspring that are well cared for. Examples include elephants, whales, and humans. The majority of animals fall between these two extremes. Indeed we can look at the situation as a life-history spectrum. So the teleological functionalist could argue (against the charge of chauvinism) that a pigeon has many more offspring in its lifetime than does a chimpanzee. Therefore, the pigeon can get away with a cheap-and-cheerful disgust mechanism, whereas the chimpanzee needs something more sophisticated.

Similarly, manufactured goods aimed at markets in which fashion frequently changes, tend to be inexpensive and have a short life history. Examples include Christmas toys, including toy robots. Manufactured goods aimed at stable, long-lasting markets, tend to be well designed, robust, and expensive. Examples include furniture, motor cars, and certain types of robot. Innovation is desirable but should be undertaken with care. The extra research and development required could endanger the long-term success of the robot (see also Chapters 1 and 2). So in considering the life-history strategy of a robot it is important to consider the type of market that it is aimed at, and where it is to be placed in the spectrum. If the robot is to compete with other toys, it needs to be cheap and cheerful. If it is to compete with humans for certain types of work, it needs to be robust and competent.

Functionalism and Robotics

The *functional stance* opens the door to the possibility of robot minds. What matters to functionalists is the *role* played by a given material state of affairs. This state is usually thought of as being a brain-state, but this is not strictly necessary. What matters is that there is some state that can influence behaviour. Components of this state could be in the brain, in other parts of the body, or in the external world. Recall the ants and termites mentioned in Chapter 1. Much of their 'memory' is deposited in the environment, giving rise to the phenomenon of *stigmergy*. The functionalist does not worry about the hardware responsible for the behaviour. It can be brain-matter, or silicon-matter. There are, of course, many differing interpretations of what a computational theory of mind consists of,[37] but basically it consists of some sort of *symbol manipulation,* and digital computer programs lend themselves to this type of exercise. But, as we have seen (above), there are problems with this approach. There is the *frame problem* and the *symbol grounding problem,* and these problems persist. One way out of this situation is to circumvent these problems by abandoning the idea of a purely symbolic approach. For example, why not use the computer to simulate brain activity?

Throughout the twentieth century scientists modelled the brain in terms of the current technology. Early in the century the brain was likened to a telephone exchange. With the advent of digital computers it became possible to endow the model brain with explicit representations and the *representational* (and realist) view became fashionable. With advances in computer power and knowledge of brain structure, it became possible to simulate networks of 'neurons'. This type led to the development of *connectionism.* Connectionism is a kind of *neurocomputing* that involves simulated nerve cells of various types and complexity. These are arranged in a network by means of 'synaptic' links involving simple arithmetic values representing synaptic strength, or more complex semantic information. Where the aim is to mimic nerve cells of the real brain the artificial neurons are usually complex, but when the aim is to use the network as a means of computing, they are usually quite simple. Large networks of neurones (or *nodes*) and synapses (or *arcs*) can be used for computational purposes. Thus connectionism is a brand of 'brain-style' modelling loosely based on neuroscience, and is not meant to simulate the actual workings of a brain.

Connectionists reject the assumption that information is stored in particular places in the brain. In connectionist models the memory is distributed. Storage and retrieval is possible because each trace is defined by its own pattern of activated memory elements.

167

Complex computations can be carried out through the concurrent action of a large number of independent processing units, each reacting only to its own local set of inputs; the whole results in *parallel distributed processing*.

Connectionism is a departure from classical artificial intelligence, and this has led to a lot of argument amongst computer scientists, but connectionism also has philosophical implications.[38] In particular, representations in a connectionist system are not discrete but are distributed, and even superimposed. Thus the same units and connections serve many different representational roles. Other ways of saying the same thing (more or less) are that representations, which may be deemed to have a causal role according to philosophical theory, may *supervene* on the connectionist network, or that the representational properties are *emergent* properties of the network, or that the connectionist system is *holistic* in nature.

While connectionism has had considerable success in areas such as pattern recognition (both visual and linguistic), it has not had much impact in the more strictly cognitive areas. This may be because the representations found within connectionist networks are typically not explicit representations, such as beliefs (in the realist sense) and intentions. In other words connectionist networks are better suited to dealing with *knowledge how*, rather than *knowledge that*.

In this chapter we have come a long way. At the outset, you (the reader) were asked to take some sort of philosophical stance, and it was assumed that the only stance relevant to the alien mind was some sort of materialism. What we were looking for is a materialist view that does not imply eliminativism and does not exclude animals and robots that have no language. We then addressed the problem of whether, or how, mental events could be causal agents. This took us into discussion of realist and functionalist accounts of mental phenomena in humans, animals, and robots. Our responses to these enquiries depend partly upon what we think the mind of an animal or robot is for. In other words what use would it be for such aliens to have minds? We take up this question in the next chapter.

8

MENTAL AUTONOMY

In Chapter 1 we saw that self-sufficient robots require a degree of energy autonomy and motivational autonomy. Autonomy implies freedom from outside control. What does this mean? *Energy autonomy* implies that the robot's energy supply is free from outside control, and that the robot is able to gain its energy by itself, from sunlight, or by foraging for a suitable energy source. The degree of energy autonomy depends upon the number of resources that the robot requires for survival. Like a plant or animal, a robot is likely to require other commodities in addition to energy, such as water and oil. So the completely self-sufficient robot would have to be able to find all its 'nutritional' requirements by itself.

Whereas energy autonomy implies that the robot is free from outside control with respect to its needs, *motivational autonomy* implies that the robot is free with respect to its 'wants'. Like an animal, a well-designed robot will tend to want whatever it needs. Not only does this apply to the 'nutrients' necessary for survival, but also the safety, territory, and freedom of choice necessary for useful work (e.g. it would be advantageous for a slug-catching robot to be territorial, because slugs removed from a productive area are soon replaced by others[1]). Similarly, animal motivation is aimed at those needs necessary for survival and reproduction, such as food, water, safety, and territory, plus the freedom to choose a mate. The degree of autonomy depends upon the number of resources that are addressed motivationally.

We now come to the question of *mental autonomy*. The mentally autonomous robot would be one that is free from outside control of its mental states. Clearly, a robot that had no mental states could have no mental autonomy. Suppose that, for the time being, we accept that robots can embody mental states. What would be implied by mental autonomy? In the cases of energy autonomy and motivational autonomy, there is no suggestion that the robot has 'a mind of its own'. All that is implied is a degree of freedom from outside control that allows the robot to decide *by itself* when to switch from one activity to another. The decisions made by such robots are entirely the result of procedures based upon information about the robot's internal state and its registration of external stimuli. The designer of this type of robot must set things up in such a way that the robot can cope with any contingency likely to arise in its environment. Of course, the designer chooses the environment within which the robot is to operate. This may be an office environment, a marine environment, the planet Mars, or whatever environment the robot sponsors think is appropriate for deploying self-sufficient robots.

Now, in this chapter we want to ask another question—could a robot decide *for itself* when to switch from one activity to another? A robot could do this only if it had some kind of self.

The Extended Self

In biologist Richard Dawkins' book called *The Extended Phenotype*, he points out that

few people have trouble understanding that there is, in principle, no difference between genetic control of morphology and genetic control of behaviour... bower bird species with especially splendid bowers tend to have relatively drab plumage, while those species with relatively bright plumage tend to build less elaborate and spectacular bowers.... It is as though some species have shifted part of the burden of adaptation from bodily phenotype to extended phenotype.[2]

Dawkins points out that the webs characteristic of particular species of spider, and the 'houses' characteristic of particular species of caddis fly, are no less the products of natural selection than the animals themselves.

Similarly, the uses that a person or animal characteristically makes of features of the external environment are no less products of themselves as are the uses that they make of their internal memories. In the words of philosopher Andy Clark,

A short anecdote helps to set the stage. Consider the expert bartender. Faced with multiple drink orders in a noisy and crowded environment, the expert mixes and dispenses drinks with amazing skill and accuracy. But what is the basis of this expert performance? Does it all stem from finely tuned memory and motor skills? By no means... the experts select and array *distinctively shaped glasses* at the time of ordering. They then use these persistent cues to help recall and sequence the specific orders. Expert performance plummets in tests involving uniform glassware, whereas novice performances are unaffected by any such manipulations.[3]

The distinctively shaped glasses are part of the bartender's extended self.

When someone dies, parts of their extended self are left behind—their shopping list, for example. The person, when alive, created the shopping list, and did so as an extension of part of themselves, their memory in particular. A shopping list is not a copy of all its creator knows about the items on the list. It is a catalyst that comes into action when needed. When they look at the list they are reminded of certain items, and they are reminded of why they put those items on the list. Once the person who made the list is dead, these memories cannot be retrieved. The list cannot be used by another person in the way that it could have been used by the person who made it. The shopping list was part of this person's extended self.

Of course, we are not always aware of the entirety of our extended selves. I may make a shopping list and then forget that I have done it. In fact, I am not always aware of things that I know in the ordinary sense. In Chapter 4 we noted that people can be the recipient of experience, and know it. Thus a person has self-knowledge about their own experiences. For example, I can say that I had a dream, meaning that I know (believe or remember) that I had a dream. If my spouse has nightmares and I don't have nightmares, then it makes sense for me to wonder *what it is like* to be a person who has nightmares. It makes sense, because I believe that other people have the mentality to have nightmares. When my dog, Border, is asleep, she sometimes appears to be dreaming. Does it make sense for me to ask *what is it like* to dream like a dog? It makes sense only if I believe that my dog has the mentality to be the subject of dream-like experiences. When my dog dreams she exhibits dream-like behaviour (vocalisations and rapid-eye-movement), but this does not necessarily mean that she is the *subject* of dream experiences. To have the requisite mentality, my dog must not only have the experiences, but she must be *aware* that she has them.

We are not always aware of the things that we are aware of. For example, I used to ask my students if they had ever looked out of the window when travelling on a train. Of course they had. Had they noticed that objects in the foreground seem to move in the

173

opposite direction to the train? Of course, they had. Had they noticed that objects in the middle ground seem to be stationary? Yes they had. Were they aware that objects in the far distance seem to move in the same direction as the train? No they were not aware of this, but, upon recollection they could confirm that it was so—they just had not noticed it at the time. In other words, they remember seeing things that they had not noticed at the time. Then our conversation would turn to the question of why distant objects seem to move in the same direction as the train, but that psychological question does not concern us here. What concerns us here is a philosophical question. How can somebody be aware of something that they had not noticed?

Philosopher and psychologist Nicholas Humphrey addresses this question.[4] He points out that when a person sees red light projected onto a white screen, they have the experience of *seeing red*, and this experience has two components:

(1) a *propositional* component (the person develops an intentional attitude *about* the situation, e.g. they *believe that* they are seeing a white screen illuminated with red light); and

(2) a *phenomenal* component (the person is the *subject* of the experience of seeing red, in the sense that the person is the author of *visual qualia* pertaining to the *red sensation*).

The first component has to do with *rationality* and the second with *subjectivity*. The first component has to do with the person's knowledge and beliefs about the situation, and the second component relates to their hedonic (like/dislike) and emotional (arousal/calmness) responses to the red sensation.

Interestingly, the students who were able to recall that (to their surprise) distant objects viewed from a train do seem to move in the same direction as the train had not developed a propositional attitude to this phenomenon. Their recall was entirely subjective.

Similarly, if a bright red patch of light projected onto a screen is suddenly removed, leaving a bright white screen, most viewers who continue to look at the screen will experience green-blue sensations (complimentary to red), and if they watch for about two minutes these coloured patches will again change in colour and shape (these are called *after-images*). Surprisingly, many students have never experienced after-images, because they did not *know* that to experience such sensations they must continue to look at a blank surface (or close their eyes) for a number of minutes. In other words, many commonplace *subjective* experiences depend upon the subjects being in the right (curious) frame of mind.

Now, what about other animals? Do non-human animals have subjective experiences of this type? As an undergraduate, I discovered that the apparent green-blue that we experience in contrast to red (a colour illusion that can be generated in a number of ways) is also treated as green by chickens. In other words, chickens trained to approach a green object to obtain a food reward will also approach an objectively white object that appears subjectively to be green to humans. The chickens have the same colour illusion as we do. This does not show that the chickens have the same *subjective experience* as we do, but it does show that they can associate an internally generated phenomenon with reward.

Nicholas Humphrey found that rhesus monkeys placed in a chamber bathed in red light became anxious and fidgety, whereas when in a chamber bathed in blue light they were relatively calm. Given a choice, the monkeys strongly preferred a blue chamber to a red one. However, this preference disappeared when the monkeys were provided with interesting thinks to look at. In other words 'they had no preference for things in the world being blue over things in the world being red.'[5] Humphrey suggests that the monkeys could switch their attention away from their subjective feelings to objective matters. All ten monkeys in his experiments preferred blue to green to yellow to red, similar to the preferences of most people.

Wherever there is a subjective experience there must be a subject (see Chapter 4). So the question is—can non-human animals be subjects of experience? One way to find an answer to this question is to investigate whether animals can remember things about themselves. The student on the train says (when prompted) *what it is like* to be on a train, and by apparently recalling what it is like can see the apparent-movement illusion that had previously gone unnoticed. Let us go back to Border and her dreams. If Border can remember having a dream, then she must have experienced the dream and been aware of it. So one way to investigate self-awareness in animals is to ask whether they can remember anything about themselves. This line of reasoning has led some scientists to study animal memory as a way of investigating their self-awareness. As we saw in Chapter 6, studies of *metacognition* in animals, using matching-to-sample tests, indicate that some dolphins and primates seem to know when they do not know which symbol to choose. However, it could be argued that such metacognition tests are an *indirect* way of monitoring an animal's awareness of its own knowledge. It could be that inability to discriminate correct from incorrect responses induces a stress-related biochemical change, and that the animal simply learns to take the escape (don't know) option when prompted by the presence of a particular chemical in the bloodstream. In other words, the 'metacognition' tests do not distinguish between memory proper (a representation in the brain) and biochemical prompting that acts as an external 'memory' in much the same way that a shopping list does.

In Chapter 6 we saw that animals learn to avoid novel dangerous foods and to consume novel beneficial food on the basis of general sensations of sickness or health, rather than on the detection of specific chemicals in the food. This raises the possibility that animals are capable of *experiencing* general sensations of sickness or health. Of course, some information about the animal's bodily state is picked up by the brain, but this information does not have to be very specific. All that is needed is a simple yes/no (go for it/avoid it) message that is associated with the novel food. In other words, two different molecules, present in the blood, could *label* the perception of the novel food. The animal's behaviour suggests that it *knows that* the food is dangerous/beneficial, but this 'knowledge' does not have to be represented in the brain.

Suppose Border had a dream one night, and as a result of the dream a particular chemical was released into her bloodstream. By the next night the chemical is still in her bloodstream, and part of her brain is sensitive to the chemical, but only when she is asleep. The chemical now causes the brain to re-create the dream. Border does not remember the dream in the ordinary sense of remember, but the chemical in her blood causes the dream to be repeated. The dream is simply a procedure triggered by the chemical. Taking a *realist stance*, Border has no self-knowledge and does not remember her dream. Taking a *functionalist stance*, it is *as if* Border remembers her dream, and the chemical plays the *role* of the memory. The realist is relying on an *argument from anatomy*—arguing that because there is no explicit representation of the dream in the brain, Border has no self-knowledge (of the dream). To the functionalist, the anatomy is irrelevant— all that matters is that *something* enables Border to repeat the dream.

Animal brains obtain information from two environments:

(1) They obtain information from the external environment through the senses of vision, hearing, olfaction, etc.
(2) They obtain information from their internal environment by detecting chemical changes (chemoreception), pressure and tension changes (mechanoreception), etc.

Both these environments offer potential depositories for information. Humans deposit information in the external environment in the form of writing, pictures, etc. Other animals do the same in the form of structures (e.g. nests), chemical deposits (pheromones), etc. Recall how ants and termites (Chapter 1) systematically alter the external environment in a way designed (by nature) to influence the behaviour of others—a process called *stigmergy*. This idea has been taken up by roboticists in designing robots that show collective behaviour, by human marine navigators,[6] and by users of the World Wide Web dedicated to cooperating on certain projects. Some scientists also have suggested that animals make use of the state of their internal environment in a stigmergic manner. Neuroscientist Antonio Damasio has suggested that success/failure, leading to reward/punishment, sets up an array of 'somatic markers', bodily states (biochemical in nature) that act as a kind of memory of past events (in a qualitative sense) and are detectable by the brain.[7] Neuroscientist Jaak Panksepp takes a similar position: 'I advocate the position that the roots of the self go back to specific . . . sensory-motor action circuits within the mammalian brain which can generate a primitive sort of intentionality.'[8] In animal behaviour studies, it is commonplace to take account of the animal's internal (motivational) state, and it has been suggested that the reason that animals do not suffer from the *frame problem* is that they are sensitive to those aspects of bodily state that indicate danger, such as proximity to lethal boundaries.[9] Thus, it seems that biological scientists of various types are in favour of the idea that part of an animal's memory resides in its body (outside the brain), and that awareness of the bodily state is akin to awareness of (at least some aspects of) self. However, scientists are not philosophers.

Many philosophers maintain that phenomenal awareness (what it is like) necessarily involves some kind of mental representation. For philosopher Bill Lycan 'the mind has no special properties that are not exhausted by its representational properties.'[10] Similarly, Michael Tye holds that pain consists of sensory representation whose *content* fixes the phenomenal character (i.e. the subject *knows that* it has a pain).[11] For David Rosenthal, 'a neural state will be conscious if it is accompanied by a thought about the state.'[12]

Other philosophers, including Daniel Dennett and Andy Clark doubt that fully fledged explicit representation is necessary for phenomenal awareness.[13] If I have a general feeling of being slightly unwell, does this mean that I *know* that I am unwell? I may be perfectly well, but just *feel* unwell. If I say 'I am unwell' it must be true (it could be argued), because I have *first-person authority*, but is this *necessarily* true? It can't be true *just because* I said it, because I could be malingering. Even if I said I *feel* unwell I could be malingering and it would be difficult for a doctor to contradict me. But if I said *I know* I am unwell, a doctor could contradict me. The doctor could justifiably say, after examining me, that they are confident that I am perfectly well. It may seem obvious that there is a difference between feeling unwell and being unwell, because a person can be unwell without being aware of it. However, it is not clear that someone can truthfully say that they feel unwell when they are not unwell. The problem is confounded by the fact that the more knowledge one has about medical matters the more one's feelings and anxieties are coloured by such knowledge. So it could be argued that a person could not truthfully say that they *knew* that they were unwell, although they could justifiably say that they *believed* that they were unwell. Their *reasons* for believing that they were unwell could be (a) that they *feel* unwell, and (b) that they *believe* that they have a certain medical condition. If they were convinced by a doctor that they did not have the medical condition (i.e. they altered their belief), then it would be entirely possible that they no longer felt unwell. Here we are close to the position taken by philosophers like Daniel Dennett and Andy Clark: basically that *feeling* is prior to *knowing* and that our awareness is partly the result of our culture.[14] For example, when I have a

general sensation of being unwell, I may, like the animals mentioned in Chapter 6, enter a state of quiescence, avoid novel situations, etc. If I am subjectively aware of this general sensation, then
I may think 'I am unwell', or 'I might be unwell', depending upon
my attitude to the idea of being unwell. In other words, my mental
attitude stems from my feeling of being unwell. I may then think, if
I am a stoic, that it will soon pass; or I may think, if I am a
hypochondriac, that I have cancer. The important thing is that I
think *that* something is the case as a result of *feeling* unwell, and my
subjective feeling stems from my general sensation of illness.

An animal may have general sensations of illness and then,
procedurally, do something about it. Another animal may have
the same general sensations, and as a result may subjectively feel
unwell. Yet another animal (a human) may have the same general
sensations, and may subjectively feel unwell (although an animal
with a human brain would probably not have the same subjective
experience as an animal with a non-human brain). The human
animal could procedurally do something in response to feeling
unwell, but could also do something intentionally. The question
is, could an animal do something intentionally, without having the
subjective feeling of illness? For this last possibility to be the case,
the animal would have to act appropriately, in the intentional sense,
without being subjectively aware of being ill.

Whereas some philosophers maintain that knowing is necessary
for feeling (see above), we are here suggesting that you cannot
know about your feelings unless you already experience them.
Your knowledge about your feelings can generate new feelings,
but some feelings must be there to start with. Andy Clark does
not entirely agree with Dennet's view that

In order to be conscious—in order to be the sort of thing it is like
something to be—it is necessary to have a certain sort if informational

organisation . . . [one] that is swiftly achieved in one species, ours, and in no other . . . My claim is not that other species lack our kind of *self-consciousness* . . . I am claiming that what must be added to mere responsivity, mere discrimination, to count as consciousness *at all* is an organisation that is not ubiquitous among sentient organisms.[15]

In other words Dennett is implying that some animals can be sentient (have feelings) without having self-awareness. Andy Clark prefers to allow other species some intentional states, albeit with rudimentary (by human standards) content.[16]

Basically, among philosophers, there is no consensus in sight when it comes to the question of qualia, or phenomenal awareness in animals. But what about robots? Could robots have feelings? Could there be something that it is like to be a robot? For engineers Igor Aleksander and Barry Dunmall, this is an axiomatic question. They maintain that 'it is necessary for certain mechanisms to be present in an agent to create a form (albeit minimal) of consciousness.' Provided that these mechanisms are recognisable through an analysis of the structural and functional characteristics of a given agent, and provided the analysis is computationally realisable, then it should be 'possible to transfer the understood mechanisms into computational agents and thus create a system with "machine" consciousness'.[17] Engineers Owen Holland and Rod Goodman claim that 'a robot able to deal intelligently with the complexities of the real world will have to engage in planning, and that this requirement will inevitably demand the creation of an internal model not just of the world, but of many aspects of the embodied agent itself.'[18] Computer scientist Stan Franklin has devised a system, called IDA, that performs a real-world task in real time. Franklin 'can see no convincing arguments against a claim for phenomenal consciousness in IDA'.[19] There are many, highly competent, computer scientists and roboticists who are willing and able to provide conscious inanimate machines. If we think that something is lacking in their prototypes, then they will be only too happy to supply the missing ingredients (given a little time). So what should be on our wish list?

The Wish List

Many scientists and philosophers have written about consciousness in recent years. It has become fashionable. So what is the answer? First of all, if you have a theory of consciousness that you wish to promote, the thing to do is to define consciousness in a way that suits you. There are as many views of consciousness as there are articles and books about it. But we are not interested in consciousness here. Consciousness is a human hang-up. What we are interested in is whether aliens (animals and robots) have *any kind* of self-awareness, and whether the kind of self-awareness that they have could give us *good reason to ascribe* (see Chapter 5) mental properties. In other words, are there aliens that do have minds of some sort? Remember that to have a mind, the agent must have both *rationality* and *subjectivity* (see Chapter 5).

We are not interested in (human) consciousness, because we are dealing with aliens. We are prepared to consider whether aliens can have some (alien) kind of self-awareness, but we do not want to call this consciousness, because aliens could not have human consciousness. The reason that we are not interested in consciousness is that we want to maintain clarity between the concept of a human mind and the concept of an alien mind.

As far as robots are concerned, what should be on our *minimal* wish list? What properties of the robot would enable us to *ascribe* mentality to it? Firstly it must be a rational agent, in the sense that we can adopt the *intentional stance* towards it. This is no problem, provided that the robot has been properly designed with a particular market in view, and is not simply a laboratory plaything. Even our mindless security robot (Chapter 2) can jump this hurdle. The security robot has a niche in a real world situation, it is ecologically viable, and we can point to criteria by which we can judge whether its behaviour is rational (in the circumstances). We can legitimately adopt the intentional stance towards it. Secondly, we would wish our robot to have some kind of *subjectivity.* There must be something that it is like to be the robot. This requirement is more problematical, but we can make a start by asking what properties of selfhood would *give us good reason to ascribe subjectivity* to a robot.

Let us now see whether we can identify some aspects of selfhood that are *not* really necessary for us to conclude that we have good reason to ascribe mentality to robots. For example, is it necessary for the mind of a robot to reside entirely within the body of the robot? From a *realist stance* the answer might be yes. For some, the property of *metacognition,* which comes from having an *internal model* of the world, would provide good reason to suppose that the robot had some kind of self. Those that take this view would locate the internal model within the body of the robot.[20] That is why it is called an internal model. However, if we accept the view that an extended self is possible, then we are not constrained to the body of the robot. The robot could have part of its brain elsewhere. For example, the security robot could have part of its brain in its 'kitchen' (Chapter 2). More importantly, the robot 'self' could be a distributed system, a possibility that would not be a problem from a *functionalist stance.* Some philosophers apply this kind of thinking to the human mind. For example, Andy Clark poses this question— 'Can it be literally true that the physical system whose whirrings and grindings constitute *my* mind is a system that includes (at times) elements and operations that leap outside my physical (biological) body?'[21]

Is it necessary for the robot self to be unitary? Although we tend to think of our own selves in unitary terms (e.g. *I* think this, *I* feel happy, *I* like the colour red), most philosophers distinguish among various aspects of self. As we saw in Chapter 6, they usually distinguish between three different aspects of the self: (1) awareness of oneself as a material body; (2) awareness of oneself as the author of actions; and (3) awareness of one's own thoughts. Although, historically, some have argued that the self is unitary, 'all we have is an *explanation* of why, groundlessly, we consider ourselves to know ourselves as unitary consciousness.'[22] What we want to know about our robot is whether it could have *any* aspect of selfhood. In particular, could it have *phenomenological awareness* that would enable us to say that there is something that it is like to be this robot? So part of the answer is that it is not necessary for the robot self to be unitary in the sense that it possesses all aspects of the human self. Moreover, the system that provides the robot with awareness of its own body could be entirely separate from the system that (say) makes the robot think that it is the author of its own actions. As we saw in Chapter 5, for a robot to be able to imitate a human, or another robot, it must have some kind of 'machine self', and it is a short further step to imagine a robot that knows something about its machine self.

Is it necessary for the robot to be self-sufficient? Not really, after all children and invalids are not self-sufficient, and we have no problem ascribing selfhood to such people. However, once we accept the possibility of an extended self, there is something of an *identity* problem. For example, the security robot is self-sufficient, but only if we include the robot kitchen as part of the identity of the robot. Without the kitchen, the security robot would not be self-sufficient. Part of the robot self, if it were to qualify for selfhood, would presumably be its kitchen. The robot would have an extended self. But what if a number of security robots shared the same kitchen? Presumably there would be some self-overlap. There is a question about the identity of the robot, but does that matter? We can agree to share part of ourselves with others, especially part of our extended selves, such as tools, hats, or even computers.

Once we accept that the robot self does not have to be a property of the robot body, and does not have to be unitary, we have more or less abandoned a *realist stance* and adopted a *functionalist stance*. What we are interested in is whether there is *anything* about the robot that plays the *role* of at least part of what we normally think of as the self. For example, we might want to say that, provided the robot has the necessary sensory information, its knowledge of the state of its own body (temperature, limb orientation, etc.) constitutes an *awareness* of part of its self. It would not be difficult to endow a robot with such abilities. Biologist Holk Cruse distinguishes between systems with an internal perspective and systems without such perspective. The former require an internal world model, the basis of which is a model of the agent's own body. He argues that the content of the internal model (which includes the body model) is what we experience as a first-person perspective. 'In other words, we do not have the experience, we are the experience.'[23]

As we saw in Chapter 6, all animals have some kind of *self-reference* that enables them to determine the positions of external objects in relation to themselves, and such mechanisms can be entirely *procedural*, a matter of *know-how*. As we saw in Chapter 5, robots can imitate people and other robots. They do this by relating their perception of their own bodies to their perception of the body they are imitating. Does this mean that they are *aware* of their own bodies? If by 'aware' we mean that they have explicit knowledge of their bodies, then this would not be difficult to arrange in a robot. To have an explicit representation (or set of explicit representations) of its own body, a robot would require some kind of self-monitoring system. But this is commonplace these days. Even your

185

PC has a self-monitoring system. So, in this sense, robot could be self-monitoring, or self-aware, and it could report on its internal state (e.g. I am managing/I am not managing to copy this persons movements).

Our robot could not only be aware of itself as a material body, but could report on its whereabouts (using GPS). The robot could be questioned by its owner (e.g. Where are you now? What are you doing?) To answer, the robot would have to consult 'itself' but it would have no language. It could simply use a look-up table. (When decimal coinage was introduced into the UK in 1970, shopkeepers were issued with look-up tables to help them to convert from the old system to the new.) On receiving the word 'where' the robot would look-up 'whereabouts', and report its coordinates; upon receiving the word 'doing' the robot would look up 'current activity', and report accordingly. Is this very different from what we do? Some philosophers think not and others think it is. So let us give the robot designer a little philosophical interrogation:

Q. The robot's orientation mechanisms and activity-monitoring mechanisms are entirely procedural?

A. Yes they are.

Q. So the robot has no knowledge of where it is or what it is doing?

A. Yes it does. It has *symbols* representing these things.

Q. Do these symbols have a role to play?

A. Yes they do. They enable the robot to report to its employer.

Q. But the symbols do not have a role to play in the orientation and activity-monitoring?

A. No, they do not, they are *excluded*, and if they did we would have a case of overdetermination.

Q. Would you agree that the robot does not have self-awareness, because the symbols are not necessary for the task in hand? They do not have a *machine function*?

A. Maybe not, but they do have a *teleological function,* because they enable the robot to report to its employer, and that is important for its survival in the market place.

Now let us ask whether a robot could be aware of itself as the author of actions. As we saw in Chapter 6, people are not always aware of themselves as the author of actions. In some cases it is clear that the person (morally) should have been aware of their actions (e.g. eating a banana in the street and throwing the skin on the pavement). However, the question that we are interested in now is whether a robot could conceivably be aware of itself as the author of its actions. Well, the first question is: does the designer of the robot need to endow the robot with the ability to produce actions (i.e. behaviour that is preceded by an intent)? There are those who think that a robot could do very well without any actions (i.e. all its behavioural output is procedural), and nobody would notice the difference. Be that as it may, the designers may want the robot to be capable of actions, because they want it to be *accountable* for its behaviour.

People are taken to be accountable for their actions if they are the cause of the action, and could have done otherwise. Philosopher Daniel Dennett notes that 'The "could have done otherwise" principle has been debated for generations' and has been criticised by many heavyweight philosophers, including Immanuel Kant, William James, and Dennett himself.[24] To say that a person, or a robot, 'could have done otherwise' begs the question whether 'would have done otherwise, had circumstances been different' would be better. The question now is whether the person, or robot, can be held accountable for the circumstances. Suppose our security robot allowed a car in the car park to be blocked in by another car (i.e. the robot did not follow the normal procedure on this occasion). Normally, the robot follows the procedure of checking that each car has sufficient space in front of it, placing a note on any car that is blocking the way, and reporting this car to the office by radio. These tasks are entirely procedural, but on this occasion the procedure was not carried out, and the owner of the blocked car complained. Who is to blame, the robot or its designer?

Let us question the designer:

Q. Why did the robot overlook the blocked car?

A. Because it ran out of time. The robot has a lot of jobs to do, and they take time. If things are very busy there may not be enough time for the robot to do all the jobs.

Q. Could the robot have done otherwise?

A. It could have postponed a visit to the kitchen to refuel, and dealt with this car instead.

Q. Why did it not do that?

A. Because it is programmed to take into account the risk of running out of fuel. Running out of fuel is serious, whereas allowing a car to be blocked is not so serious.

Q. So this is a matter of *values*?

A. Yes, it is.

Q. Final question, did the robot know that a car was blocked?

A. No, it had not discovered it, and if it had done so it would have followed the procedure automatically. It is an automaton, and knows nothing.

Now let us consider a human traffic warden. They follow a laid-down procedure that involves systematically patrolling the street, and leaving a ticket on any car that does not have a valid parking permit. All this takes time, especially writing out the ticket. A person who shall be nameless notices that the warden down the road is busy, parks illegally (blocking an exit), and nips into a shop to buy a paper. There is a queue in the shop and buying the paper takes longer than expected. In the meantime a car coming out of the exit backwards has hit his car, the driver not expecting the exit to be blocked. The warden is nowhere in sight, having nipped into another shop to buy some chocolate. If the warden had not taken this time off the street, then the accident might have been prevented. The warden is accountable because he/she knew that taking (unauthorised) time off the job involved a small risk of an incident on his/her patch.

Comparing the security robot and the warden, the issue of accountability hinges on both knowledge and values. The warden values, and takes pride in, the job. The warden values his/her health and believes that chocolate is good for health. The warden is aware of the possible consequences of actions taken in relation to these two values. The robot has been endowed with values relating to the trade-off between time spent patrolling and time spent refuelling, but the robot has no knowledge of the consequences of its actions. Moreover, the robot's values are really the designer's values, whereas the warden's values are an aspect of the warden's self as the author of actions. To hold the robot accountable for its actions, we would have to be convinced that its values were its own values (but see below).

Values

Every self-sufficient agent, whether animal or robot, has some built-in primitive values. Usually, these have to do with crossing lethal boundaries, such as overheating and running out of fuel. Usually they are related to automatic mechanisms, or procedures for preventing the state of the animal or robot from crossing such boundaries. Thus most birds start panting when their brain temperature reaches a certain level, and most motor cars have a fan that cuts in automatically when the engine temperature reaches a certain level. These values are put there by the designer.

In addition to built-in values, there are *emergent values* in animals, and even in robots. It helps if the robot can learn. Like animals, successful robots must be able to adapt to environmental change. It is well established that animals can learn to associate two events if the relationship between them conforms to what we normally call a causal relationship.[25] Thus, animals can learn that one event (the cause) predicts another event (the effect), or that one event predicts that another event (non-effect) will not occur. They can also learn that certain stimuli predict no consequences in a given situation, or that a class of stimuli (including the animal's own behaviour) is causally irrelevant. The conditions under which these types of associative learning occur are those that we would expect on the hypothesis that animals are designed to attune themselves to the causal relationships in their environment. Thus the animal must be able to distinguish potential causes from contextual cues, and for this to occur there must be some surprising occurrence that draws the animal's attention to particular events, or the events must be (innately) relevant to particular consequences. If these conditions are not fulfilled, contextual cues may overshadow potential causal events, or learning may be blocked by prior association with an irrelevant cue. Thus the conditions under which associative learning occurs are consistent with our common-sense views about the nature of causality.

Robot learning algorithms abound in the literature, and animal-like learning can be achieved in artificial neural-networks.[26] For example, imagine a wheeled robot equipped with collision detectors that inform it about collisions with obstacles, and also equipped with range finders that provide information about the distance to obstacles. Suppose that there is no pre-wired connection between these two types of information about the environment. The naïve robot will bump into obstacles, from time to time, then back up and move off in another direction. If the robot were able to make an association between collisions and the proximity of obstacles as detected by the range finders, then it could begin to learn to avoid obstacles before colliding with them. In one experiment, such a robot was provided with a simple association mechanism (technically called a Hebbian learning mechanism) that allowed the robot to combine sensory inputs.[27] The robot keeps moving until it bumps into an obstacle. It then performs a reflex disengagement manoeuvre. Each collision triggers an association between the collision sensors and range finders, with which the robot is equipped. Soon the avoidance movements initially triggered by physical collisions are replaced by avoidance movements triggered by range finders. In other words, the robot learns to avoid obstacles before contacting them.

As the robot gains experience it slowly shifts from collision-driven behaviour to range-finder driven behaviour, and thus starts anticipating obstacles. This anticipatory behaviour is *emergent*, because there is no component of the system designed to do antici-pation per se. The associations formed between specific sensory inputs and responses are driven by learning criteria provided by a *predefined value system*, which is a kind of 'teacher' guiding the learning process. In a sense the learning is 'supervised' by the value system in interaction with the environment.[28] Learning re-quires feedback about success and failure, and this feedback must be based upon an immutable set of *values*, as students of animal learning realised some time ago. Thus, in order for learning to be adaptive (i.e. of advantage), the (predefined) value system must reflect certain characteristics of the ecological niche, within which the animal or robot is designed to operate. So, to learn to avoid obstacles the robot must 'know' that collision with obstacles is 'bad', whilst avoidance of obstacles is 'good'.

A basic value system, combined with a learning mechanism, can produce new values that act as constraints on the behaviour of the robot. For example, a bomb-disposing robot would have values relating to proximity to a bomb, values relating to the time that a bomb was likely to explode, and values relating to danger to humans. If the robot learned that bombs of a certain type were likely to explode at any moment, then the values (risks) relating to time would be paramount, and the robot would act as quickly as possible to defuse the bomb. If the bomb was of a different type (e.g. a land mine), then the time element of the value system would be downgraded, and time would be spent warning people about the bomb, and defusing the bomb slowly and carefully. If the employers of the robot were confident that it had the right value system, or system of priorities, then they could 'trust' the robot to carry out its duties without human supervision.

Scientifically, values refer to the size of a variable or parameter. The weightings given to certain critical parameters in a system provide the values that we are interested in. For example, an incubating herring gull will quit its nest when an intruder comes within a certain distance (it is endangering the eggs, but it will have many future opportunities to breed). The distance that triggers this response (the flight distance) progressively diminishes as the hatching date approaches, and increases thereafter. The weighting (value) given to the nest reaches its maximum at the point of hatching and decreases thereafter, as the chicks become more and more able to fend for themselves.

Confidence in the value system is all important in robot design, especially for autonomous robots. That is why roboticists are paying attention to it.[29] However, value systems are important for another reason. In Chapter 1 we saw that the idea of *emergent functionality* appears in both animal behaviour and robotics.[30] Self-organisation occurs in social insects and in their robotic equivalents.[31] It has also been advocated and developed at the cognitive level in robots.[32] However, such developments must not be allowed to imply that 'anything goes'. A successful self-organising robotic system must be kept within bounds by a *value system*. Otherwise the robot would not be tailored to its ecological niche, and would not be successful in the marketplace. Imagine a situation where a robot may have cognitive freedom to the extent that its designer would not be able to tell what was going on in its 'mind', yet the designer must remain confident that the robot will not do anything 'stupid'. The designer is no longer in control, but by virtue of the value system embodied in the robot, the designer should be willing to hand over 'responsibility' to the robot. Unless we are willing to hand over 'responsibility' to robots, their useful future will be limited. We will really need robots to carry out certain types of duty, in outer space, the deep ocean, radioactive areas, and other places that are dangerous for humans. The question is: can it be done? No doubt the necessary technology is available, but is it conceivable philosophically?

Self-sufficient robots that operate by rules-of-thumb based upon optimal decision theory, and variants thereof, can be made and in this respect they are similar to animals (see Chapter 2). Provided that the robots are sufficiently well engineered and robust, the designer can be confident that they will 'stick to the rules'. However, once the designer introduces aspects of self-organisation, with a view to achieving emergent functionality, then various problems arise.

Self-organisation at the behavioural level, such as is seen among social insects, and in robots modelled upon them, pose no particularly philosophical problems for the designer. Provided the designer has correctly anticipated the implications of the design, there should be no surprises. Self-organisation at the (mental) representational, or cognitive, level does pose problems for the designer, because the designer must somehow keep the behaviour of the robot 'within bounds', even though it has some 'freedom of thought'. The designer can attempt to do this by endowing the robot with a suitable value system.

Once a robot becomes autonomous and free of human control, who is responsible for its actions? If a robot is *causally responsible* for a state of affairs, in the sense that it brought it about either directly or indirectly, then there arises questions of *legal responsibility* and *moral responsibility.* To be legally responsible is to fulfil the requirements for accountability under the law. To be morally responsible, an agent usually has a moral obligation, and fulfils the criteria for deserving blame or praise. As things stand, a robot could be causally responsible for some event, but it could not be legally or morally responsible, because it could not be the recipient of *desert*. For a robot to be given what it deserves, it would have to be given something that mattered to it, and it would have to have some understanding of the significance of its deserts.

Let us go back to the traffic warden, who is supposed to follow a laid-down procedure that involves systematically patrolling the street. The warden nips into a shop to buy some chocolate. During the time off the street there is an accident that the warden could have prevented. The warden is accountable because he/she knew that taking (unauthorised) time off the job involved a small risk of an incident on his/her patch. When the warden is called to account he/she will probably be asked for an explanation—what was the *reason* for going into the shop? We are able to ask people to give reasons, but we are unable to ask animals. This is not only a matter of language. Animals do not *have* reasons (of this type), because they do not need them. They do not have a lifestyle that involves reason-giving.

Let us go back to Betty the Caledonian Crow (Chapter 5): It could be argued that Betty is able to solve the problem of obtaining food with a straight piece of wire, because she is capable of practical reasoning. (She might reason to herself something like this—*I cannot pull up the food item with this probe because the probe does not grip the food in any way. Therefore, I need a tool that I can fasten onto the food item. The simplest such tool is a hook. So perhaps I can alter this probe to make it into a hook.*) Such reasoning would require a fairly sophisticated cognitive mechanism, and there is little doubt that Betty would benefit from such a mechanism. But even if Betty realises the *reason* why the probe is inadequate, this does not signify that she could give this reason as an explanation of her behaviour. It is likely that her practical reason is domain-specific, and not part of the more complete type of rational system found in humans.

Now it could be that we would want (some) robots to be accountable for their behaviour. So maybe accountability should be on our wish list. In comparing the security robot and the warden (above) we noted that the robot's values are really the designer's values, whereas the warden's values are an aspect of the warden's self as the author of actions. To hold the robot accountable for its actions, we would have to be convinced that its values were its own values. Now wait a minute:

Q. Are we saying that the robot has values by virtue of its design, and therefore should not be accountable for its actions?

A. Yes, we are.

Q. Are we saying that a person has values that are part of its self, and therefore the person should be accountable?

A. Yes, we are.

Q. But some of the person's values (such as phobias, disgust reactions, loyalty to kin) are most certainly the result of design (by natural selection), so why should the person be held accountable for these?

A. What people are held accountable for is a matter of *social convention*. For example, in many societies men are held accountable if they do not pull their economic weight and provide for their families, whereas in other societies men who do not provide are not held accountable, or blamed.

Q. Do you mean that it could be a matter of social convention that a particular type of robot be held accountable for its actions?

A. Yes, it could. Many things could be a matter of social convention, but of course, the robot would have to be *capable* of being accountable.

Let us look at another example. Deep ocean currents can be mapped using a flock of about six robots by dropping them into the ocean.[33] As it descends, each robot records sensory information such as salinity, temperature, pressure, and the presence of specific chemicals, along with the distance between itself and the other robots (it is not necessary to monitor the bearing of other robots). Once at a predefined depth the robots start ascending and still continue collecting data until they reach the surface. Back on the surface, they communicate the collected data to a base computer in a ship or on land, through satellite or other means. The base computer collects the data from every recovered member of the flock and this is used to construct a 3D map of the oceanic currents. This is done by computing the way in which the flock was distorted by the underwater currents. The flock distortion is calculated from the records that each robot keeps of its distance from the other robots. For this system to work the robots must remain within communication distance of each other. To do this they need a certain amount of manoeuvrability.

These robots are automata that work collectively. Data from a number of robots are necessary to compute the flock distortion, but if a robot goes missing it does not really matter. Underwater, the robots can communicate with each other by sonar, but once underwater their communication with the base computer is cut off (because radio signals cannot be sent through seawater). So they lose contact with humans once they are in the sea. There is no way that humans can control the behaviour of the robots when they are underwater. The robots are autonomous in the sense that they have to manage their on-board energy supply and make decisions by themselves. The human operators can have confidence in the robots, provided they have set the right parameter values. In particular the robots must ensure that the flock stays together, and to do this they must use some of their precious energy. Therefore, like the security robot, these robots have to trade off competing priorities. Working together, the robots can provide valuable information about deep ocean currents, their temperature, salinity, and any chemicals that they contain.

Now, would it not be even better if such robots could use their initiative? After all, they may come across something important and interesting, such as currents containing radioactive substances, a new kind of animal, or whatever. It might be useful in such circumstances for a robot to zoom to the surface and report as quickly as possible. The problem is that to use its initiative a robot would have to 'break the rules'. It would have to abandon the flock. It would have to risk failure due to lack of fuel. It would have to decide for itself whether such departures would be worthwhile. Note that it would have to decide *for itself* and not simply *by itself*. What does this imply?

It would imply that the robot had some kind of self, not necessarily a unitary self (it is afterall part of a flock), and probably an extended self. It would be self-monitoring, but so would its automaton counterpart. It would have to be aware of itself as the author of actions, because we would want it to be accountable. We would want to know *its* reason for breaking away from the flock. An engineer could say that all we need to do is to look into its brain, but it is quite likely that we will never recover the robot. We can communicate with it as it floats on the surface, but recovering it is another matter in the extensive ocean. (It is only the size of a bucket, and not all that expensive, so recovery is probably not worth the cost.) To have a reason for acting, the robot would have to have some limited cognitive ability (like Betty the crow), but to *give* a reason for acting it would have to have some limited mentality. Moreover, to act on its own initiative, for its own reasons, would imply that the robot had some *mental autonomy*. Of course, we would hope that its *values* were such that it would not do anything stupid.

In this chapter we have seen that animals, including humans, and robots can have extended selves, in the sense that part of their 'memory' resides outside the body, and that stigmergy is thus a universal behavioural phenomenon. It is clear that people are sometimes aware of these external memories, but sometimes they simply serve as reminders of things that would otherwise have been forgotten. When it comes to animals, the scientific evidence is inconclusive, but there is some philosophical argument in favour of the view that an agent cannot know about its own feelings unless they are subjectively experienced. In other words, they cannot know that something is the case about themselves without having some sort of subjectivity.

On the other hand, it is conceivable that a robot could have some sort of intentionality, and could give an account of its 'reasoning' and its 'actions'. To accomplish this, it would not be necessary for the robot to have any phenomenological awareness of its 'self'. It may be programmed to refer to its machine self, but there would be nothing that it is like to be such a robot. However, there are some scientists and engineers that are confident that they can, and will, produce robots that are 'conscious' in the sense that they do have phenomenological awareness and 'emotions'. The question is: do you want one? Would you buy one? Suppose you were sold such a robot, on the understanding that it had true 'feelings about itself'. How would you know whether you had been sold a pup? This is very much a case of buyer beware. How *could* you know; i.e. on what basis could you know? This is a question that we must address.

EPILOGUE

THE ALIEN MIND

Where to begin? Let us begin at the beginning. You may have wondered why, at the beginning of this book, so much space was devoted to robots, their development and evolution. The reason is that to understand the mind of an alien, to understand how it works, one must understand what it is for. Many animals have no mind, they are automata. To have a mind, and especially to have language, is expensive. A bigger brain is needed, and brains are expensive to develop, to train, and to run. Bigger brains mean bigger bodies and fewer, more expensive, offspring. Fewer offspring mean less future genetic influence. So many animals do not need minds, thank you, they are doing very well as they are.

For robots, it is different. Their mode of development and reproduction is different from that of most animals. Robots have a symbiotic relationship with people, analogous to the relationship between aphids and ants, or domestic animals and people. Robots depend on humans for their reproductive success. The designer of a robot will flourish if the robot is successful in the marketplace. The employer of a robot will flourish if the robot does the job better than the available alternatives. Therefore, if a robot is to have a mind, it must be one that is suited to the robot's environment and way of life, its ecological niche.

Philosophically, these considerations have certain consequences. They imply that the animal mind and the robot mind will not be like the human mind. They imply that philosophical weight should be given to the teleological consequences of any theory of the animal or robot mind. What are we to conclude from this?

First of all, let us look at the situation objectively by comparing robots with animals. There are many scientists and philosophers who reckon that they have good reason to ascribe some kind of mentality to some animals. Let us look at some of these reasons. There are some animals that can recognise themselves in a mirror or film—so can some robots.[1] There are some animals that can imitate vocalisations and behaviour of others—so can some robots.[2] There are some animals that seem to demonstrate reasoning—so can some robots.[3] There are some animals that can perform complex feats of navigation—so can some robots. Some animals seem to indicate that they are in pain or feel ill—so can some robots.[4] There are some animals that can apparently remember whether they know something (metacognition)—so can some robots.[5] In fact probably all the phenomena that have been cited as evidence that animals have some kind of mentality have also been demonstrated in robots. This exercise does not imply that any of this evidence is sufficient/insufficient, or uncontroversial, but it does raise one important issue. The robots that can match animals in the various respects cited above are all man-made. They are machines that work in a machine-like way, without any neural apparatus. Therefore, those features of animal behaviour that can be simulated by robots can be accounted for in an entirely mechanistic manner. This does not mean that the animals in question work in the same way as the robots, but it does show that mentalistic scenarios are not necessary to account for the behaviour. Indeed, you might be inclined to think that whether aliens do (or do not) have minds is an empirical matter, and we might as well simply wait for science to tell us the answer. Why bother with the philosophy?

Consider the following two problems. In scenario I a man is manning the points on a railway line. He is making sure that the points are not moved, because he knows that there is another man working on the line ahead. If the points were switched this man would be killed. He now receives a call on his mobile phone to say that a train is coming and, unless he switches the points now, three men (that he did not know about) working on the (other) line will be killed. Should he switch the points and kill one man, or do nothing and allow three men to be killed? Most people agree that it is better to kill one man to save three.

In scenario II, a doctor has a patient who is terminally ill. He could let him die naturally, or he could hasten his death. He receives a call for help from another doctor who has three patients, one who urgently needs a liver transplant, one who urgently needs a heart transplant, and one who urgently needs a lung transplant. If they don't receive these transplants they will die. If the doctor hastens the death of (kills) his patient he can donate his organs to the other three patients and save their lives. Surely it is better to sacrifice one life to save three. Most people agree that it is better to kill one man to save three in scenario I, but do not agree with this solution in scenario II.

Leaving aside the reasons that these people give for their logical inconsistency, it is clear that these are philosophical and not purely empirical matters. So what? So what is the difference between punishing Border for stealing the cat's food, in the hope that she will not do it again, and blaming and shaming a human visitor for doing the same thing? The normal answer would be that Border did not commit the crime voluntarily (assuming that we believe this to be empirically correct), whereas the human did act voluntarily in full knowledge that she was doing wrong. (Again we assume that this interpretation is empirically correct.) So we have two animals that show the same behaviour (albeit for different 'reasons'), yet we blame one and not the other. Why we blame one and not the other is a philosophical question (about how we ought to behave) and not an empirical one.

It is true that, in recent decades, philosophers have moved more and more towards a naturalistic viewpoint, looking to science to provide some of the answers. However, it is also true that scientists are involving themselves more and more in philosophy. Indeed, we have the somewhat bizarre scenario of scientists taking different philosophical stances towards the same empirical situations, primarily the behaviourist versus cognitive stances (Chapter 4), and realist versus functionalist stances (Chapter 6). The stances that they adopt are consistent with the evidence, but it is clear that they do not adopt their chosen stance for empirical reasons, since the evidence is also fully consistent with the alternative stance.

Theories about the human mind abound in the literature. There is some theorising about animal minds, and most of this is based upon the idea of evolutionary psychological continuity—the idea that the human brain has evolved through various stages that are similar to the brains of other species existing today.[6] There are a number of problems with this approach. Firstly, it seems odd to argue that the animal mind is somewhat like the human mind, when there is so much disagreement about the human mind. Secondly, the evolutionary continuity argument does not tell us where, along the line (if there is a line), certain mental capacities evolved. So far, the attempts that have been made to demonstrate language capacity, reasoning capacity, or intentional capacity in animals have been a signal failure. Why is this? The answer is that it is difficult. It is not difficult to demonstrate that certain animal abilities conform to certain theories or philosophical stances. The difficulty is that they usually conform to more than one of these.[7] Thirdly, there is an element of chauvinism in the evolutionary continuity approach. Too much attention is paid to the similarities between certain animals and humans, and not enough to the fit between the animal and its ecological niche. If an animal has a mind, it has evolved to do a job that is different from the job that it does in humans.

Theories about possible robot minds also abound in the literature. One problem in this area is not chauvinism, but liberalism: anything goes. When I first became interested in robotics I visited, and worked in, various laboratories around the world. I was extremely impressed with the technical expertise, but not with the philosophy. They could make robots all right, but they did not seem to know what they wanted their robots to do. The main aim seemed to be to produce a robot that was intelligent. But an intelligent agent must be intelligent about something. There is no such thing as a generalised animal, and there will be no such thing as a successful generalised robot.

Another problem is that the technology tends to drive the agenda. We have these computers in which we can program symbol systems; therefore we can explain the mind in terms of symbol systems. We have this technology that can produce artificial neural networks; therefore we can explain the mind in terms of connectionism. We have this technology that can produce miniaturised, 'mind components'; therefore we can use these to replace/interact with bits of the human mind. It must be said that, given the time and money spent over the past fifty years on robotics and related

203

disciplines, we are not much nearer to knowing what we want to know. I remember, in my early robotics days, attending an inaugural lecture in which the new engineering professor said that his aim was to produce a robot that was as intelligent as a sheep. I was absolutely convinced that he had no idea what 'intelligent as a sheep' meant.

That is the downside, now for the upside. You can make up your own mind. You can start by adopting a philosophical stance, and a quick reminder may help here.

Anthropomorphism—The behaviour of animals and machines can be interpreted in terms of human folk psychology.
Materialism—Everything in the world is material, made up of some combination of matter and energy (alternatives are idealism and dualism).
The intentional stance—Anything that behaves in a 'rational' way is behaving 'as if' it had mental states.
Behaviourism—Invoking mental states is not necessary in explaining observed behaviour.
Eliminative materialism—Explanations in terms of mental states will eventually be eliminated by explanations in physical terms.
Naturalism—Everything in the world is part of nature and will eventually be explained in scientific terms.
Realism—Mental states really do exist and take up space in the brain.
Functionalism—Any state of affairs that plays the role of a mental state is a mental state, whether it be in the brain or not.

Of course, each philosophical stance has its downside. If you adopt a comfortable anthropomorphic stance, you are lazy. If you do not adopt a materialist stance, you must figure out how mind and body marry. If you adopt an eliminativist stance, you are a reductionist, with all that that entails. It is up to you to face the consequences of any philosophical stance that you choose to adopt.

Once you have adopted a particular stance you will form opinions about certain issues. For example, when my dog, Border, is sleeping and showing signs of dreaming, I sometimes adopt the lazy anthropomorphic stance and attribute dreams to my dog. If I were to adopt a realist stance, I might ascribe dreams to my dog, having good reason to do so (e.g., being a realist, I believe that dreams take place in the brain, and I have reason to believe that these dreams are mental events, and that the dog subjectively experiences these mental events). I would then have to be prepared to say what my reasons were, and to defend them.

Let us see whether we can apply all this to the traffic robot introduced in the Preface. It wears a policeman's cap on its spherical head, has two protruding lens-like eyes, and has a whistle for a mouth. Its head swivels on a thin neck, supported by a torso that rotates on a pedestal. Two long arms direct the traffic: the hands on the ends of them point to, beckon, and stop the traffic in the time-honoured manner.

Unlike the security robot, the traffic robot does not have to worry about energy. It is supplied with energy by the taxpayer, through its pedestal. However, it does have to earn its living by doing a good job, directing the traffic, avoiding accidents wherever possible, and dealing with emergencies. In directing traffic it must try to keep the traffic moving as fast and as smoothly as possible. It awards itself bonus points for each vehicle that passes it per unit time. It has no legs, so if a vehicle stalls, or is involved in an accident, it must sort things out while remaining on its pedestal.

To do all this, the robot is equipped with binocular vision and binaural hearing. So it can judge the distance of objects by vision and the direction of sounds by hearing. It has special camera-eyes for reading number plates. These are mounted at the side of each incoming road, so there is no way that a vehicle can slip past without being detected. It has a multitone whistle and in addition to the normal

205

traffic-directing blasts, it can play tunes. It does this at the dead of night, when there is no traffic. It can also play ironic tunes directed at certain unfortunate drivers (we leave this to your imagination). It has long arms and hands that can perform all the necessary movements. Moreover, it has information feedback from all its effectors, and it can remember all the movements and directions that it made on any particular occasion in the past. Like the security robot, it has a range of devices to deter and protect itself from vandals.

The traffic robot can communicate with drivers by whistle, with pedestrians by voice, and with the emergency services by radio. It can videotape incidents and transmit the information to headquarters. It can filter out speech from background noise, and so can record messages spoken to it by people. It has no language, so it cannot hold an ordinary conversation. The question is: does it have a mind? The next question is: does it need a mind? If it needs a mind, it can have one (we have the technology).

The traffic robot has values. It has values relating to its body, its well functioning, or 'health'. It has values relating to its job, the smooth and safe flow of traffic. It has values relating to security, including its communications with the security services and emergency services. The traffic robot also has motivation towards keeping itself at a good working temperature, towards avoiding injury, towards its work. It also has 'anxieties' or 'phobias', of fire, smoke, and dust. The traffic robot also has 'feelings'. It feels 'pain' if injured, or as a result of wear-and-tear (creaking joints). It feels 'unwell' if it has a virus. It feels 'happy' if things are going well.

Much of the work of the traffic robot involves automatic control of the traffic. It does not have to 'think' to do this. It works like an automaton, following procedures. However, it does have to 'think' in emergency situations. Although the robot has a 'rule book' of procedures to follow in emergency situations (e.g. inform the authorities, divert traffic around stalled vehicles), there are times when it must use its initiative. It can deploy a certain amount of reasoning power to untangle traffic jams. It can decide to abandon the 'rule book' in certain situations. It has a certain amount of cognition.

Does all this mean that the robot has intentionality? Does it have beliefs, desires, and intentions? The technical experts will say, 'If you want the robot to have such mental states, we can provide them (given time). But do we (as designers) want this? If so, why do we want it?'

Some philosophers would argue that to endow a robot with mental states is impossible, but others would argue that if human mental states exist, they are material things, part of our machinery, and therefore there is no reason (in principle) why they should not be provided in a machine such as a robot. It all depends upon one's philosophical stance.

Let us suppose that what we want for our robot is technically possible. What would we want, and why? One quality that we would want is accountability. We would want the robot to be accountable for its actions, not to blame it, or punish it, but to help us understand the circumstances of particular unusual situations. For example, suppose the robot stopped all the traffic on a particular road, causing chaos:

Q. What was the reason for stopping all the vehicles?
A. I saw a pedestrian knocked down by a vehicle.
Q. Why did you not follow the usual procedure, and allow traffic to filter past the site of the incident?
A. Because I saw a pedestrian knocked down, but I could not see the body, so I thought that the body might have been taken up into a vehicle.
Q. But why stop all the traffic?
A. Because that vehicle must still be there, for the authorities to investigate.

207

Not only does accountability allow the robot to give a reason for its actions, it also allows it to give an account of its reasoning. In other words, the robot is able to provide an explanation. Surely this ability would be very desirable in a policeman on traffic duty, and therefore it would be desirable in a traffic robot.

Now, to give a reason, the robot would have to have a reason, and to have a reason it would have to have intentionality. But is this enough for us to conclude that the robot has a mind?

Few informed philosophers would deny that, given that all this is possible, the robot would have intentionality. Not only would it conform to the intentional stance, behaving as if it was rational, but it would actually be rational, in either the realist or functionalist sense. However, we have set ourselves a hard target, by asserting that, to have a mind, an agent must have both rationality and subjectivity.

There are some philosophers who would assert that our robot (as described so far) is like a zombie. A philosophical zombie is a hypothetical being that is indistinguishable from a normal human being except that it lacks *conscious experience* or *qualia* or *sentience*. For example, when a zombie is poked with a sharp object it does not feel any pain. It behaves as if it does feel pain, but it does not actually have the experience of pain as a person would.

Because zombies are exactly like us in all physical respects but have no subjective experiences there can be 'nothing it is like' to be a zombie. Although few people think zombies exist, many philosophers hold they are at least conceivable. If zombies are possible, then it follows that conscious experience is not physical. If your concious experience were a physical property, then your zombie twin would also have it.

To a materialist all subjective experience arises from physical systems. The philosopher David Chalmers argues that when experience arises from a physical system, it does so in virtue of the system's functional organisation:

Specifically, I defend a principle of organizational invariance, holding that experience is invariant across systems with the same fine-grained functional organization. More precisely, the principle states that given any system that has conscious experiences, then any system that has the same functional organization at a fine enough grain will have qualitatively identical conscious experiences. A full specification of a system's fine-grained functional organization will fully determine any conscious experiences that arise.[8]

Currently, philosophers seem to take up one of three positions:

1. Zombies are possible, and therefore conscious experience cannot be accounted for in physical terms (a dualist stance).
2. Zombies are not possible, because everything in the universe can be accounted for in physical terms (a materialist or physicalist stance).
3. If zombies are possible, then consciousness must be epiphenomenal, caused by physical events but having no effect upon them, and therefore having no effect upon behaviour.[9] Philosopher Robert Kirk holds that such epiphenomenalism is inconceivable, therefore zombies are inconceivable.[10]

Conciousness is an intrinsic property of the human brain, so a zombie with a human brain would have conciousness, but a zombie with a brain made of some other material (e.g. silicon-based) may not have comciousness. A silicon-based zombie would be a zombie in the functionalist sense, but not in the realist sense (note that this special pleading about the nature of the human brain is very similar to the position taken by Searle (see Chapter 7).

The zombie debate is important, because it raises the possibility that the traffic warden does have subjective experiences (of pain, etc.) and it has a double that does not have such experiences. If materialism/physicalism is true, it cannot be the case that the traffic robot has subjective experiences while its physically identical double does not. Even if it were the case, we could not tell the difference between one robot that has subjective experiences and an identical one that does not, because their behaviour and responses to inter-rogation would be the same (this argument also applies to zombies). If we cannot tell the difference between these two cases, then we cannot tell (in principle) whether our traffic robot has subjective experiences. Therefore we cannot tell whether there is something that it is like to be the traffic robot. Even if the robot's designer asserts that the robot has been provided with everything necessary for it to have subjective experiences, we cannot tell whether this is true.

If this type of argument applies to robots and to zombies, then does it apply to other people? Peter Strawson would say we cannot doubt that other people have subjective experiences, because a necessary condition of ascribing states of consciousness to oneself is that one be able to make sense of their ascription to others.[11] And a necessary condition of ascribing states of consciousness to others is to be able to identify them as individuals of the same type as oneself. (This seems somewhat like a social convention—do as you would be done by.)

So where are we now? Earlier, we came to the conclusion that for an alien to have a mind, it must have both rationality and subject-ivity, but we have now come to the conclusion that we cannot tell whether an alien has subjectivity. Clearly, for an alien to have a mind like ours it must have subjectivity, but an alien would not have a mind like ours, because it is not a human. An alien would have an alien mind. An animal would have a mind suited to its lifestyle, and a robot should have a mind suited to its lifestyle. So do we have good reason to ascribe mentality to our traffic robot? We certainly have good reason to ascribe rationality. It exhibits rational behav-iour, the designer says that it is capable of reasoning, and it can give reasons for its decisions (it is accountable). Although logically we cannot tell whether it can feel pain (etc.), any more than we can with other people, sociologically it is in our interest (i.e. a matter of social convention) for the robot to feel accountable, as well as to be accountable. That way we can think of it as one of us, and that also goes for the dog. How do you feel about that, Border?

GLOSSARY

A guide to the meaning of technical terms as used in this book

ACCESSIBILITY   The ability to obtain resources as a function of skill, etc. (strictly a limit on the rate that an agent can obtain resources from the environment).

ACTION   A philosophical term for behaviour caused by a mental state, such as an intent. However, some philosophers regard habitual movements as actions, even when they are not apparently caused in this way.

ACTION SELECTION   A roboticist's term for the mechanism by which incipient 'behaviours' are selected for overt expression.

ANIMAL ECONOMICS   The application of economic principles to animal behaviour.

ANOMALOUS MONISM   A form of monism that denies that the mental can be reduced to the physical.

ANTHROPOMORPHISM   The attribution of human qualities to non-human entities.

ARTIFICIAL INTELLIGENCE   The science of making machines do things that would require intelligence if done by humans.

ASCRIPTION   Assigning a quality to a person, animal, or machine, with good reason.

ATTRIBUTION   Assigning a quality to a person, animal, or machine.

AUTOMATON   A machine that behaves in a procedural manner.

AUTONOMY   Freedom from outside control.

AVAILABILITY   The ability to obtain resources as a function of their abundance in the environment.

BASIC CYCLE   The cycle of work – find fuel – refuel shown by animals and energy-autonomous robots.

BEHAVIOURAL STABILITY   The stability of the basic cycle. This implies that the animal or robot does not succumb to irrecoverable debt of any vital resource.

BEHAVIOURISM   A school of psychology, and a philosophical stance, that accounts for behaviour in terms of observable phenomena, without invoking mental entities.

CHAUVINISM   Discriminating in favour of a particular category of agent, such as a particular species of animal.

COGNITION   Thinking that requires manipulation of explicit knowledge.

COLLECTIVE BEHAVIOUR   Behaviour, involving a number of participants, that is essentially self-organising, there being no direct communication between the participants. There is, however, indirect communication via the environment.

COMMUNICATION   The transmission of information from one individual to another, which is designed to influence the behaviour of the recipient.

COMPUTATIONAL THEORY OF MIND   A body of theory that equates symbol manipulation in a digital computer with the workings of the human mind.

CONNECTIONISM   A kind of neurocomputing that involves simulated nerve cells of various types and complexity.

DECEIT   Communication that benefits the sender at the expense of the receiver.

DECISION VARIABLES   The variables upon which decisions are based; e.g. in deciding between chalk and cheese, their hardness might be a decision variable.

DECLARATIVE KNOWLEDGE   Explicit knowledge that people can speak about.

DEMAND FUNCTION   An economic concept expressing the relationship between the price and consumption of a commodity. When applied to

213

animals the price is usually represented by energy/time spent on the relevant activity.

DESIGN STANCE   A philosophical stance that judges issues on the basis of design criteria on the basis of what ought to be the case in the circumstances.

DISPOSITIONS   A philosophical term for a non-mental causal agent.

DUALISM   A philosophical stance which holds that mind and matter are two distinct things, and that the one cannot be accounted for in terms of the other.

ELIMINATIVE MATERIALISM   A materialistic philosophical stance that claims that folk psychology is flawed and will eventually be eliminated by being reduced to explanations in terms of physics.

ELIMINATIVISM   A philosophical stance that holds that mental phenomena play no part in determining human behaviour.

ENERGY AUTONOMY   Freedom from outside control of energy supply; i.e. the agent obtains its own energy.

EPIPHENOMENON   A phenomenon that plays no causal role in a system.

EXCLUSION PROBLEM   A question of whether the physical properties that realise mental properties exclude the latter from causal relevance.

EXPLICIT KNOWLEDGE   Knowledge involving explicit representations, or knowledge that something is the case.

EXPLICIT REPRESENTATION   Information made obvious in a physical manner, and is not simply part of a procedure.

FEEDBACK CONTROL SYSTEM   A system in which the independent variable x is influenced by the dependent variable y. If the latter tends to increase the former, then positive feedback exists. If the latter tends to reduce the former, then negative feedback exists. Such systems are often goal-directed.

FEELINGS   The subjective experience of what it feels like to be subject to certain stimuli, or to be another agent.

FIRST-PERSON AUTHORITY   A person is said to have first-person authority with respect to the content of their own mind, whereas others (third persons) can access this content only indirectly.

FITNESS   A biological and mathematical concept that indicates the ability of genetic material to perpetuate itself during the course of evolution.

FIXED ACTION PATTERN   Activities that have a relatively fixed pattern of coordination.

FOLK PSYCHOLOGY   A philosopher's term for the subject matter of our everyday understanding of one another in psychological or mental terms, such as belief, desire, and intention.

FRAME PROBLEM   A problem that arises because many of the possible consequences of a planned action are not really relevant to the decision whether to perform the action. The problem is to distinguish among the relevant and irrelevant consequences.

FUNCTION (*BIOLOGICAL*)   The contribution to fitness of an item.

FUNCTIONALISM   The view that certain entities, including some mental ones, are best described in terms of the functional role that they play within a system.

GOAL ACHIEVING   Recognising a goal once it is arrived at, even though the process of arriving at the goal is largely a matter of environmental circumstances.

GOAL-DIRECTED   A system that involves an explicit representation of the goal-to-be-achieved that is instrumental in guiding the behaviour.

GOAL-SEEKING   Seeking a goal without the goal being explicitly represented within the system.

HOLISM   The idea that the elements of a system have significance by virtue of their interrelations with each other.

ICONS   Signs that resemble the things that they represent; e.g. a thermometer icon represents temperature.

IDEALISM   A philosophical stance that holds that reality is confined to the contents of our own minds.

IDENTITY THEORY   A theory holding that mental states are identical to physical states of the brain.

IMPLICIT   Information available for use by a competent user.

INCLUSIVE FITNESS   A measure of fitness based upon the number of an animal's genes present in subsequent generations, rather than the number of offspring.

INCORRIGIBILITY   Although your judgements about your mental content might be wrong, you cannot be corrected by others, because you count as the highest authority.

INDICES   Signs causally related to what they represent (e.g. smoke is a sign of fire).

INTELLIGENT BEHAVIOUR   Behaviour judged to be intelligent (by some criterion) regardless of the mechanism responsible for the behaviour.

INTENTIONAL STANCE   A philosophical stance holding that any system whose behaviour can be explained in intentional terms (i.e. in terms of beliefs, desires, etc.) is (prima facie) a system endowed with mental properties.

INTENTIONALITY   That property of the mind by which it is directed at, or about, objects and states of affairs in the world. It includes such mental phenomena as belief, desire, intention.

KINAESTHETIC VISUAL MATCHING   The ability to relate visual information about bodily movement with the corresponding movements of one's own body.

KNOWLEDGE HOW OR KNOW-HOW   Knowing how to do something, such as ride a bicycle.

KNOWLEDGE THAT   Explicit knowledge, or knowledge that something is the case.

LANGUAGE OF THOUGHT   A form of symbol manipulation postulated to be the vehicle for mental representations, the contents of which are our thoughts and experiences.

LIBERALISM   Obtaining results that are far too easy to come by from the initial starting assumptions. In other words, if functionalism ends up ascribing minds to things that don't have them, it is liberal.

LIFE-HISTORY STRATEGY   Evolutionary strategy relating to the expenditure of energy (on growth and reproduction) throughout the lifetime of an individual.

MACHINE FUNCTIONALISM   The view that mental processes can be realised in different physical ways, such as a human brain, octopus brain, or a robot 'brain'.

MARKET VIABILITY   Pleasing the robot's employer, thus encouraging others to buy the robot.

MATERIALISM   The view that everything in the world, including mental states, is made of matter, or explainable in physical terms.

MENTAL AUTONOMY   Freedom of control of mental processes; i.e. the agent thinks for itself.

MENTAL STATE   A state having intentional characteristics; i.e. it is about something, or refers to something.

MENTAL STATE ATTRIBUTION   Attributing mental states to other beings.

METACOGNITION   The ability to monitor the state of one's own knowledge.

MICROECONOMIC LAWS   The laws of consumer economics (e.g. those relating to demand) that may also be applied to animals and robots.

MINIMAL RATIONALITY   Rational behaviour instigated by a thought process, or reason, as opposed to rational behaviour that is reflex or structural.

MONISM   The claim that reality is made up of only one kind of substance; i.e. that the mental and the physical are substantially the same.

MOTIVATION   A set of internal reversible processes that influence behaviour.

MOTIVATIONAL AUTONOMY   Freedom of control of motivation; i.e. the agent generates its own motivation.

NATURAL REPRESENTATION   Information-bearing.

NATURALISM   A philosophical stance which holds that everything there is belongs to the world of nature, and so can be studied by the appropriate (scientific) empirical methods.

NEUROCOMPUTING   Computing based upon simulation of nerve cell networks.

NORMATIVE RATIONALITY   Doing something for good reasons.

217

OPTIMAL   The best that can be achieved in the circumstances (by some criterion).

OPTIMALITY CRITERION   The criterion by which an outcome (of behaviour or of design) is judged to be optimal.

ORGANISATIONAL INVARIANCE   Experience is invariant across systems with the same fine-grained functional organisation.

PHENOTYPE   The bodily expression of genetic influence.

PHILOSOPHICAL STANCE   A philosophical viewpoint, or starting point, in a philosophical argument.

PHYSICALISM   A modern version of materialism.

PLEASURE   A proposed optimality criterion for human and animal behaviour, assumed (by some) to be a mental state.

PLURALISM   The view that the world is made up of more than one substance (e.g. mind and matter).

PROCEDURAL   Relating to a fixed procedure.

PROCEDURAL KNOWLEDGE   Knowledge relating to a procedure or skill, such as riding a bicycle. Also called knowledge how or know-how.

PSYCHOLOGICAL CONTINUITY   The view that there is continuity across species with respect to mental abilities.

QUALIA   A philosophical term given to subjective qualities, such as the way coffee smells, the way a cat's purr sounds, the way coriander tastes, and the way it feels to receive an electric shock.

RATIONALITY   Being logical and consistent in behaviour, economics, or thought.

REACTIVE   Behaviour determined solely by reaction to external stimuli.

REALISM   When applied to mental states, realism asserts that those states really do exist (and take up space) in the brain, as opposed to being emergent functions of the brain, or of entities outside the brain.

REASONING   Logical thinking.

REDUCTIONISM   The idea that all explanation of happenings in the world can (in principle) be reduced to explanations in terms of physics.

REPRESENTATION   Something that stands for, or provides information about, something else.

SELF   A supposed entity that is entirely subjectively experienced.

SEMANTIC   To do with meaning.

SIGN   Construct by which an organism affects the state of another. A sign is an explicit representation that is a proxy for an object, property, or event.

SIGNAL   The physical embodiment of a message.

SITUATED   Actions taken in the context of particular concrete circumstances and dependent upon the situation at the time.

STIGMERGY   The production of behaviour that is a direct consequence of the effects produced in the local environment by previous behaviour.

SUBJECTIVITY   Having knowledge of being the recipient of experience.

SUPERVENIENCE   A supposed property of mental states, such that supervenient (mental) properties go hand-in-hand with base (physical) properties, without being reducible to them.

SURVIVAL VALUE   The survival of a trait within a population, depending upon the action of natural selection.

SYMBOL   Arbitrary label that is not a straightforward proxy for an object. When an explicit representation takes the form of a symbol, it leads the agent to conceive of the object.

SYMBOL MANIPULATION   Manipulation of symbols, in a brain or in a computer, in a meaningful (semantic) way.

TELEOLOGICAL   Relating to purpose or function.

TELEOLOGICAL FUNCTIONALISM   Functional explanations in a biological or behavioural context, rather than the logical or mathematical context favoured by machine functionalists.

THEORY OF MIND   Weak theory of mind is the same as mental state attribution. Strong theory of mind is a theory relating to the possible mind of another being.

TOKEN   A physically identifiable bearer of information.

TOKEN IDENTITY   A situation in which every instance of a mental state is identical with the corresponding instance of a physical state.

TOLERANCE   The ability to tolerate extreme values of environmental factors, such as temperature.

TRADE-OFF   The balancing of priorities so that an optimal compromise is achieved.

TYPE IDENTITY   A situation in which every type of mental state is identical with a type of physical state.

UTILITY   The quantity maximised in the process of rational decision-making.

VALUE SYSTEM   A system of parameters that sets boundaries to the behaviour of an agent.

ZOMBIE   A philosophical zombie is a hypothetical being indistinguishable from a normal human being except that it lacks conscious experience, qualia, or sentience.

ENDNOTES

Preface: Traffic Robot

1. We are animals ourselves, but we normally distinguish between humans and other animals, and we will follow this practice in this book. *Anthropomorphism* is the attribution of human qualities to non-human entities. It is usually regarded as an aspect of human nature. However, it plays the same role as a philosophical stance, in that the assumptions (albeit tacit) provide the platform for the view that is taken. For example, if I see a dog standing by the door making little whining noises, I may say (or think), 'The dog wants to go out and believes I will let him out.' If I drive into a car-washing machine, and see a blinking red arrow, I may say (or think), 'The machine wants me to back up, and believes that I will thus get the car into a good position to be washed.' Leaving aside the question of whether it is conceivable that the dog, or the machine, could have such beliefs, my mode of thinking is a perfectly normal, everyday, mode of human thinking. That humans attribute human characteristics to gods, animals and machines is well documented. In some cases they are well aware that some kind of metaphor is being used, in other cases not. Further reading: J. S. Kennedy, *The New Anthropomorphism* (Cambridge: Cambridge University Press, 1992).

Chapter 1: Mindless Machines

1. See Preface n. 1.

2. Further reading: L. Suchman, *Plans and Situated Actions*. (New York: Cambridge University Press, 1987).

3. Further reading: R. Beckers, O. Holland, and J. L. Deneubourg, 'From Local Actions to Global Tasks: Stigmergy and Collective Robotics', in R. Brooks and P. Maes (eds) *Artificial Life, IV* (Cambridge, MA: 1994), 181–9; MIT Press, O. Holland, 'Gathering and Sorting in Insects and Robots', in O. Holland, and D. McFarland, (eds) *Artificial Ethology* (Oxford: Oxford University Press, 2001), 77–92; O. Holland and C. Melhuish, 'Stigmergy, Self-organisation, and Sorting in Collective Robotics', *Artificial Life*, 5 (2) (1999), 173–202; C. Melhuish J. Westby, and C. Edwards, 'Using Templates for Defensive Wall Building with Autonomous Mobile Ant-Like Robots', in *Proceedings of Towards Intelligent Mobile Robots*, Technical Report Series, Department of Computer Science, Manchester University, Report UMCS-99-3-1.

4. Further reading: O. Holland, 'The Evolution of Animal-Like Mobile Robots', in O. Holland and D. McFarland (eds), *Artificial Ethology* (Oxford: Oxford University Press, 2001), 14–41.

5. Further reading: I. Kelly, 'The Design of a Robotic Predator: The SlugBot', *Robotica*, 21 (2003):399–406; C. Glover, 'Reinvasion of Cleared Areas by the Slug Deroceras reticulatum', Project report for MSc in crop protection, University of Bristol, 1998; I. D. Kelly, C. Melhuish, and O. Holland, 'The Development and Energetics of SlugBot, a Robot Predator', in *EUREL: European Advanced Robotics Systems Masterclass and Conference*, University of Salford, Manchester, UK, 12–14 April 2000, vol. ii.

6. A fuel cell is a device that produces electric current direct from a chemical reaction between continuously supplied materials, such as the gases emanating from the fermentation or digestion of organic matter.

7. Further reading: I. Ieropoulos, C. Melhuish, and J. Greenman, 'Artificial Metabolism: Towards True Energetic Autonomy in Artificial Life,' in *Proceedings of the 7th European Conference in Artificial Life (ECAL 2003)*, September 2003, 792–799; S. Wilkinson, ' "Gastronome"—A Pioneering Food Powered Mobile Robot', in *Proceedings of the 2000 IASTED International Conference on Robotics and Applications*, Paper 318-037, August 2000.

8. D. Dennett, *Elbow Room, the Varieties of Free Will Worth Wanting* (Oxford: Oxford University Press, 1984), 51–2.

Chapter 2: Design of Animals and Robots

1. For further reading see Charles Darwin, *On the Origin of Species by Natural Selection* (London: John Murray, 1859); and Richard Dawkins, *The Blind Watchmaker* (London: Longman, 1986).

2. The seminal papers are W. D. Hamilton, 'The Genetical Theory of Social Behaviour' (I and II), *Journal of Theoretical Biology*, 7 (1964): 1–16; 17–32.

3. A good account of the importance of genetics in the process of domestication is given by Jared Diamond in *Guns, Germs and Steel* (London: Vintage, 1998).

4. Briefly, the success of a biological design is measured by the success of the genes that produce it, and this depends upon the ability of those genes to increase their representation in the population in the face of competition from rival genes. How does this relate to product design? Suppose a variety of products is under consideration. They vary in the period required for development, in the chance of failure in the market place, and in the expected returns from sales if the product is successful. The development period refers to the period before any return is achieved on investment. For animals, this is the period between birth and reproduction, and for products it is the period prior to the time that financial returns accrue to the investors. The success of animal design is evaluated by the net rate of increase of the genes coding for it (i.e. the return on investment by the parents). The success of product design is measured in terms of the net rate of increase of the money invested in it. Some animals have a short life and produce all their offspring in one go. Others have long adult life, and have repeated breeding seasons that produce offspring each time. Some products are designed for a one-off sales period (e.g. Christmas toys), while others are designed to be produced at a steady rate for a given period. Some animals experience a roughly constant mortality rate, and their collective breeding performance is likely to follow a negative exponential curve. Similarly, product sales might be expected to decline with time, as a result of market competition and loss of market appeal. For further reading see D. McFarland, 'What It Means for Robot Behaviour to be Adaptive' in J. Meyer and S. Wilson (eds), *From Animals to Animats* (Cambridge, MA:

MIT Press, 1991), D. McFarland, 'The Biology of Behavior: Criteria for Success in Animals and Robots', in L. Steels (ed.), *The Biology and Technology of Intelligent Autonomous Agents* (Berlin: Springer-Verlag, 1995), 1–20, and O. Holland, 'The Evolution of Animal-Like Mobile Robots', in O. Holland and D. McFarland (eds), *Artificial Ethology* (Oxford: Oxford University Press, 2001), 14–41.

5. See Diamond, *Guns, Germs and Steel*, n. 3 above.

6. Evolved systems develop by a process of progressive variation of previous evolved systems, all of which were good enough to ensure that their owners bred successfully. This variation may take the form of adding components to an existing system, thus creating a functional unit or module. Examples can readily be seen in the evolution of limbs, and their control systems, that function in locomotion. However, evolution is also parsimonious, because additional structures impose additional costs, both capital costs and maintenance costs. Biological systems grow, development necessarily building on what has previously been developed. Moreover, such development often proceeds while the system is functioning. To be functionally accurate and precise over the lifetime of the animal, growing systems must be adaptable in themselves, and in relation to other systems. In addition, they must be capable of being fine-tuned after the initial growth has taken place. Analogously, the design of conventionally engineered systems is subject to economic considerations. The extent to which these impose constraints on what can be produced is not generally appreciated by those outside the profession. For example, designs intended for mass production must take account of the necessity of producing spare parts in the future, and some products must meet international quality and performance standards. Owen Holland provides an extended discussion of the design processes of animals and robots in Holland, 'The Evolution of Animal-Like Mobile Robots.' Cited above.

7. See D. McFarland and E. Spier, 'Basic Cycles, Utility and Opportunism in Self-Sufficient Robots', *Robotics and Autonomous Systems,* 20 (1997), 179–90.

8. Decisions among mutually exclusive behavioural alternatives, such as sitting, standing, and walking, which cannot be performed simultaneously, must involve some kind of *common currency* in terms of which chalk and cheese can be compared (e.g. chalk and cheese could be compared in terms of density, hardness, etc). (In technical terms, there must also be a mathematical function, the *currency function*, that specifies the relationship between the currency and the decision variables. The role of the currency function is to translate all the decision variables into a single value (a real-valued function), so that all possible decisions can be ranked along a single scale.)

9. R. Zach, 'Shell Dropping: Decision Making and Optimal Foraging in North-western Crows,' *Behaviour*, 68 (1979), 106–17.

10. B. Heinrich, *Bumblebee Economics* (Cambridge, MA: Harvard University Press, 1979).

11. Ibid.

12. Useful references are J. H. Kagel, R. C. Battalio, H. Rachlin, and L. H. Green, 'Demand Curves for Animal Consumers,' *Quaterly Journal of Economics*, 96 (1981), 1–15; M. S. Dawkins, 'Battery Hens Name Their Price: Consumer Demand Theory and the Measurement of Ethological "needs." ', *Animal Behaviour*, 31 (1983), 1195–205; M. S. Dawkins, 'From an Animal's Point of View: Motivation, Fitness, and Animal Welfare'. *Behavioral and Brain Sciences*, 13 (1990), 1–61; A. I. Houston, 'Demand Curves and Welfare'. *Animal Behaviour*, 53 (1997), 983–90.

13. For an account see D. McFarland and T. Bosser, *Intelligent Behaviour in Animals and Robots* (Cambridge, MA: MIT Press, 1993).

Chapter 3: Interpreting Behaviour

1. Ivan Petrovich Pavlov's (1849–1936; Nobel Laureate, 1904) work on conditional reflexes laid the foundations of our modern understanding of animal learning.

2. The concept of intentionality was originally used by medieval scholastic philosophers. It was reintroduced into modern philosophy by Franz Brentano (1838–1917). Brentano's thesis states that intentionality is the mark of the mental, and only mental states are intentional. In other words, one cannot believe, wish, or hope without believing or wishing something.

3. See Preface n. 1.

4. *Realism* implies that things exists independently of the mind, as opposed to *idealism* that asserts that the same things exist only in the mind. When applied to mental states, realism asserts that those states really do exist (and take up space) in the brain, as opposed to being emergent functions of the brain. In referring to robot 'mental' states, realism would imply that the state could be physically identified within the robot hardware.

5. A good account of the history of behaviourism is given by Robert Boakes in *From Darwin to Behaviourism* (Cambridge: Cambridge University Press, 1984).

6. The philosopher Karl Gustav Hempel (1949) held that a person's physical behaviour provides a large part of the evidence for ascribing particular mental states to that person. Another philosopher often classified as an analytical behaviourist is Gilbert Ryle, who argued against the idea that actions are the result of complex mental processes, and introduced the notion of agential behavioural dispositions. For Ryle, 'overt intelligent performances are not clues to the workings of minds, they are those workings' (G. Ryle, *The Concept of Mind* (London: Hutchinson, 1949), 58). Unlike Hempel, Ryle did not seek to eliminate mental concepts altogether. He always treated behaviour as fully intentional. However, at the same time he suggests that the mind consists of patterns of behaviour, and can be reductively identified with behaviour. Thus Ryle was not an *eliminative behaviourist* like Watson and Skinner, but other philosophers have subsequently taken an eliminative stance towards the mind.

7. Alex Byrne, Behaviourism, in Samual Guttenplan (ed.), *A Companion to the Philosophy of Mind* (Oxford: Blackwell, 1994).

8. Rene Descartes (1596–1650) believed that a person's judgements about their own mental states are infallible. Other philosophers have taken the view that they are incorrigible. However, recent psychological evidence suggests that people can be frequently wrong about the claims they make about their reasons for action, or about their perceptions. Some patients with brain damage, such that they are cortically blind and deny seeing things, nevertheless guess correctly when asked to do so, a phenomenon called 'blindsight' (see R. Nisbet, and T. de Ce. Wilson, 'Telling More Than We Know: Verbal Reports on Mental Processes',

Psychological Review, 84 (1977), 231–59, and L. Weiskrantz, *Consciousness Lost and Found* (Oxford: Oxford University Press, 1997).

9. Dualism is the doctrine that mind and matter are two distinct things, and that the one cannot be accounted for in terms of the other. Descartes was the most notable proponent of this view. Dualism gives rise to the question of how the mind is attached to the body, often called the *mind–body problem*. The main problem is to explain how, if immaterial mind is distinct from material body, the two interact causally, as they evidently must.

10. Temple Grandin and Catherine Johnson, *Animals in Translation* (London: Bloomsbury, 2006), 6.

11. Dogmatism is often applied to belief in religious doctrine, irrespective of reason or evidence. In such cases the doctrine comes from scripture, or from religious authority. Dogmatism is characteristic of any kind of argument by appeal to authority, if it is assumed that the authority cannot be questioned. First person authority suffers from this problem. Dogmatism sanctions belief that is unjustified by reason, and this attitude leads to intolerance of contradictory views. Thus it is difficult for a dogmatist to take part in philosophical discussion. We are here concerned with dogmatism as a refusal to engage in rational argument. To engage in meaningful philosophical discourse, it is necessary that some starting assumptions be agreed by all parties. Any argument based purely upon intuition, or introspection, is open to the accusation that it is not an argument in which others can engage. Dogmatists are incorrigible insofar as their philosophical stance is based, in part, upon their own private experience, whether it be religious, spiritual, or whatever. Because their private experience is inaccessible to other people, questions of credibility are bound to arise in philosophical discussions with dogmatists.

12. Key references are P. M. Churchland, 'Eliminative Materialisn and Propositional Attitudes', *Journal of Philosophy*, 78 (1981), 67–90; P. S. Churchland, *Neurophilosophy: Towards a Unified Science of the Mind/Brain* (Cambridge, MA: MIT Press, 1986); P. M. Churchland, *A Neurocomputational Perspective: The Nature of the Mind and the Structure of Science* (Cambridge, MA: MIT Press, 1989).

13. For a good account of the main approaches to folk psychology see Barbara Von Eckhardt, 'Folk Psychology and Scientific Psychology', in Guttenplan (ed.), *A Companion to the Philosophy of Mind*, 300–7.

14. The main proponent of folk-psychology realism is Jerry Fodor, 'Computation and Reduction', in *idem, Representations* (Cambridge, MA: MIT Press, 1981); J. Fodor, *Psychosemantics* (Cambridge, MA: MIT Press, 1987). The anti-realists include S. P. Stich, *From Folk Psychology to Cognitive Science: The Case against Belief* (Cambridge, MA: MIT Press, 1983); and Churchland, 'Eliminative Materialism and Propositional Attitudes'. In between stand D. Dennett, The *Intentional Stance* (Cambridge, MA: MIT Press, 1987), and B. Von Eckhardt, *What is cognitive science?* (Cambridge, MA: MIT Press, 1993).

15. See, for example, J. T. Tedeschi, S. Lindskold, and P. Rosenfeld, *Introduction to Social Psychology* (St Paul, MN: West Publishing, 1985); R. d'Andrade, 'A Folk Model of the Mind', in D. Holland and N. Quinn (eds), *Cultural Models of Thought and Language* (Cambridge: Cambridge University Press, 1987); and C. Lutz, 'Goals and Understanding in Ifaluk Emotion Theory', in Holland and Quinn (eds), *Cultural Models of Thought and Language*.

16. If it is not a theory, as some philosophers maintain (e.g. R. Gordon, 'Folk Psychology as Simulation', *Mind and Language*, 1 (1986), 158–71; R. Gordon, 'The Simulation Theory: Objections and Misconceptions', *Mind and Language*, 7 (1992), 11–34; A. Goldman, 'Interpretation Psychologised', *Mind and Language*, 4 (1989), 161–85; A. Goldman, 'In Defense of Simulation Theory', *Mind and Language*, 7 (1992), 104–19), then it cannot be a false theory and there is no point in trying to eliminate it (S. P. Stich, and S. Nichols, 'Folk Psychology: Simulation or Tacit Theory?', *Mind and Language*, 7 (1992), 35–71).

17. See K. Wilkes, 'Functionalism, Psychology and the Philosophy of Mind'. *Philosophical Topics*, 12 (1981), 1; and K. Wilkes, 'Pragmatics in Science and Theory in Common Sense', *Inquiry*, 27 (1984), 4. Other philosophers also argue that folk psychology must remain autonomous with respect to physical or neuro-scientific theories. See, for example, T. Horgan and J. Woodward, 'Folk Psychology Is Here to Stay', *Philosophical Review*, 94 (1985), 197–225.

18. For the view that neuroscience is not the appropriate level at which to discuss psychological matters, see R. N. McCauley, 'The Role of Cognitive Explanations in Psychology', *Behaviorism* (subsequently *Behavior and Philosophy*) 15 (1987), 27–40; and R. McCauley (ed.). *The Churchlands and Their Critics* (Oxford: Blackwell, 1996).

19. For the view that scientific progress requires us to believe not only that all our past scientific theories are false, etc., see T. Rockwell, *Beyond Eliminative Materialism: Some Unnoticed Implications of Churchland's Pragmatic Pluralism*, presented at the American Philosophy Association Meeting (Pacific division) in San Francisco 1995 (with commentary by John Bickle). Available at: http://www.california.com/%7Emcmf/beyondem.html

20. Paul Churchland's response to Rockwell is to advocate a 'pluralistic form of pragmatism' (Churchland, *A Neurocomputational Perspective*, 194). This position is developed at greater length in Chapters 15 and 17 of P. M. Churchland and P. S. Churchland, *On the Contrary* (Cambridge, MA: MIT Press, 1998). However, L. Laudan, 'A Confutation of Convergent Realism', *Philosophy of Science* 48 (1981), 19–49, has argued that scientific realism, as it was commonly defined, could not be defended once we admitted that new scientific theories eliminated old ones. And although Paul Churchland continues to refer to himself as a scientific realist, he clearly accepted Laudan's views: 'So many past theories, rightly judged excellent in their time, have since proved to be false. And their current successors, though even better founded, seem but the next step in a probably endless and not obviously convergent journey' (Churchland, *A Neurocomputational Perspective*, 140). 'It is expected that existing conceptual frameworks will eventually be replaced by new and better ones, and those in turn by frameworks better still, for who will be so brash as to assert that the feeble conceptual achievements of our adolescent species comprise an exhaustive account of anything at all?' (ibid. 52). For a comprehensive review of this whole debate see the article by Rockwell on eliminative materialism at http://philosophy.uwaterloo.ca/MindDict/eliminativism.html

21. D. Dennett, *Brainstorms* (Brighton: Harvester Press, 1981).

22. Ibid. 271.

23. D. Dennett, 'Intentional Systems in Cognitive Ethology: The "Panglossian Paradigm" Defended', *Behavioral and Brain Sciences* 6 (1983), 343–90.

24. D. Dennett, 'Do Animals Have Beliefs?' in H. L. Roitblatt and J. Meyer (eds) *Comparative Approaches* to *Cognitive Science* (Cambridge, MA: MIT Press, 1995), 111–18.

25. Functionalism is discussed in Chapter 7. Basically, it is the view that certain entities (mental or physical) are best described in terms of their function or role within a system. Thus *capacitance* is a measure of energy storage, whether it be in an electrical, mechanical, or biological system. It stores potential energy when its effort level is raised by influx of a flow variable. The capacitance is measured in terms of displacement per unit effort. In a mechanical system the capacitance may be the compliance of a spring, in which case the effort variable is force, and the flow variable is velocity. In an electrical system the effort variable is voltage and the flow variable is current. A functional entity, such as capacitance, or pain for that matter, is defined solely in terms of its role in the system, and not in material terms. Thus, for some functionalists, it would be possible for a machine to be in pain. It would not matter, to them, that the machine had no nervous tissue, like that found in the human brain. All that would matter would be the functional role played by pain within the system.

26. Dennett, *Brainstorms*, as n. 21.

27. Many ground-nesting birds perform distraction displays. For further details see A. F. Skutch, *Parent Birds and Their Young* (Austin: University of Texas Press, 1976); C. A. Ristau, 'Aspects of Cognitive Ethology of an Injury-Feigning Bird: The Piping Plover', in M. Bekoff and D. Jamieson (eds), *Readings in Animal Cognition* (Cambridge, MA: MIT Press, 1996), 79–89.

28. What is meant here is intentional action (see Chapter 6). Unfortunately, there is some terminological confusion between the terms intentional (deliberate action), intentionality (aboutness, a mental property), and Dennett's intentional stance (a way of viewing behaviour).

230

Chapter 4: Beyond Automata

1. G. Ryle, *The Concept of Mind* (London: Hutchinson, 1949).

2. J. O'Leary-Hawthorne, 'Belief and Behavior', *Mind and Language,* 8 (1993), 461–86 and D. Davidson, 'Rational Animals', *Dialectica, 36* (1982), 318–27, believe that the only evidence that someone has this or that explicit knowledge comes from their utterances. Others such as J. Bennett, *Linguistic Behaviour,* 2nd edn (Cambridge: Cambridge University Press, 1990) and D. Dennett, *The Intentional Stance* (Cambridge, MA: MIT Press, 1987), accept other types of evidence.

3. There are problems with Anthony Dickinson's terminology. Dickinson believes that the capacity for *goal-directed action* is the most fundamental behavioural marker of cognition. By goal-directed action he means those *actions* mediated by *instrumental knowledge* of the causal relationship between the action and the outcome or goal, *and* the current goal or incentive value of the outcome. For most workers in this area, all actions are goal-directed (for a discussion of goal-directed see Chapter 1, and for a discussion of action see Chapter 6), so Dickinson's terminology is confusing. By *instrumental knowledge*, Dickinson presumably means *explicit* knowledge, or knowledge *that* a particular action will have a particular outcome.

4. Key references are E. Spier and D. McFarland, 'Learning to Do without Cognition', in R. Pfeifer, B. Blamberg, J. Meyer, and S. Wilson (eds), *Animals and Animats* (Cambridge, MA: MIT Press, 1998), v. 38–47, and Dimitrios Lambrinos, 'Navigation in Desert Ants: The Robotic Solution', *Robotica,* 21 (2002), 407–26.

5. Key references are A. Dickinson, 'Actions and Habits—The Development of Behavioural Autonomy', *Philosophical Transactions of the Royal Society of London, Series B, 308* (1985), 67–78; A. Dickinson and G. Dawson, 'Incentive Learning and the Motivational Control of Instrumental Performance', *Quarterly Journal of Experimental Psychology,* 41B (1989), 99–112; C. Heyes and A. Dickinson, 'The Intentionality of Animal Action', *Mind and Language,* 5 (1990), 87–104.

6. As n. 4.

7. D. Dennett, *The Intentional Stance* (Cambridge, MA: MIT Press, 1987), 256.

8. Ibid. 259.

9. D. McFarland, 'Rational Behaviour of Animals and Machines', *Bielefeld Zif Conference Papers on Prerational Intelligence*, 2 (1994), 133–43; A. Kacenlic, 'Meanings of Rationality', in S. Hurley and M. Nudds (eds), *Rational Animals?* (Oxford: Oxford University Press, 2006), 87–106.

10. Ibid.

11. F. Dretske, 'Minimal Rationality', in Hurley and Nudds (eds), *Rational Animals?*, 107–16.

12. B. McGonigle and M. Chalmers, 'On the Genesis of Relational Terms: A Comparative Study of Monkeys and Human Children', *Anthropologia Contemporanea*, 3 (1980), 236; B. McGonigle and B. Chalmers, 'Monkeys Are Rational!' *Quarterly Journal of Experimental Psychology*, 45B (1992), 198–228; C. Allen, 'Transitive Inference in Animals: Reasoning or Conditioned Associations?', in Hurley and Nudds (eds), *Rational Animals?*, 175–85.

13. S. Lea, 'The Psychology and Economics of Demand', *Psychology Bulletin* 85 (1978), 441–66; H. Rachlin, *Judgement, Decision and Choice,* Freeman, 1989); D. McFarland and T. Bosser, *Intelligent Behaviour in Animals and Robots* (Cambridge, MA: MIT Press, 1993), chapter on utility.

14. Notably T. Nagel, 'What Is It Like to Be a Bat?', *Philosophical Review,* 83 (1974), 435–50. For an overview of subjectivity, see N. Norton, 'Subjectivity', in S. Guttenplan (ed.), *A Companion to the Philosophy of Mind* (Oxford: Blackwell, 1994), 568–75.

15. See Chapter 3 n. 2.

Chapter 5: Mental Possibilities

1. D. Dennett, *The Intentional Stance* (Cambridge, MA: MIT Press, 1987); T. Nagel, 'What Is It Like to Be a Bat?', *Philosophical Review,* 83 (1974), 435–50.

2. D. Premack, and G. Woodruff, 'Does the Chimpanzee Have a Theory of Mind?', *Behavioural and Brain Sciences*, 4 (1978), 515–26; R. Byrne, *The Thinking Ape* (Oxford: Oxford University Press, 1995), 100, 143–4.

3. See Preface n. 1.

4. For an overview see Gabriel Segal, 'Belief (Z)', in S. Guttenplan (ed), *A Companion to the Philosophy of Mind* (Oxford: Blackwell, 1994), 146–52. The seminal false-belief study is that of H. Wimmer and J. Perner, 'Beliefs about Beliefs: Representation and Constraining Function of Wrong Beliefs in Young Children's Understanding of Deception', *Cognition*, 13 (1983), 103–28.

5. I. Eibl-Eibesfeldt, *Human Ethology* (New York: De Gruyer, 1989); A. Fernald, 'Four-Month Old Infants Prefer to Listen to Motherese', *Infant Behavior and Development*, 8 (1985), 181–95.

6. Ibid.

7. D. Dennett, *Brainstorms* (Brighton: Harvester Press, 1981), 273.

8. Byrne, *The Thinking Ape* (Oxford: Oxford University Press, 1995).

9. Ibid. 140.

10. On the general subject of teaching in animals see T. Caro and M. D. Hauser, 'Is There Teaching in Non-human Animals?', *Quarterly Review of Biology*, 67 (1992), 151–74. Note also that there is a more recent report of teaching in ants: N. Franks and T. Richardson, 'Teaching in Tandem-Running Ants', *Nature*, 439 (2006), 153.

11. Byrne, n. 8, 143; R. S. Fouts, D. H. Fouts, and T. E. van Cantfort, 'The Infant Loulis Learns Signs from Cross-Fostered Chimpanzees', in R. A. Gardner, B. T. Gardner, and T. E. van Cantfort, (eds), *Teaching Sign Language to Chimpanzees* (Albany: State University of New York Press, 1989), 280–92.

12. C. Boesch, 'Teaching in Wild Chimpanzees', *Animal Behaviour*, 41 (1991), 530–2.

13. Ibid.

14. As n. 10.

15. G. W. Allport, *Pattern and Growth in Personality* (New York: Holt, Rinehart and Winston, 1961), 536.

16. S. T. Parker, R. W. Mitchell, and M. L. Boccia (eds), *Self-awareness in Animals and Humans* (Cambridge: Cambridge University Press, 1994).

17. C. Wynne, *Animal Cognition* (London: Palgrave Macmillan, 2001), 23.

18. A. Alissandrakis, C. L. Nehaniv, K. Dautenhahn, and J. Saunders, 'Evaluation of Robot Imitation Attempts: Comparison of the System's and the Human's Perspectives', in K. Dautenhahn and C. L. Nehaniv (eds), *Imitation in Animals and Artifacts* (Cambridge, MA: MIT Press, 2002).

19. P. Strawson, *Individuals* (London: Methuen, 1959); *idem, Freedom and Resentment* (London: Methuen, 1974); A. Narayanan, *On Being a machine*. (Chichester: Ellis Horwood, 1990,) ii. 30, 104.

20. Ibid.

21. Ibid.

22. W. Kohler, *The Mentality of Apes* (New York: Harcourt Brace, 1925).

23. Key papers are J. Chappell and A. Kacelnik, 'Tool Selectivity in a Non-primate: The New Caledonian Crow (*Corvus moneduloides*)', *Animal Cognition*, 5(2002), 71–8; B. Kenward, A. A. S. Weir, J. Chappell, and A. Kacelnik, 'Tool Manufacture by Naïve Juvenile Crows', *Nature*, 433 (2005), 121; A. A. S. Weir, J. Chappell, and A. Kacelnik, 'Shaping of Hooks in New Caledonian Crows', *Science*, 297 (2002), 981.

24. A. Kacelnik, 'Tool-Making Crow', *Earth and Sky*, 9 November 2002 [radio interview]. Available at: http://wwwZ.earthsky.org/radioshows/45663/toolmakingcrow

25. The video of Betty is available at http://users.ox.ac.uk/~kgroup/trial7_web.mov

Chapter 6: The Feeling of Being

1. P. Rozin, 'Specific Aversions as a Component of Specific Hungers', *Journal of Comparative and Physiological Psychology*, 64 (1967), 237–42; P. Rozin and J. Kalat, 'Specific Hungers and Poison Avoidance as Adaptive Specializations of Learning', *Psychological Review*, 78 (1971), 459–86.

2. Relevant references for trade-off in animals include D. Stephens and J. Krebs, *Foraging Theory* (Princeton, NJ: Princeton University Press, 1986); M. Balasko and M. Cabanac, 'Motivational Conflict among

Water Need, Palatability, and Cold Discomfort in Rats', *Physiology and Behaviour,* 65 (1998), 35–41; M. Cabanac, 'Conflicts and Strategy in a Cold Environment', *Journal of Thermal Biology,* 9 (1984); 63–6; D. J. McFarland, and A. Houston, *Quantitative Ethology: The State Space Approach* (London: Pitman Books, 1981); M. Cababac and K. G. Johnson, 'Analysis of a Conflict between Palatability and Cold Exposure in Rats', *Physiology and Behaviour,* 31 (1982), 249–53; M. Milinsky and R. Heller, 'Influence of a Predator on the Optimal Foraging Behaviour of Sticklebacks (*Gasterosteus aculeatus*)', *Nature,* 275 (1978), 642–4; R. M. Sibly and D. J. McFarland, 'On the Fitness of Behaviour Sequences', *American Naturalist* 110 (1976), 601–17; N. B. Davies and A. I. Houston, 'Owners and Satellites: The Economics of Territory Defence in the Pied Wagtail *Motacilla alba*', *Journal of Animal Ecology,* 50 (1981),157–80.

3. Balasko and Cabanac, 'Motivational Conflict among Water Need, Palatability, and Cold Discomfort in Rats'. (As quoted above)

4. Milinsky and Heller, 'Influence of a Predator'; Sibly and McFarland, 'On the Fitness of Behaviour Sequences'; Davies and Houston, 'Owners and Satellites'. See n. 2.

5. Cabanac's work on humans includes M. Cabanac, 'Performance and Perception at Various Combinations of Treadmill Speed and Slope', *Physiology and Behaviour,* 38 (1986), 839–43; M. Cabanac and J. Leblanc, 'Physiological Conflict in Humans: Fatigue vs. Cold Discomfort', *American Journal of Physiology,* 244 (1983), 621–8; M. Cabanac, 'Palatability vs. Money: Experimental Study of a Conflict of Motivations', *Appetite,* 25 (1995), 43–49; M. Cabanac, 'Money versus Pain: Experimental Study of a Conflict in Humans', *Journal of the Experimental Analysis of Behavior,* 46 (1986), 37–44; K. G. Johnson and M. Cabanac, 'Human Thermoregulatory Behavior during a Conflict between Cold Discomfort and Money', *Physiology and Behaviour,* 30 (1983), 145–50; M. Cabanac, 'La maximisation du plaisir, response a un conflit de motivations', *C.R. Seances Acad. Sci Paris),* 309 (1989), 397–402.

6. Cabanac, 'Performance and Perception at Various Combinations of Treadmill Speed and Slope'. (Quoted in n. 5.)

7. Cabanac and Leblane, 'Physiological Conflict in Humans'. See n. 5.

8. Cabanac, 'Palatability vs. Money'. See n. 5.

9. Ibid.

10. Cabanac, 'Money versus Pain'; Johnson and Cabanac, 'Human Thermoregulatory Behavior'. See n. 5.

11. Cabanac, 'La maximisaton du plaisir'. M. Cabanac, 'Pleasure: The Common Currency', *Journal of Theoretical Biology*, 155 (1992), 173–200.

12. Ibid.

13. E. A. Madsen, R. J. Tunney, G. Fieldman, H. Plotkin, R. I. M. Dunbar, J. Richardson, and D. McFarland 'Kinship and Altruism: A Cross-Cultural Experimental Study', *British Journal of Psychology*, 98 (2007), 339–59.

14. A. Dickinson, 'Actions and Habits—The Development of Behavioural Autonomy', *Philosophical Transactions of the Royal Society of London, Series B*, 308 (1985), 67–78; A. Dickinson and G. Dawson, 'Incentive Learning and the Motivational Control of Instrumental Performance', *Quarterly Journal of Experimental Psychology*, 41B (1989), 99–112; C. Heyes and A. Dickinson, 'The Intentionality of Animal Action', *Mind and Language*, 5 (1990), 87–104.

15. D. McFarland, *Problems of Animal Behaviour* (Harlow: Longman, 1989); F. Wemelsfelder, *Animal Boredom* (Utrecht: Elinkwijk, 1993).

16. S. T. Parker, R. W. Mitchell, and M. L. Boccia (eds), *Self-awareness in Animals and Humans* (Cambridge: Cambridge University Press, 1994); I. Howard and B. Templeton, *Human Spatial Orientation* (London: Wiley, 1966); P. Michel, K. Gold, and B. Scassellati, 'Motion-Based Robotic Self-Recognition', *Proceedings of 2004 IEEE/RSJ International Conference on Intelligent Robots and Systems*, Sendal, Japan, 2004.

17. Ibid.

18. J. Allen, 'Towards a General Theory of Action and Time', *Artificial Intelligence*, 23 (1984), 123–54, esp. 126.

19. Functional equivalence is discussed in M. Montefiore and D. Noble (eds), *Goals, No Goals and Own Goals* (London: Unwin-Hyman, 1989), 284–8.

20. There is a huge philosophical literature on action and intention. For a start, consult S. Guttenplan (ed.), *A Companion to the Philosophy of Mind* (Oxford: Blackwell, 1994).

236

21. D. Premack and G. Woodruff, 'Does the Chimpanzee Have a Theory of Mind?', *Behavioural and Brain Sciences*, 4 (1978), 515–26; R. Byrne, *The Thinking Ape* (Oxford: Oxford University Press, 1995).

22. Dickinson, 'Actions and Habits', Dickinson and Dawson, 'Incentive Learning'; Heyes and Dickinson, 'The Intentionality of Animal Action'.

23. S. Shettleworth and J. E. Sutton, 'Do Animals Know What They Know?', in S. Hurley and M. Nudds (eds), *Rational Animals* (Oxford: Oxford University Press, 2006), 235–46.

24. See Chapter 3 n. 11 on the issue of dogmatism.

25. R. Crisp, 'Evolution and Psychological Unity', in M. Bekoff and D. Jamieson (eds), *Readings in Animal Cognition* (Cambridge, MA: MIT Press, 1996), 309–21.

Chapter 7: The Material Mind

1. Stephen Schiffer, 'Thought and Language', in S. Guttenplan (ed.), *A Companion to the Philosophy of Mind* (Oxford: Blackwell, 1994), 593.

2. Ibid.

3. D. Davidson, 'Mental Events', in L. Foster and J. W. Swanson (eds), *Experience and Theory* (Amherst, MA: University of Massachusetts Press, 1970), 79–101. See also 'Davidson, Donald' and J. Kim, 'Supervenience', in Guttenplan (ed.), *A Companion to the Philosophy of Mind*, 231–6 and 575–83.

4. Ibid.

5. S. Hurley, 'Making Sense of Animals', in S. Hurley and M. Nudds (eds), *Rational Animals?* (Oxford: Oxford University Press, 2006), 138–74; quote from 141.

6. See n. 3.

7. T. K. Darlington, K. Wager-Smith, M. F. Ceriani, *et al.*, 'Closing the Circadian Loop: CLOCK-Induced Transcription of Its Own Inhibitors per and tim', *Science*, 280 (1998), 1599–603.

8. D. Katzenberg, T. Young, L. Finn, *et al.*, 'A CLOCK Polymorphism Associated with Human Diurnal Preference', *Sleep*, 21 (1998), 569–76.

9. D. Lewis, 'Reduction of Mind', in Guttenplan, *A Companion to the Philosophy of Mind*, 412–31.

10. J. Fodor, *Psychosemantics: The Problem of Meaning in the Philosophy of Mind* (Cambridge, MA: MIT Press, 1987); *idem, A Theory of Content and Other Essays* (Cambridge, MA: MIT Press, 1991).

11. F. Dretske, *Explaining Behaviour: Reasons in a World of Causes* (Cambridge, MA: MIT Press, 1988), 264; *idem,* 'Minimal Rationality', in Hurley and Nudds (eds), *Rational Animals?*, 107–15.

12. J. Searle, 'Minds and Brains without Programs', in C. Blakemore and S. Greenfield (eds), *Mindwaves* (Oxford: Blackwell, 1987), 215, 217, 223, 220. See also A. Narayanan, *On Being a Machine,* ii: *Philosophy of Artificial Intelligence* (Chichester: Ellis Horwood, 1990), 40–55.

13. Ibid. 222.

14. Fodor, See n. 10. A Theory of Content.

15. Searle, 'Minds and Brains without Programs', 214–15. See n. 12.

16. Ibid. 210.

17. J. R. Searle, 'Minds, Brains and Programs', *Behavioural and Brain Sciences*, 3 (1980), 417–28.

18. 'Searle, John R.', in S. Guttenplan (ed.), *A Companion to the Philosophy of Mind* (Oxford: Blackwell, 1994), 546.

19. A. Clark, *Mindware* (New York: Oxford University Press, 2000).

20. M. Minsky, *Semantic Information Processing* (Cambridge, MA: MIT Press, 1968), 130.

21. For accounts of early robot evolution see O. Holland, 'The Evolution of Animal-like Mobile Robots', in O. Holland and D. McFarland (eds), *Artificial Ethology* (Oxford: Oxford University Press, 2001), 14–41, and A. Clarke, *Being There* (Cambridge, MA: MIT Press, 1998); quote from 21.

22. D. McFarland and T. Bosser, *Intelligent Behaviour in Animals and Robots* (Cambridge, MA: MIT Press, 1993). The argument is 'in optimised (well-designed) single-task systems there is no formal (mathematical) difference between the goal-directed principle and a maximisation principle. Both are designed to achieve equivalent performance criteria. In optimised multi-task systems, however, there is necessarily some trade-off among the decision variables, and this requirement is incompatible with the goal-directed principle. Moreover, this discord occurs in any system capable of more than one activity (where activities are defined as mutually exclusive outputs), even though the different activities may seem to be designed to fulfil the same task' [pp x–xi]. In other words, sense–think–act cycles are goal-directed and they offer a poor design for multitask robots (see Chapter 1).

23. D. Kirsh, 'Today the Earwig, Tomorrow Man?', in M. Boden (ed.), *The Philosophy of Artificial Life* (Oxford: Oxford University Press, 1996), 237–61; R. Brooks, 'Intelligence without Representation', *Artificial Intelligence*, 47 (1991), 139–59.

24. J. McCarthy, 'Programs with Common Sense', *Proceedings of the Teddington Conference on the Mechanisation of Thought Processes* (London: HMSO, 1959).

25. D. Dennett, 'Cognitive Wheels: The Frame Problem of AI', in Z. W. Pylyshin (ed), *The Robot's Dilemma: The Frame Problem in Artificial Intelligence* (Norwood, NJ: Ablex Publishing, 1987).

26. D. McFarland, 'Animals as Cost-Based Robots', in M. Boden (ed), *The Philosophy of Artificial Life* (Oxford: Oxford University Press, 1996), 179–205.

27. S. Harnad, 'The Symbol Grounding Problem', *Physica*, D42 (1990), 335–46.

28. M. Taddeo and L. Floridi, 'Solving the Symbol Grounding Problem: A Critical Review of Fifteen Years of Research', *Journal of Experimental and Theoretical Artificial Intelligence*, 17 (2005), 419–45.

29. T. Deacon, *The Symbolic Species* (London: Allen Lane).

30. See Chapter 3 n. 25.

31. H. Putnam, 'Minds and Machines', in S. Hook (ed.), *Dimensions of Mind* (New York: Collier Books, 1960); J. Fodor, *Psychological Explanation* (New York: Random House, 1968); see also H. Putnam, 'The Meaning of "meaning" ', in K. Gundeson (ed.), *Language, Minds and Knowledge*. Minnesota Studies in the Philosophy of Science, Vol. 7 (Minneapolis: University of Minesota Press, 1975).

32. Epiphenomena are by-products of relevant causal processes. For example, a robot that moves around displaces molecules of air as a by-product of its activity. This phenomenon is not a relevant cause or consequence of the robot's movement. In philosophy of mind, epiphenomena are subjective states, such as a pain or a memory, that, supposedly, have no causal efficacy. Philosophers who claim that certain sensations are epiphenomena have the problem of explaining their role. For example, if I burn my hand on the stove, I experience pain. I withdraw my hand, hold it under the cold tap, and then consider some kind of medication. An epiphenomalist would claim that the hand withdrawal was a reflex, that I put my hand under the cold tap as a result of my knowledge of physics, and I considered medication as a result of my knowledge of health matters. At no point did the pain have a role. The problem for such a view is to explain how such a sensation as pain can exist (be experienced) if it plays no causal role and has no biological function. In other words, in what way is it a by-product of the situation?

33. Ibid.

34. See especially W. Lycan, *Consciousness* (Cambridge, MA: MIT Press, 1987).

35. P. Rozin and A. A. Fallon 'A Perspective on Disgust', *Psychological Review*, 94 (1987), 23–41.

36. Ibid.

37. Relevant references include A. Narayanan, *On Being a Machine*, ii. 30; P. Smolensky, 'Computational Models of Mind', in Guttenplan (ed.), *A Companion to the Philosophy of Mind*, 176–85; Clark, *Mindware*.

38. Ibid.

Chapter 8: Mental Autonomy

1. See Chapter 2 n. 12.

2. R. Dawkins, *The Extended Phenotype* (Oxford: Oxford University Press, 1982), 199–200.

3. A. Clark, *Mindware* (New York: Oxford University Press, 2000), 34–7, 141.

4. N. Humphrey, *Seeing Red* (Cambridge, MA: Belknap Press, 2006).

5. Ibid. 22.

6. E. Hutchins, *Cognition in the Wild* (Cambridge, MA: MIT Press, 1995).

7. A. Damasio, *The Feeling of What Happens* (New York: Harcourt Brace, 1999).

8. J. Panksepp, 'The Pernicious Substrates of Consciousness', *Journal of Consciousness Studies*, 5 (1998), 566–82.

9. D. McFarland, 'Animals Are Cost-Based Robots', in M. Boden (ed.), *The Philosophy of Artificial Life* (Oxford: Oxford University Press, 1996), 179–205.

10. W. Lycan, 'Consciousness as Internal Monitoring,' in N. Block, O. Flanagan, and G. Guzeldere (eds), *The Nature of Consciousness* (Cambridge, MA: MIT Press, 1997), 755.

11. M. Tye, 'A Representational Theory of Pains and Their Phenomenal Character', in Block, Flanagan, and Guzeldere (eds), *Nature of Consciousness*, 333.

12. D. Rosenthal, 'A Theory of Consciousness', in Block, Flanagan, and Guzeldere (eds), *Nature of Consciousness*, 741.

13. Clark, *Mindware*, 181 (see also 154), D. Dennett, *Brainchildren: Essays on Designing Minds* (Cambridge, MA: MIT Press, 1998), 417–20.

14. Ibid.

15. Dennett, *Brainchildren*. See n. 13.

16. Clark, *Mindware*. See n. 3.

17. I. Alexsander and B. Dunmall, 'Axioms and Tests for the Presence of Minmal Consciousness in Agents', in O. Holland (ed.), *Machine Consciousness* (Exeter: Imprint Academic, 2003), 8–18.

18. O. Holland and R. Goodman, 'Robots with Internal Models,' in Holland (ed.), *Machine Consciousness*, 77–109.

19. S. Franklin, 'IDA: A Conscious Artifact?', in Holland (ed.), *Machine Consciousness*, 47–66.

20. Holland and Goodman, 'Robots with Internal Models'. See n. 18.

21. Clark, *Mindware*. See n. 3.

22. K. Morrison, 'The Self', in S. Gutenplan (ed.) *A Companion to the Philosophy of Mind* (Oxford: Blackwell, 1994), 553.

23. H. Cruse, 'Feeling Our Body: The Basis of Cognition?', *Evolution and Cognotion*, 162 (1999), 2.

24. D. Dennett, *Elbow Room* (Oxford: Oxford University Press, 1984), 131.

25. D. McFarland and T. Bosser, *Intelligent Behavior in Animals and Robots* (Cambridge, MA: MIT Press, 1993).

26. Ibid.

27. P. Vershure, B. Krose, and R. Pfeifer, 'Distributed Adaptive Control: The Self Organization of Structured Behavior', *Robotics and Autonomous Systems*, 9 (1991), 181–96.

28. Xiao Huang and Juyang Weng, 'Value System Development for a Robot', *Neural Networks, IEEE Proceedings*, 4 (2004), 2883–8.

29. Ibid.

30. L. Steels, 'Towards a Theory of Emergent Functionality', in J. Meyer and S. Wilson (eds), *From animals to animats* (Cambridge, MA: MIT Press, 1991).

31. McFarland and Bosser, *Intelligent behaviour in Animals and Robots*, 272–6; 289–92. See n. 25.

32. Clark, *Mindware*, Chapter 7 n. 3.

33. D. McFarland and E. Honary, 'Flock Distortion: A New Approach in Mapping Environmental Variables in Deep Water' *Robotica*, 21 (2003), 365–83.

Epilogue: The Alien Mind

1. S. T. Parker, R. W. Mitchell, and M. L. Boccia (eds), *Self-awareness in Animals and Humans* (Cambridge: Cambridge University Press, 1994); I. Howard and B. Templeton, *Human Spatial Orientation* (London: Wiley, 1966); P. Michel, K. Gold, and B. Scassellati, 'Motion-Based Robotic Self-Recognition', *Proceedings of 2004 IEEE/RSJ International Conference on Intelligent Robots and Systems*. Sendal, Japan, 2004.

2. C. Wynne, *Animal Cognition* (London: Palgrave Macmillan, 2001); A. Alissandrakis, C. L. Nehaniv, K. Dautenhahn, and J. Saunders, 'Evaluation of Robot Imitation Attempts: Comparison of the System's and the Human's Perspectives', in K. Dautenhahn and C. L. Nehaniv (eds), *Imitation in Animals and Artifacts* (Cambridge, MA: MIT Press, 2002).

3. W. Kohler, *The Mentality of Apes* (New York: Harcourt Brace, 1925); J. Chappell and A. Kacelnik, 'Tool Selectivity in a Non-primate, the New Caledonian Crow (*Corvus moneduloides*)', *Animal Cognition*, 5 (2002), 71–8; B. Kenward, A. A. S. Weir, J. Chappell, and A. Kacelnik, 'Tool Manufacture by Naïve Juvenile Crows', *Nature*, 433 (2005), 121; A. A. S. Weir, J. Chappell, and A. Kacelnik, 'Shaping of Hooks in New Caledonian Crows', *Science*, 297 (2002), 981.

4. S. Shettleworth and J. E. Sutton, 'Do Animals Know What They Know?', in S. Hurley and M. Nudds (eds), *Rational Animals?* (Oxford: Oxford University Press, 2006), 235–46.

5. Ibid.

6. R. Crisp, 'Evolution and Psychological Unity', in M. Bekoff and D. Jamieson (eds), *Readings in Animal Cognition* (Cambridge MA: MIT Press, 1996), 309–21.

7. See Chapters 7 and 8 of Hurley, S. and Nudds, M. (eds) *Rational Animals*. Oxford University Press, 2006.

8. D. Chalmers, 'Facing up to the Problem of Consciousness', *Journal of Consciousness Studies*, 2 (3) (1995), 200–19; and *idem*, *The Conscious Mind: In Search of a Fundamental Theory* (New York Oxford: Oxford University Press, 1996). According to Chalmers, 'A physical system *realizes* a given functional organization when the system can be divided into an appropriate number of physical components each with the appropriate number of possible states, such that the causal dependency relations between the components of the system, inputs, and outputs precisely reflect the dependency relations given in the specification of the functional organization. A given functional organization can be realized by diverse physical systems. For example, the organization realized by the brain at the neural level might in principle be realized by a silicon system. . . . Strictly speaking, for the purposes of the invariance principle we must require that for two systems to share their functional

organization, they must be in corresponding states at the time in question; if not for this requirement, my sleeping twin might count as sharing my organization, but he certainly does not share my experiences. When two systems share their organization at a fine enough grain (including the requirement that they be in corresponding states), I will say that they are *functionally isomorphic* systems, or that they are *functional isomorphs*. The invariance principle holds that any functional isomorph of a conscious system has experiences that are qualitatively identical to those of the original system. ... It follows that we have good reason to believe that the principle of organizational invariance is true, and that functional organization fully determines conscious experience.' ('Facing up to the problem of Consciousness').

9. See Chapter 7 n. 32.

10. R. Kirk, *Zombies and Consciousness* (Oxford: Clarendon Press, 2005).

11. P. Strawson, *Individuals* (London: Methuen, 1959); *idem, Freedom and Resentment* (London: Methuen, 1974).

FURTHER READING

Darwin, C., *On the Origin of Species by Natural Selection* (London: John Murray, 1859).

Dautenhahn, K., and C. Nehaniv, *Imitation in Animals and Artefacts* (Cambridge, MA: MIT Press, 2002).

Dawkins, R., *The Blind Watchmaker* (London: Longman, 1986).

Heyes, C. M., 'Theory of Mind in Nonhuman primates', *Behavioral and Brain Sciences*, 21 (1998), 101–34.

Holland, O., 'The Evolution of Animal-Like Mobile Robots', in O. Holland and D. McFarland (eds), *Artificial Ethology* (Oxford: Oxford University Press, 2001), 14–41.

Holland, O., 'Gathering and Sorting in Insects and Robots', in O. Holland and D. McFarland (eds), *Artificial Ethology* (Oxford: Oxford University Press, 2001), 77–92.

Kennedy, J. S., *The New Anthropomorphism* (Cambridge: Cambridge University Press, 1992).

Pfeiffer, R., and J. C. Bongard, *How the Body Shapes the Way We Think: A New View of Intelligence* (Cambridge, MA: MIT Press, 2006).

Suchman, L., *Plans and Situated Actions* (New York: Cambridge University Press, 1987).

INDEX